THE WILD BUNCH

THE WILD BUNCH

*Sam Peckinpah, a Revolution in
Hollywood, and the Making of
a Legendary Film*

W. K. STRATTON

BLOOMSBURY PUBLISHING
NEW YORK · LONDON · OXFORD · NEW DELHI · SYDNEY

BLOOMSBURY PUBLISHING
Bloomsbury Publishing Inc.
1385 Broadway, New York, NY 10018, USA

BLOOMSBURY, BLOOMSBURY PUBLISHING, and the Diana logo are
trademarks of Bloomsbury Publishing Plc

Library of Congress Cataloging-in-Publication Data
Names: Stratton, W. K., 1955– author.
Title: The wild bunch : Sam Peckinpah, a revolution in Hollywood, and
the making of a legendary film / W. K. Stratton.
Description: New York : Bloomsbury Publishing Inc., 2019.
Identifiers: LCCN 2018024992 | ISBN 9781632862129 (hardback) |
ISBN 9781632862143 (e-book)
Subjects: LCSH: Wild bunch (Motion picture) | Western films—United States—
History and criticism.
Classification: LCC PN1997.W536133 S77 2019 | DDC 791.43/72—dc23
LC record available at https://lccn.loc.gov/2018024992

2 4 6 8 10 9 7 5 3 1

Typeset by Westchester Publishing Services
Printed and bound in the U.S.A. by Berryville Graphics Inc., Berryville, Virginia

To find out more about our authors and books visit www.bloomsbury.com and
sign up for our newsletters.
Bloomsbury books may be purchased for business or promotional use. For information on
bulk purchases please contact Macmillan Corporate and Premium Sales Department at
specialmarkets@macmillan.com.

For Brad Morelli and Gene Lehmann, my brothers
from different parents, and remembering Bill Lehmann,
Frank Parman, John Kelso, and Gentleman Jim Brewer

We were born of risen apes, not fallen angels, and the apes were armed killers besides. And so what shall we wonder at? Our murders and massacres and missiles, and our irreconcilable regiments?

—ROBERT ARDREY, *AFRICAN GENESIS*

I'm not made to philosophize, I don't have the heart for it. My heart is more like a machine for making blood to be spilled in a knife fight.

—CAMILO JOSÉ CELA, *LA FAMILIA DE PASCUAL DUARTE*

The essential American soul is hard, isolate, stoic, and a killer. It has never yet melted.

—D. H. LAWRENCE, *STUDIES IN CLASSIC AMERICAN LITERATURE*

We've got to start thinking beyond our guns. Those days are closing fast.

—WILLIAM HOLDEN AS PIKE BISHOP, *THE WILD BUNCH*

CONTENTS

THE *WILD BUNCH* ROLL CALL

Photo by Bernie Abramson, courtesy of Tonio K.

Pike Bishop's Gang

Pike Bishop	William Holden
Dutch Engstrom	Ernest Borgnine
Freddie Sykes	Edmond O'Brien
Lyle Gorch	Warren Oates
Tector Gorch	Ben Johnson
Angel	Jaime Sánchez
Crazy Lee	Bo Hopkins
Buck	Rayford Barnes

Bounty Hunters

Deke Thornton	Robert Ryan
Coffer	Strother Martin

T.C.	L. Q. Jones
Ross	Paul Harper
Jess	Billy Hart

Railroad Boss

Harrigan	Albert Dekker

Mexican Federal Army Troops

General Mapache	Emilio Fernández
Zamorra	Jorge Russek
Herrera	Alfonso Arau
Yolis (soldadera)	Yolanda Ponce

Angel's Village

Don José	Chano Urueta

Mapache's Women

Teresa	Sonia Amelio
Lilia	Lilia Castillo

Women in Pike Bishop's Flashbacks

Aurora	Aurora Clavel
Elsa	Elsa Cárdenas

Germans

Mohr	Fernando Wagner
Ernst	Ivan J. Rado

Temperance Union

Wainscoat	Dub Taylor

American Army Troops on Train

McHale	Stephen Ferry

PREFACE

The butchery occurred in the Quảng Ngãi Province village of Sốn Mỹ on March 16, 1968. American soldiers of the Twenty Third Infantry Division believed two hamlets harbored Viet Cong fighters in retreat after the Tet Offensive of two months earlier. The commander of the company sent in to root out Viet Cong told his men that all villagers who had not departed for the market by seven A.M. were likely Viet Cong or VC sympathizers and should be killed. Heeding orders to destroy anything walking, crawling, or growing, Charlie Company soldiers slaughtered men, women, children, and infants that morning. Some women were gang-raped before they were shot. Bodies were mutilated. All told, between 350 and 500 Vietnamese died in what became known in the United States as the Mỹ Lai Massacre. Meanwhile, in a Mexican town thousands of miles from Sốn Mỹ, Sam Peckinpah was shooting a film that would confront the violence in the human soul to a degree unlike any movie before it while also dealing with many other weighty matters.

It was called *The Wild Bunch*.

INTRODUCTION

Son of Liberty Valance

In the years following World War II, Guthrie, Oklahoma, boasted four movie theaters. The Cimarron was a low-rent venue, mostly showing Westerns produced by Poverty Row studios. Kids packed it for Saturday-afternoon matinees. Up the block sat the State, a notch above the Cimarron in status. It showed its share of Westerns but also second-run features. As the town's first-run movie house, the Melba was Guthrie's most prestigious theater. Out by the airport was the Beacon Drive-In, its name inspired by the signal beam rotating above the runway.

Guthrie's population hovered for decades around the ten thousand mark. It may seem remarkable, from a twenty-first-century perspective, that a town that size could be home to four cinemas. Guthrie was, however, more rule than exception. Thousands of movie theaters operated in cities and towns across the United States at the midpoint of the twentieth century, providing entertainment and escapism to millions nightly.

But America was changing. Sharing the same Guthrie streets with the theaters were furniture and appliance stores. Facing outward from their display windows were console televisions showing programming from Oklahoma City stations. Guthrie's farmers, stockmen, oil-field roughnecks, housewives, and furniture-factory workers gathered in front of the plate glass to stare at the fuzzy black-and-white images. It is safe to assume that no one in Guthrie owned a TV at the end of the war. By the time I was born there ten years later, there were more homes with a television than without. The effect on Guthrie's cinemas was, well, dramatic. The Cimarron and the State disappeared, leaving just the Melba and the Beacon Drive-In.

It was at the Beacon that I discovered the movies.

Money never ran deep for my family. This was especially true early on, when the five of us lived in a ten-by-fifty-foot trailer house, and every dime had to be carefully accounted for. The Beacon allowed my parents to load my stepbrothers and me into the Chevy station wagon and enjoy an evening out for a couple of bucks. For that, the whole family gained admission to the drive-in with enough change left over to buy popcorn and RC Colas at the concession stand. There were downsides, though. The Oklahoma nights typically were clammy and hot during summer, leaving moviegoers craving the air-conditioning of an indoor theater such as the Melba. The images on the screen usually seemed to be slightly out of focus. Sometimes the projectionist, whose day job was running the town's icehouse, fell asleep, and someone would have to go rouse him when it was time to change reels. Such shortcomings paled against the wonders projected on that giant screen: previews of coming attractions, newsreels, cartoons, features, sometimes a double feature. Even viewed from a backseat through a bug-spattered windshield, movies at the Beacon were grander than anything on TV.

Westerns were a standard offering at the Beacon. That was fine by me. I had deep roots in the West, and even as a small kid I was fascinated by anything involving men and women on horseback in wide-open spaces. Most of the television I watched fell into the Western category: *The Rebel* starring Nick Adams; *Wanted: Dead or Alive* starring Steve McQueen; *The Rifleman* starring Chuck Connors, a former Cubs first baseman; and *Maverick* starring Oklahoma native son James Garner. Best of all was *Have Gun—Will Travel*, the saga of a knight without armor in a savage land, as Johnny Western sang in the theme song. Richard Boone as Paladin combined sophistication and ruggedness, equally at home in San Francisco's finest salons or the desert's roughest terrains. He was as cool as James Bond and, like Britain's greatest spy, he could outfight and outshoot anyone. And, again like 007, he could make women swoon.

These shows made for fun viewing and, like most of the Westerns I saw at the Beacon, they danced around something elemental in American mythology. Usually, though, they never went much beyond shallow entertainment. However, one sticky Beacon evening in the summer of 1962, I bore witness to art for the first time.

Mind you, I was just six years old when I watched *The Man Who Shot Liberty Valance* at the drive-in, perhaps a precocious six-year-old, but a six-year-old nevertheless. That movie dealt with themes that were light-years beyond me. Still, it captured my interest from the very beginning and never turned me loose. In some childlike way, I understood that the characters played by Lee Marvin, Lee Van Cleef, and Strother Martin were pure evil, and they scared the dickens out of me. I understood in some equally basic way that Vera Miles's character, Hallie, did not marry the man she truly loved. I also understood that heroes aren't always what they're cracked up to be. Finally, I understood—again, in some naïve way—that the story had some deeper meaning. Fifteen years later, as a college student reading A. C. Bradley on Shakespearean tragedy, I understood just what that deeper meaning was.

I remember I had a difficult time sleeping after I saw *The Man Who Shot Liberty Valance* for the first time. I lay on my bunk bed in the swelter of our trailer house, replaying the movie in my young mind. For weeks thereafter, *The Man Who Shot Liberty Valance* was all I could talk about. Little did I realize that I was not alone. A young cinephile at the University of Illinois at Urbana-Champaign, Roger Ebert, would come to believe that the movie was one of director Ford's self-contained masterpieces, one of his "most pensive and thoughtful."[1] In Italy, a nascent filmmaker named Sergio Leone declared *The Man Who Shot Liberty Valance* his favorite Ford picture, "the only film where Ford learned about something called pessimism."[2] Years passed before I learned who Ebert and Leone were, but Gene Pitney's pop hit with the same title as the movie became my favorite song for a while. I'd feel chills every time I heard the *huasteco*-style fiddle intro on the radio.

The Man Who Shot Liberty Valance changed my life.

No one I knew was a serious moviegoer, so I had no role models for becoming one. For whatever reason, the Melba became a refuge for me. Sometimes I'd see as many as three features a week, hunkered down in the musty seats, my shoes sticking to a floor coated by generations of spilled sodas and Milk Duds ground underfoot. The Melba had been around forever, first as a vaudeville house called the Pollard, then as a silent-film venue, and finally, in the late 1920s, as Guthrie's first sound cinema. By the time I began "going to the show" at the Melba, little had been updated since the era of Al Jolson. I loved its out-at-the-elbows charm.

I saw all kinds of features at the Melba: biker pics from American International. Roger Corman's renderings of Edgar Allan Poe short stories with Vincent Price as the star. Spy spoofs starring Dean Martin and James Coburn. Cop dramas. Action-adventure flicks. *Godzilla* films from Japan. Horror films from England. Stupid entries in the *Beach Party* series. Ponderous historical costumers. Beatles movies and a bunch of lesser entries in the rock 'n' roll film genre. Dramas that took themselves all too seriously. Comedies that strained too hard in their attempts to be wacky. Disney features sterile enough to placate the most pious of Campbellite preachers.

And, of course, there were always more Westerns. Plenty of them.

I was a kid in the 1960s and into the mid-1970s. In this period it very much seemed as if the center of American culture could not hold any longer, and the world that I'd grown up in might fly apart. In terms of movies, the center shattered. Innocence was sure enough drowned. That turned out to be a good thing. Many movies began to brim with passionate intensity. Extraordinary creativity was occurring everywhere movies were being made, especially so in Hollywood. We moviegoers sat in movie houses such as the Melba and watched as barriers to nudity, the language that grown-ups actually used, and realistic portrayal of violence fell to the wayside.

Teenagers such as myself were supposed to be protected from what I was seeing. The puritanical Motion Picture Production Code had set the standards for American morality in cinema since 1934. It was hopelessly outdated by the 1960s, and Jack Valenti, the onetime LBJ special assistant who had become president of the Motion Picture Association of America, ripped it asunder. It bore the "odious smell of censorship,"[3] he said, in one of the great understatements of the time. The MPAA replaced it with a system of movie ratings with age restrictions that went into effect in 1968.

My mother believed that I was mature beyond my years when it came to such things as literature, movies, and art, even if I was hopelessly immature in other ways. Mom thought she was a better judge than the MPAA of what movies I should and should not see. She had known the owner of the Melba since they were in high school together, and she made a deal with him. Anytime I showed up at the theater, he and his employees could assume that it was okay with her for me to be there and should admit me. Because of that agreement, I skirted the system and watched movies meant for grown-ups. And so, in the summer of 1969, I settled in at the Melba to watch a picture that changed my life to a far greater degree than *The Man Who Shot Liberty Valence* ever had.

I was preparing to enter the eighth grade. A year earlier, the Guthrie public schools had been desegregated, and interracial violence had become a daily part of my life. Knives were not uncommon in my junior high. We students there heard about a beloved teacher at the high school who'd been hit in the head with a brick during a fight. At our school, just stepping into one of the boys' restrooms was risky, likely as not to involve thrown punches and kicks.

Moreover, I'd begun drinking a little—beer and vodka were never difficult to find—and smoking weed whenever possible. I was also stealing my mother's cigarettes every chance I got. And I was a shoplifter and, on a couple of occasions, a petty burglar. On top of all that, I'd discovered the sweet pleasures of keeping company with girls while attending parties and slow dancing endlessly to "Hey Jude." My grades were not as good as they might have been. My relationship with my parents was often icy. It was in this phase of life that I saw Sam Peckinpah's *The Wild Bunch* for the first time.

I had taken in challenging films in the ragged old Melba. Yet nothing compared to what I saw that night. For one thing, this picture looked different, looked better than any other movie I'd seen. The visual impact was stunning, something like stepping into an Old Master's painting hanging in a museum and remaining inside it for two hours. The stars' faces were as familiar as canned vegetables—William Holden, Robert Ryan, Edmond O'Brien—yet their performances in *The Wild Bunch* were much different from, much darker than, anything I'd ever seen them in before. Ernest Borgnine was also one of the stars. I knew him best as the scamp Lieutenant Commander Quinton McHale from one of the inanest TV sitcoms in history (and that's saying a lot). Nothing seemed goofy about him in *The Wild Bunch*. On the contrary, his character was multidimensional, sometimes pleasant, lovable, but at other times with a merciless and psychotic threat punctuated by a giggle even more ominous than Strother Martin's in *The Man Who Shot Liberty Valance*. Martin also appeared in *The Wild Bunch*. His character, Coffer, made Floyd from *Liberty Valance* come off as harmless as an elm leaf. Martin and longtime Peckinpah collaborator L. Q. Jones formed a duo devoted to nastiness quite unlike anything else in the movies, a Laurel and Hardy team joined together by Satan himself.

As a moviegoer from north of the Rio Grande, I'd been programmed to accept ethnic Italians, Jews, or Anglos to fill the roles of Mexicans in movies. Hollywood had served up Wallace Beery, Telly Savalas, and Yul Brynner as Pancho Villa. *Yul Brynner!* With one exception, *The Wild Bunch* had actual Mexicans playing Mexican characters. As for that exception, it was played by a native Spanish speaker, a Puerto Rican named Jaime Sánchez. The number of Mexicans in the picture dwarfed the number of Los Angeles gringos. Dozens and dozens of Mexican faces show up in *The Wild Bunch*. Again, this was different from anything I'd ever seen on the big screen. The groundbreaking films of Sergio Leone had prepared me for a West that was grimy, a West where people seldom bathed and looked like it, a West where flies lit and crawled on people's faces. *The Wild Bunch* took it further. Billy Bob Thornton said it was the first American film to take you down into the dust.[4] Exactly.

And then there was the violence.

I'm looking at a set of comments taken from audience reaction cards gathered at a test screening of *The Wild Bunch*: *I have never seen blood squirt out of humans like in this movie. This movie was TOO DAMNED BLOODY!! One big bloody mess. No story, just gore, filthy, repulsive = blood, blood, blood! Truly a product of our sick society. It's great for morbid people. It stunk!!!! Christ have mercy. Whatever happened to the old John Wayne movies? I'm aghast. Your film leaves me shaky. I can't say more.*[5]

It certainly left me shaky. After the final shoot-out, after the last exchange of dialogue between Robert Ryan and Edmond O'Brien, after the credits rolled to the tune of "Las Golondrinas," I stepped out of the theater into the night, my heart beating as if I'd just been running hundred-yard sprints. I still feel that way any time I watch *The Wild Bunch*. *This picture is burnt in my brain*, reads one of the audience reaction cards. *I don't think I'm gonna ever forget it.* That sentiment has been shared by millions of people since *The Wild Bunch* premiered in June 1969. And it's certainly burnt in my brain.

The Wild Bunch's bloodletting has been trumped many times during the past fifty years, yet the psychological impact of the film's violence has not diminished. There is much, much more than just carnage, however. *The Wild Bunch* is about men out of their time, the catastrophic effect of technology on the human soul, loyalty, honor and dishonor, failure and success, good and evil, and, finally, redemption. It dealt with change—change that was not good, change that diminished the human spirit. It pushed the boundaries of realism in moviemaking, including the violence but also in character development—the men it portrayed were savage yet vulnerable, and, when backed into a corner, able to do the right thing. It overhauled long-standing clichés from Western films, made them new and interesting. Its storytelling is complex. It has become a classic film, not just in America but worldwide; if anything, it is appreciated more in Europe than in the United States. It is clearly the greatest Western ever made, besting Ford's *The Searchers*, Howard Hawks's *Red River*, and other claimants to the title. Why? The significance of the story and its construction, the cinematography, the acting from top to bottom, the soundtrack—all are excellent, absolutely first-rate. *The Wild Bunch* is one of the best movies of any sort ever made, ranking with Orson Welles's *Citizen Kane* and Akira Kurosawa's *Rashomon*. A moderate box-office success when it was released fifty years ago, *The Wild Bunch* has become one of Warner Bros.' biggest all-time money earners as it found new audiences with the expansion of home video markets in the late twentieth and early twenty-first centuries.

The picture, however, would never have been filmed had not circumstances come into precise alignment. It was the product of a nation torn by divisions unseen since the Civil War, a nation that was sacrificing thousands of its young to a war in Southeast Asia, a nation where decades-old racial strife had exploded into fiery violence in its cities and towns, a nation numbed by political assassinations, a nation where a youthful generation was wholesale rejecting values held by their parents.

It was the product of a burgeoning city, Los Angeles, which had displaced, at least for a time, New York as America's cultural center—the place where the American dream was manufactured and disseminated as movies, rock 'n' roll records, TV shows, and pop art. ("No offense," Ken Kesey told Tom Wolfe one day during the late 1960s, "but New York is about two years behind.")[6] And the film also was the product of a movie industry in turmoil. The studio system had become a beached whale exhaling its last gasps as young filmmakers were forging a whole new kind of American cinema, one that drew at least as heavily from foreign pictures as from native traditions. At the same time, the picture also was very much a product of those traditions, including the hoariest of them all, the Western.

Above all else, it was the product of the intellect, the creative sensibilities, and the heart of its director, Sam Peckinpah. Around the time of the release of *The Wild Bunch*, Kris Kristofferson, who would become Peckinpah's friend and collaborator, wrote a song called "The Pilgrim, Chapter 33." The chorus includes the lines *He's a walking contradiction / Partly truth and partly fiction / Taking every wrong direction on his lonely way back home.*[7] Those words could well have been written about Peckinpah. By the mid-1960s, when he was at work on *The Wild Bunch*, he had taken more than his share of wrong directions, and home still seemed far away.

He was a director with an extraordinary mastery of the nuts and bolts of film production. His work ethic was unsurpassed by any of his Hollywood peers. His artistic vision was intense, and by the time he turned forty, he had an impressive body of work behind him both in TV and movies. On a personal level, he could exhibit undying loyalty to old friends, had a soft heart for the down-and-out, and ponied up thousands of dollars to aid disadvantaged children. If he sometimes seemed most at home inside the boozy, smoky, dim interiors of Nevada whorehouses, he would also weep openly at the color explosion of a sunset high in the Sierras. "Inside, Sam was a sweet guy," his friend and fellow director

Monte Hellman told me. "But you had to go through a lot of layers of crap before you got to that sweet center."[8] Another old friend, novelist Max Evans, told me that Peckinpah was an intense man. Even Sam's leisure time was not laid-back: "Sam wasn't the kind of guy you'd just go get a hamburger with and sit around and shoot the shit," Evans said.[9]

Peckinpah subscribed to an ethos, much of it absorbed from the authentic cowboys he knew as a kid, that ran counter to the slick, hollow, and often dishonest practices of the Hollywood of his time. As a result, he made more than his share of enemies within the film industry. A heavy drinker with a temper that at times grew frighteningly dark, he gave his adversaries plenty of ammunition to use against him. He was a notoriously bad loser, and after he suffered a series of losses in the mid-1960s, he'd alienated enough Hollywood power brokers that it seemed as if his career as a film director was over. The walking contradiction found himself blacklisted, not for political reasons, but because he was a committed artist who refused to compromise his values.

Yet he returned from studio exile to achieve the most unlikely of triumphs with what he sometimes referred to as a simple story about bad men in Mexico during changing times. The story was set far from the place where Sam grew up. Still, every frame of *The Wild Bunch* reflected some piece of himself and the country that shaped him: the mountains, valleys, and flat agricultural land of Central California and the people who lived there.

But even more, it reflected his passion for Mexico, his adopted second homeland. With his first visit to Mexico City, he fell in love with the country and its people. Mexico was for him the perfect antidote to an America that had been conquered by the man in the gray flannel suit. To Peckinpah, the United States had become a nation of soul-crushing technocrats, a place where the human spirit was devalued, where freedom was easily sacrificed for the comfort of conformity, where people were all too ready to embrace totalitarianism. He held romanticized views for sure, but to him, Mexico was a saner place.

The America he knew, though changing, still embraced the tenets of the Woman's Christian Temperance Union across wide swatches of its territory. Not so in Mexico, where people accepted and celebrated cerveza, tequila, and mezcal. Mexico was a religious country, but also a place where people understood that life comprises both angels and devils. Peckinpah reveled in its people's ability to express emotions openly, something that in large measure wasn't accepted in the America where he grew up.

America's obsessions pointed toward air-conditioned automobiles, color televisions with increasingly sophisticated doodads attached, and wall-to-wall carpeting. The American heroic figure was a businessman who'd made enough money to buy a split-level in the suburbs with a swimming pool in the backyard, a man living out a life as processed and refined as white flour. Relatively few Americans knew much about actual horses, except that the animals drew flies and that their owners spent a lot of time mucking out their stalls. It seemed that most Americans understood more about adjusting the console hi-fi in the corner to provide music for their dark, wood-paneled enclaves. Opposite that console hi-fi sat the console TV, with the roof antenna adjusted just so to pick up the three network-affiliated channels and, if the weather was right, the fuzzy image broadcast by the low-wattage local NET (shortly to be rechristened PBS) station. Ensconced in these comfort lairs, Americans learned what they knew of the real world from television. The novelist Henry Miller found this condition deplorable: "Why terrifying? Because nowhere else in the world is the divorce between man and nature so complete. Nowhere have I encountered such a dull, monotonous fabric of life as here in America. Here boredom reaches its peak."[10]

To Peckinpah, Mexico was the opposite of America's sterility. To film his masterpiece, Peckinpah led an extraordinarily talented troupe of Mexican and gringo actors and crew members to a sandblasted Mexican steppe town far removed from the niceties of Hollywood or Mexico City. Here they confronted freezing predawn mornings, blistering afternoons, stinging insects, poisonous snakes, rabies-infected rodents, rutted-out roads, bad food, and sand, always sand, fouling equipment, invading clothing and bedding, turning up everywhere. On at least one occasion, filming shut down because of a blinding sandstorm. Yet in many ways it was an ideal place to shoot a movie during the first half of that dark year, 1968.

Certainly, the countryside and buildings in Parras de la Fuente, Coahuila, and at the nearby Hacienda Ciénega del Carmen were ideal for Peckinpah's purposes. Parras seemed isolated from the student riots that crippled Paris; the rumbling Soviet tanks in Czechoslovakia during the Prague Spring; the political assassinations, racial violence, and massive social unrest in the United States; the powder keg of Egypt and Israel; and the horrific and seemingly endless war in Southeast Asia. Indeed, "mere anarchy" seemed set to be "loosed upon the world," in the words of the William Butler Yeats poem.[11] Mexico was not immune. As the repressive government of Gustavo Díaz Ordaz prepared Mexico City to host the 1968 Olympics, political dissidents and other undesirable types simply disappeared. Eventually protesters would be shot and killed under Díaz Ordaz's orders at the Plaza de las Tres Culturas in the Tlatelolco section of Mexico City. The turmoil that would lead up to that shooting spree seemed far removed from Parras during the spring of 1968. It was then that Peckinpah, his cast, and his crew settled in to create their realistic masterpiece about complex characters, men outside their time who find themselves backed into a corner, the tyranny of technology, changing

Sam Peckinpah employs a trick of Sam Fuller's and starts action by firing a pistol during the filming of *The Wild Bunch* in Mexico. Photo by Bernie Abramson, courtesy of Jeff Slater.

values, the horror of gun violence, and, ultimately, deliverance. In Mexico, all the components of *The Wild Bunch* came together to create cinematic magic found in only the best motion pictures.

Everything in the world seemed far, far removed as Peckinpah and company made *The Wild Bunch*. Everything, that is, except the resonance of the bloody horror of the Mexican Revolution. It was exactly what Peckinpah wanted.

PART I

"A Wild Bunch"

1.

Roy N. Sickner was by any measure a piece of work. He was born Roy A. Cooley in Arizona, but his family relocated to Los Angeles when he was young. For all intents and purposes, he was an L.A. kid. Before his twelfth birthday, both his middle and last names changed. His near-lifelong friend Buck Holland remembered him as being a wild guy, even back in junior high school—wild, but also a hell of an athlete and a tough hombre.[1] Sickner told school friends that his father was a full-blood Apache from Tree Branch, Arizona. They bought into it, even if they were not sure where exactly Tree Branch, Arizona, was—or even if it actually existed. As he tore up the football field at Santa Monica High, he did indeed seem like some sort of latter-day Jim Thorpe. He ran faster than anyone else, he was stronger than anyone else, and he possessed a winner's spirit. He also took up skiing and was a natural at it, enough so that he turned pro for a couple of years after high school. (Skiing would remain a passion for him, and eventually on the slopes he met businessmen who helped shape his career.) Beyond his athletic prowess, Sickner could endure endless physical punishment. He kept on keeping on, even if injured, never slowing down. He also indulged in crazy high jinks that filled the whiskey hours between dusk and dawn. He grew up to be one of those 1950s guys who could booze it up all night and still show up early for work to put in a hard, full day, impressing everyone he worked with, even if word spread to use caution before accepting an offer to go out drinking with him.

As an Angeleno with athletic skills and an unbreakable constitution, Sickner found his way into his hometown's highest-profile industry. Filming movies had always required the services of stuntmen, going all the way back to the age of the silent two-reelers. When the fifties turned out to be a golden age of the Western, it upped the need for doubles willing to fall off buildings or be dragged by horses. As with most other things in his life, Sickner was a natural at it. Though he convinced his high school buddies that he was half-Apache, Sickner never became much of a horseman, at least in the estimation of his friend Holland, who joined him as a stuntman. Sickner mastered everything else. He befriended Roy Jenson, another rowdy stuntman and actor, about whom Jenson's friend Texas-born novelist James Crumley wrote, he "makes looking mean, downright rock-hard bad, look easy."[2] Sickner and Jenson developed the reputation for staging fight scenes better than anyone else in the business, using at least in part what they learned in real barroom brawls during the wee hours. By the beginning of the 1960s, Sickner was at the absolute top among the stuntmen working in Hollywood.

The major studios were all but moribund, victims of the passing of the moguls who'd built them, the assault on their audience base by TV, the anti-Hollywood sentiment of the Second Red Scare, the taxing of imported American movies by foreign markets, and the antitrust court rulings that forced the studios to sell off their theater chains. The studios also struggled to adapt to the tastes of a changing America, especially those of younger moviegoers. RKO, one of the Big Five studios, ceased production before the 1950s ended. A television production company, Desilu, owned by Desi Arnaz and Lucille Ball, bought RKO's facilities and used the soundstages that gave birth to *Citizen Kane* to churn out thirty-minute installments of idiot-box pabulum.

But the decline of the studio system brought about opportunities in Hollywood that were all but inconceivable twenty years earlier. More and more, the studios were acting as distributors for films made by independent production companies. Often, this absolved the studios of actually investing money and resources into the making of a movie, though sometimes the studios did pony up some production money. A person with Sickner's connections could put together a project and sell it to an independent production company. After that, all involved would have to chase the money, recruit the star power, and then convince a studio that their product was worthy of distribution. If all the pieces fell into place, someone could go from stuntman and bit actor to producer pretty quickly. It just required the right project. The right star connected to it. And the right set of moneymen lined up to support it.

In 1963, Sickner worked stunts on a Yul Brynner flop from United Artists called *Kings of the Sun* alongside Jenson and another friend, Chuck Hayward, who often doubled for John Wayne. While in Mexico shooting the movie, Sickner began to talk to Hayward about an idea he had for his own film. The main characters were vague, and the storyline rudimentary at best: In the 1870s, a group of gringo outlaws rob a train someplace north of the Rio Grande, then escape to Mexico with a posse hot on their heels. Mexican authorities also get involved with the chase, leading to a big shoot-out at the end. Even though the story wasn't much, Sickner described several action scenes he envisioned. Hayward liked what he heard and added some of his own thoughts to the mix. The two men left Mexico in agreement that this movie concept was something worth pursuing. Within a short time, Sickner was calling his germinating film project *The Wild Bunch*.

It is unclear exactly how Sickner arrived at that title. The term *the wild bunch* turns up in King Vidor's 1955 cowboy picture *Man Without a Star*, in which characters refer to a gang of ruffians by that name in the screenplay written by Borden Chase, himself a onetime driver for a Prohibition-era bootlegger. There's no evidence that movie influenced Sickner in any way. It's likely *the wild bunch* came from newspaper stories about real-life criminals based in Wyoming working in the late 1800s into the early 1900s. The Wild Bunch was one of the names applied to the criminal operation headed up by Robert Leroy Parker, better known to history as Butch Cassidy. The group was also known as the Hole-in-the-Wall Gang. At the time Sickner conceived of his movie, which was years before the Paul Newman/Robert Redford hit movie, Cassidy and the outlaws associated with him were not well-known beyond Wyoming old-timers and a relatively small group of Western historians. Sickner seemed to have some knowledge of Cassidy, however, and mentioned him in conversations around the time he began talking up his ideas for the movie.

Before the term the Wild Bunch was applied to Cassidy and company, newspapers used it widely as the name for an intriguing group of bank and train robbers led by Bill Doolin in Oklahoma and Indian Territories in the 1890s. This Wild Bunch, sometimes called Oklahombres or the Doolin-Dalton Gang (later celebrated by the Eagles on their *Desperado* album) grew out of the remnants of the Dalton Brothers gang following the demise of its core members on the dusty streets of Coffeyville, Kansas, in 1892. Doolin had been a respected range foreman who turned outlaw rather than surrender to advancing barbed wire and plowed fields in what is now central Oklahoma. Most of the members of this Wild Bunch were like him, cowboys driven to outlawry by changing times and the loss of open range to homesteaders, as well as the cursed advancement of technology. Government leaders and railroad men attempting to "civilize" the area gave Doolin and his compatriots no truck. To a man, Doolin's Wild Bunch were tracked down and killed by deputy U.S. marshals, sheriffs, and posses. Here, too, no evidence suggests that Sickner had this group of plains desperadoes in mind when he chose the title for his movie. Another possibility is that he lifted the title from an early 1940s novel by Ernest Haycox.[3]

Haycox was a Portland, Oregon–based author who published dozens of novels and short stories over twenty years. He distinguished himself by writing with a literary flair absent from the Western books that came before him. Slick magazines such as *Collier's* serialized his novels and paid him top dollar for his work. A young Sam Peckinpah numbered among the thousands of readers who valued Haycox's writing. Hollywood loved him, too. A dozen or so movies grew out of his stories and novels, including the seminal John Ford film *Stagecoach*. Such high-profile directors as Cecil B. DeMille and Anthony Mann also directed adaptations of Haycox's work. As someone who worked in the industry, Sickner had to have been aware of the Oregon writer's books and short stories, even if the story Haycox told in his novel *The Wild Bunch* had nothing in common with Sickner's Mexican shoot-out yarn. However Sickner arrived at *The Wild Bunch*, he could not have selected a more effective title.

Sickner began exploring the feasibility of his plans for the movie with different people. In 1964, he was hired on to double for Richard Harris in a movie being shot in Mexico, Peckinpah's *Major Dundee*. Sickner pitched *The Wild Bunch* to him on location, but Peckinpah was not in a place to be considering future films. He sat at the helm of a disaster in the making, and saving his current project was his sole concern. He would fail at that mission.

2.

Two years earlier, Peckinpah had emerged from a run in television as a wunderkind feature film director with his award-winning *Ride the High Country*. That picture had been green-lighted by its studio, MGM, as a low-budget Western with two over-the-hill stars, Randolph Scott and Joel McCrea, to serve as bottom bill on a double feature in the United States and for general release in European markets, which hungered for American cowboy movies. Peckinpah was then hardly known outside the world of series TV. He had just one uneven feature film behind him, *The Deadly Companions*. Yet, for *Ride the High Country*, he assembled an extraordinary supporting cast, enlisted a superb crew, coaxed the best performances of their careers from Scott and McCrea, worked magic in the cutting room, and, against all odds, released a Western that rivaled the best work in the genre of John Ford, Howard Hawks, Raoul Walsh, George Stevens, and Anthony Mann. In spite of the neglect MGM showed in promoting the film, *Ride the High Country* stood alongside *The Man Who Shot Liberty Valance* as the last of the great post-*Stagecoach* golden age Westerns. Its tone was at once elegiac and dark, the latter making it a harbinger of the revisionist Westerns that came later in the 1960s.

Because MGM brass considered *Ride the High Country* a throwaway, it received little promotion from distributors in America. Still, the critics loved it. In addition to glowing reviews in publications that mattered at the time—the *New York Times*, the *New York Herald Tribune*, *Life* magazine—it was named movie of the year by *Newsweek* and wound up as one of *Time*'s ten best films of the year. International critics applauded it even more. Awards poured in: Mexico's Diosa de Plata, Sweden's Silver Leaf, and the Paris film critics award among them. *Ride the High Country* also beat out Fellini's *8½* to claim the Grand Prix at the Belgian International Film Festival.

Peckinpah became a hot director around Hollywood. Jerry Bresler, a producer at Columbia, screened *Ride the High Country* for Charlton Heston, whom he was courting to star in the feature eventually released as *Major Dundee*. After watching *Ride the High Country*, Heston told Bresler that Peckinpah was the man.[4] With that, Sam found himself ramrodding a big-budget feature promising the sweep of a David Lean epic.

There were problems from the beginning.

Heston and Peckinpah agreed to the project on the basis of a treatment, not a completed screenplay. Different writers contributed to the script, but it was never quite right. Peckinpah ended up leading a company into Mexico to shoot an expensive picture with a story that fell apart in the second half. The flawed foundation doomed whatever Peckinpah might attempt to build on it.

Problems multiplied, although Peckinpah managed to put together one of his best supporting casts: James Coburn, Warren Oates, Ben Johnson, Dub Taylor, L. Q. Jones, R. G. Armstrong, Slim Pickens. He added two gifted Mexican actresses, Aurora Clavel and Begoña Palacios, both of whom eventually forged romantic links to Peckinpah. Armstrong figured out that Peckinpah's intent with *Major Dundee* was to make "*Moby-Dick* on horseback"[5] with this tale of an American incursion into Mexico while in pursuit of Apaches. Sam confessed to Armstrong that he was right. Peckinpah faced a problem. None of his lead actors (Heston, Richard Harris, Senta Berger) were up to such an undertaking.

Third-billed Jim Hutton, as in most of his films, gave an annoyingly goofball performance. Beyond that, he disrupted work behind the camera when he wasn't acting. Gordon Dawson, then still in his twenties, had been pressed into service as de facto wardrobe supervisor. One day, as Dawson hustled about, getting his work done under extreme pressure from Peckinpah, he found himself lassoed, with a guffawing Hutton at the other end of the rope. Dawson beat the ever-living shit out of Hutton, pounding him everywhere but the face—"never hit the talent in the face."[6] Such angry encounters were hardly rare on the troubled production, mostly because Peckinpah was in over his head directing an epic he was not ready to handle.

In addition, the whole film company grew exhausted and edgy because of another error Peckinpah had made. He had selected locations that were separated by hundreds of miles, stretching all the way from the U.S.

border to not far from Mexico City. Columbia boasted in a promotional film that the *Major Dundee* company was the largest accumulation of American actors, crew members, and livestock ever to make a movie in Mexico. Caravans of buses, trucks, and trailers rumbled on for hour after hour moving from one place to another, wearing down everyone's nerves. Though he did his best to cover it with gruff bravado, Peckinpah was terrified—"overwhelmed and lost and terrified, absolutely terrified," his friend Jim Silke described him years later.[7]

This bad situation was exacerbated by events Peckinpah could not control. Harry Cohn, the most tyrannical of all Hollywood moguls (no small achievement), ruled Columbia for nearly four decades, ever since cofounding the company in 1919. Cohn died unexpectedly in 1959, thrusting management of the studio into years-long turmoil as Columbia struggled to remain profitable. Just two days before the *Major Dundee* company was to leave for Mexico, Columbia axed the head of production who had okayed the picture and replaced him with Mike Frankovich. Frankovich's team determined that *Major Dundee* should not be the expensive epic originally planned. Columbia cut the budget and adjusted the shooting schedule accordingly.

From an accountant's perspective, Columbia made the correct decision. Nearly a fourth of America's movie theaters had shut down over the previous decade. Overall ticket sales had declined in the neighborhood of 12.5 percent. On top of that, the studios produced bloated epics year after year that cost fortunes to make, but audiences failed to show up for them. Only savvy producers and directors such as Roger Corman working for bare-bones companies such as American International Pictures seemed to understand the formula for releasing movies that ended up in the black with some consistency. No one at the major studios was immune from the dire economic changes hitting the industry. Even John Ford's epic *Cheyenne Autumn*—intended, at least in part, to be an apology to American Indians for the way Ford had portrayed them in earlier movies—went from road show to just another Western as the studio that produced it, Warner Bros., battled its own economic demons.

So it simply was not the right time or place for Roy Sickner to be pitching another Mexican film to Peckinpah, whose career was about to slip into purgatory. Sickner turned to another industry outlaw, whose career was headed in the other direction. His name was Lee Marvin.

3.

In 1964, Sickner's own career took off in an unexpected direction. Horsemanship may not have been his greatest talent, but he fell in easily with cowboys and gained their respect. And he looked the part. That year, he showed up at the Cheyenne Frontier Days rodeo in Wyoming—"the Daddy of 'Em All"—and the timing was just right to make his face familiar to millions of people.

The Leo Burnett agency had, through its Marlboro Man ad campaign, transformed Philip Morris's Marlboro brand from a smoke "Mild as May" marketed to women to a cigarette for the most virile of men, who, up until then, had eschewed filtered cigarettes. The campaign's cowboy image worked as Marlboro sales skyrocketed. Philip Morris went from also-ran to leading player in the American cigarette industry.

A series of men portrayed the Marlboro Man in magazine advertisements and eventually on TV. The first one was a Texas rancher, but then came a procession of male models, some of whom didn't even know how to mount a horse. One ad had showed a cowboy with his spurs on upside down, which elicited hoots from Marlboro customers in the West. The Burnett agency decided to pursue some real cowboys after that and dispatched representatives to the Daddy of 'Em All to search for them.

At the rodeo, they found just what they needed for Marlboro's slick magazine ads, billboards, and, most important, TV commercials. Sickner was among the cowboys the agency signed in Cheyenne. He would come to claim he was the first Marlboro Man, which was far from the truth by any measure. Several testosterone-soaked Marlboro Man commercials ran on national TV before Sickner appeared in one.[8] The Marlboro commercials, which often appeared during pro football broadcasts, became extremely popular. Sickner was now a recognizable figure in American pop culture. If he fibbed a bit by claiming to be the first

Marlboro Man, no one back in Hollywood seemed to challenge it. The success of the commercials helped raise Sickner's profile at the time he was pushing *The Wild Bunch*.[9]

The newly signed Marlboro Man first began talking up *The Wild Bunch* to his good friend and drinking buddy Marvin sometime in 1965. The timing was perfect. Marvin's star in Hollywood was on the rise. The next year he would strike gold by beating out heavyweight stars such as Richard Burton and Laurence Olivier to win the Oscar for Best Actor for playing a comic role in the whacked-out Western *Cat Ballou*. In the mid-1960s, Marvin held more sway than at any other point in his movie career.

No one else in the film world was remotely like Marvin. He came of age in movies and on TV at a time when antiheroic leading men—Mitchum, Brando, Dean—rose to prominence. Yet Marvin was even less like a typical movie star. He possessed not an inkling of glamour. On-screen, he looked like a man who'd never gone through the innocence of a childhood. Instead, it seemed as if he'd blown in from the desert fully formed. His cigarette-tortured voice sounded like a wicked, low rumble from deep in the earth, suggesting a volcano about to blow. Moviegoers likely assumed this white-haired pit bull of an actor had to fight for everything he ever received in life.

In fact, the opposite was true. He was a New Yorker, a product of American gentry, and he wanted for little growing up. There was trouble in Marvin's comfortable childhood, however. "My father was the classic Puritan," Marvin said. "Hold the emotions in check. Keep up appearances. Tight assed. He had feelings, but he'd never show them to you. I remember once he told me about a bunch of horses he saw in World War One. They were twisted and dead from mustard gas. He cried talking about them. He had feelings. It took something like that to bring them out."[10] But Marvin's father was also an alcoholic who when drunk and enraged beat Lee's mother.

Marvin had educational opportunities most kids could only dream of, but he squandered them. He was kicked out of exclusive school after exclusive school. Finally, he wound up at a Catholic high school in Florida. He still had a discipline problem, but he excelled at sports and acted in school plays. He then enlisted in the marines during World War II. The culture of the Corps was a good fit for him, but once he shipped out for duty in the Pacific, he learned lessons about the nightmare of war: "The war had an effect on me. I remember a native woman on one of

Lee Marvin (right) with Warren Oates at a party in 1967. Photo from the author's collection.

the islands that was carrying a dead child in her arms—and she was nine months pregnant with the next one. She was walking around in shock. A marine came up to her and said, 'Put that dead kid down.' She wouldn't do it. The marine got sore. He told her to put it down. She refused. He took out a knife and sliced her belly open. He disemboweled her. The fetus dropped out. When he put his knife back in the scabbard, he was ready to fight a war. This insanity, this raving inhumanity—it was then I suddenly knew: This is what war does to a man, what war means."[11]

Marvin was wounded during the Battle of Saipan and received a medical discharge. At loose ends back in the States, he took jobs as a plumber's helper. While repairing a toilet at a community theater in Woodstock, New York, Marvin was asked by a director to fill in for an ailing actor. Marvin agreed, and that changed everything for him. Before long, he was in L.A. working on TV shows and films. He did his best work in noir movies and Westerns, including Budd Boetticher's *7 Men from Now*. Other films he appeared in included Fritz Lang's *The Big Heat*, Marlon Brando's biker flick *The Wild One*, *The Caine Mutiny*, *Bad Day at Black Rock*, and *Raintree County*. *The Man Who Shot Liberty Valance* helped boost Marvin to leading-man status. *Cat Ballou* made him a star.

The 1950s and early 1960s in general were a time of conformity, the age of the air-conditioned nightmare that Henry Miller hated, but some Americans rejected the Eisenhower ideal all along. Their dream was not a little box of a house made of ticky-tacky stuck away in a neat suburb where the lawns were always well trimmed and the picket fences were painted a glowing white. Instead, they wanted to live wild and free—and, often as not, crazy. At the far reaches of this group were the Beats and one-percenter motorcycle clubs such as the Hells Angels. Even in everyday life they could be encountered, freethinkers who rejected society's constraints. They drank heavily, brawled, slept around, and never felt compelled to show up for church on Sunday. They had no fear of telling a boss to go to hell. In Hollywood, you could find members of that nonconformist tribe hanging out at restaurants and bars such as Chez Jay in Santa Monica or at the Raincheck Room in West Hollywood. Sickner, Marvin, Peckinpah, and young actors of the likes of Dennis Hopper, Warren Oates, and Harry Dean Stanton numbered among them.

Marvin and Sickner began boozy sessions at Chez Jay planning to hammer out a treatment of some kind for *The Wild Bunch*. Often as not, Buck Holland joined them. Much like Sickner's earlier conversations with

Buck Holland (center), playing a bounty hunter in *The Wild Bunch*. With Strother Martin (left) and Robert Ryan. Photo by Bernie Abramson, courtesy of Tonio K.

his stuntman buddy Chuck Hayward, these talks did not accomplish much in the way of story line or character development. Action sequences dominated the discussions, such as they were. Things eventually became sidetracked as the liquor flowed. A "conference" could prove to be a movable feast as Sickner, Marvin, and Holland, and maybe another friend or two, set off from Chez Jay to other nightspots.

Usually at about half past midnight, Holland, seeing that things were going nowhere, would announce that he needed to take a leak and depart for the men's room. Instead of returning for more talk and drinking, he'd head home, leaving Sickner and Marvin to caper away the rest of the night. Holland's sister, who had some skills with typing and composing sentences but little experience in developing a narrative, came into the fold. Adding her to the mix did nothing toward producing a real treatment.

It became clear to Sickner that he needed a professional writer to work with him on *The Wild Bunch*. He thought back to a young man he'd met in 1964 on the set of a Marlon Brando–Yul Brynner thriller called *Morituri*, also known as *Saboteur: Code Name Morituri*. It was filmed mostly on a boat moored off Catalina and ran 100 percent over its shooting schedule. *Morituri* was among several critical and financial blunders of Brando's during the 1960s as it almost seemed that the greatest actor in American movie history was intent on destroying his career. Sickner doubled for Brando on the film. While on the set, Sickner met Walon Green, who, though not yet even thirty years old, was already impressing people with his understanding of how dialogue and story lines function in a motion picture.

A year later, Sickner served as second unit director on *Winter A-Go-Go*, one of those wretched youth-exploitation films belched out by independent production companies and cash-strapped studios—in this case, Columbia—to rake in teenage baby-boomer dollars. *Winter A-Go-Go* transported the *Beach Party* concept to the ski slopes as a plotless, snowy teenage romp. Before production began, the producer determined—absurd as it seems, considering the quality of the film— that the screenplay needed a dialogue polish. Sickner recommended Green to give the young man a payday, but Sickner had more in mind for Green.

4.

Roughly the same age as Buddy Holly and Roy Orbison, Walon Green grew up as a member of the first rock 'n' roll generation: too young for World War II or Korea, too old to be drafted for duty in Vietnam. Though born in Baltimore, Green grew up in L.A., where his stepfather was pop composer James V. Monaco. Monaco made his name writing tunes for the *Ziegfeld Follies* in New York, then relocated to California to work in pictures. Through Monaco, Green was exposed to movie-industry people throughout his childhood. He attended public schools in Beverly Hills and was of the right age and in the right place to have been an angst-ridden 1950s teenager of the sort portrayed in Nicholas Ray's *Rebel Without a Cause*.

But Green held a wider, less self-obsessed view of life than many youths of his time. And he had cojones. When he was barely into his teen years, he talked his way into a group from the Los Angeles Museum of Natural History that traveled to Baja California to collect birds and small mammals. One night the group camped unknowingly on a tidal marsh. Green and the others were awakened by a foot of seawater that rolled in with high tide. No one was hurt, but their car sank to its axles in the wet sand. The group set out walking to find help. It took nearly six hours, but they finally found a bunkhouse on a ranch that was miles away from their stranded vehicle. One of the ranch workers spoke a little English, and once he understood the plight of the group, he mobilized a crew of other vaqueros to help the gringos. They traveled to the stuck car and, with the aid of a World War II–vintage half-track, the vaqueros freed the car. Then the ranch hands invited the yanquis to return to the ranch with them, where they fed Green and his companions and put them up in the bunkhouse. Green was moved by the kindness. "I thought, 'Jesus, these are really special people,'" Green said. "You're stuck in the mud, and they haul you out, but they want nothing for it. To them, it was just the right thing to do. That started my love affair with Mexico."[12] After that, Green returned to Mexico whenever he could and eventually went to college there.

While attending classes in Mexico City, he met the son of Antonio Ríos Zertuche, who had been a general in the Mexican Revolution under Álvaro Obregón. The elder Ríos Zertuche helped set up the ambush that took the life of *el caudillo del sur*, Emiliano Zapata. A little more than a year later, a firing squad under Ríos Zertuche's command executed Jesús Guajardo, the officer credited with killing Zapata. Green befriended the elder Ríos Zertuche and began to hear tales of the revolution, which, then as now, was largely ignored by American schools even though it was the most horrifically violent conflict ever to occur in North America, one that changed both Mexico and the United States forever. Ríos Zertuche's stories opened up a whole world to Green.

After finishing college, Green took a job in Cuernavaca with a company that installed swimming pools and water-purification systems. His work took Green to every state in Mexico. Four decades had passed since Obregón consolidated power, effectively ending the revolution, yet, during his travels, Green encountered surviving revolutionary generals and officers. Their stories were as riveting as those told by General Ríos Zertuche. A few years later, Green drew on his memories of those old men and what they must have been like in their prime when he began to dream up a fictional Huertista general he would call Mapache, a character who reflected Mexico during its darkest days.

5.

Here is a story about the Mexican Revolution.

In December 1916, Pancho Villa's troops defeated Carrancistas (followers of Villa's rival Venustiano Carranza, a future president of Mexico) defending the train station at Santa Rosalía de Camargo, in the border state of Chihuahua, roughly 150 miles south of Presidio, Texas. A number of the Carrancistas were *soldaderas*, women who were soldiers or who traveled with their soldier husbands to assist them during battle. Villa's forces took ninety *soldaderas* prisoner. As the Centaur of the North rode past the prisoners, one of the women took a shot at him. Villa was already angry. Earlier, he'd personally put a bullet through the heart of the widow of the station paymaster because she called him a son of a bitch and a murderer. Now, even more enraged by the round that nearly hit him, he demanded that the *soldaderas* name the woman who fired the gun. One old woman screamed that the shot came from all of them: They all wanted him dead. Villa announced that if they all wanted him dead, then all of the *soldaderas* would die. His soldiers sprang into action, gunning down the ninety women. Legend holds that the women screeched hideously, but not a one out of fear or agony. Instead all howled oaths of revenge on Villa, on his children, and on his children's children.[13] The killing of the women at Santa Rosalía was hardly the only incident of unspeakable violence during the Mexican Revolution, during which death came fast and easy. Around a tenth of the population of Mexico died in the warfare. The catastrophic carnage still resonated in the country forty years later when Green listened to the blood-soaked stories of old men.

The revolution began in reaction to the three-decade dictatorship of Porfirio Díaz. He had been a hero in the war to end the French intervention, which war had as its goal returning Mexico to a republican form of government. Díaz had little taste for democracy or fair elections. He strong-armed his way to the presidential throne in the spring of 1877. Once he seized power, he brutally eliminated any domestic threat to his rule while he courted American and European capitalists. Díaz considered himself more than just *el presidente* as he became fixated on kings and emperors, in particular the German kaisers, and the trappings of his government began to resemble an imperial court. Díaz even wore an elaborate mustache and connected sideburns that was very much in keeping with the fashion of the German royalty. Each time Díaz was inaugurated for yet another term as president of Mexico, celebrations occurred from the court of the mikado in Japan to the palace of the emperor in Vienna.

During the Porfiriato, Mexico embarked on a dizzying program of laying railroad tracks and stringing electric and telephone lines, nearly all of it financed by American dollars or European capital. The small group of Mexicans who profited greatly from the investments became known as the *científicos*, men who worshipped at the altar of technological and scientific advancement, regardless of any collateral human suffering. The workers who drove the rail spikes and shoveled ore in the mines were considered expendable by the arrogant engineers in charge. All that concerned the *científicos* was progress as defined by more railroads, more machinery, more mines, and more power lines. That virtual slaves made up the labor force manifesting the progress meant nothing to the *científicos*. These technocrats were the most favored in Díaz's ruling class. They and their women strolled the stylish boulevards in Mexico City wearing the latest fashions from Germany and France as they hobnobbed with Díaz, his closest advisers, high-ranking clerics (the Catholic Church in Mexico was among the richest in the world, even as the poorest of the poor filled its parishes; bishops lived the opulent lives of princes), and visitors from Berlin and Munich. That the *científicos* were loathed by the perhaps 90 percent of the population trapped in poverty caused Mexico's ruling elite no alarm. Díaz, his *federales*, and his *rurales* were there to protect them.

Mexico reached a breaking point early in the twentieth century as the oppression of Díaz's autocracy became too much for the country's rank and file to bear. In spite of all the progress introduced by the *científicos*, impoverished workers grew ever poorer. Issues of class and racism, well entrenched in Mexican society, reached a crisis point. *Indios*, many of whom did not even speak Spanish, had long been discriminated against. The intrusion of foreigners in Mexican life, particularly by *los yanquis* but also by Europeans and Asians, was widely resented. *México para los mexicanos* became a slogan among the exploited people of the country as the great powers of Europe moved toward what would become the World War. Voices of revolution began to resound, coming from within Mexico but also from exiles in cities such as San Antonio, El Paso, Los Angeles, and even St. Louis. Another election rigged to reinstall Díaz for yet another term was too much. An unlikely revolutionary, an *hacendado* from Parras de la Fuente in southern Coahuila, led the movement that overthrew Díaz. Francisco Madero's armed revolt forced Díaz from office in the spring of 1911. In June, Madero entered Mexico City with huge crowds chanting *"¡Viva Madero!"* By November, he had become president.

But plenty of *científicos* and others loyal to the Porfiriato remained in Mexico, and they were anxious for a return to the good old days. The massive federal army Díaz assembled was still intact, if battered; for the most part, its officers held Madero in quiet disdain. Most ominous for the success of Madero's tenure in office was outrage over Díaz's defeat in American corporate boardrooms. Capitalists in the United States were not willing to give up profits from south of the border without a fight. Madero hardly had time to take office before American politicians and businessmen were quietly considering ways to replace him.

Madero did not enact massive change, but from the day he took office, he began to put in place policies that outraged gringo capitalists. Early on he nationalized the T.O. Ranch, an outfit in Chihuahua so massive that it dwarfed Texas's fabled King Ranch. It was owned by Chicago-based businessmen in the meatpacking industry, and about two hundred Texas cowboys were among the outfit's four hundred hands. Once the T.O. acreage began to be redistributed to Mexican farmers and ranchers, the Texas cowboys found themselves suddenly unemployed. On the ranch, they'd lived as if it were still the 1800s. Now they were cast into a world of rapid technological transformation. Unable to find a place for themselves in changing times, many became outlaws, rustling cattle and robbing banks and trains.

Madero's presidency began to unravel because of pressure from Díaz loyalists and from radical revolutionaries who thought he acted too slowly on behalf of the working poor. The American government also wanted him gone so that Mexico could return to being a safe haven for U.S. capital investments. Insurgency broke out in the north, and to crush it Madero turned to an opportunistic sociopath who was both an alcoholic and a cocaine addict, Victoriano Huerta.

Huerta had been a general in Díaz's army and a member of the strongman's unofficial court at Chapultepec Castle. Historian Barbara W. Tuchman described him as possessing "a flat nose, a bullet head, a sphinx's eyes behind incongruous spectacles [often with darkened lenses], and a brandy bottle never far from hand."[14] Alcohol and cocaine had already fouled the health of his eyes—he was typically seen wearing sunglasses, indoors and out—and he was beginning to show the symptoms of cirrhosis of the liver, the disease that eventually killed him. After Díaz fell, Huerta pledged fealty to Madero. Madero accepted it, a decision that cost the new president his life. After crushing Madero's opponents in the north, Huerta began plotting with American State Department officials to overthrow the president he'd pledged to support.

Huerta's great ally during the campaign in the north was Pancho Villa. On his own, Villa and his troops routed insurgent forces in Parral, then joined with Huerta's Federal Army to reclaim the major city of Torreón for Madero. Huerta named Villa an honorary brigadier general as a reward for his service, but saw in Villa a threat who had to be eliminated.

Huerta was right to be concerned about the man born as José Doroteo Arango Arámbula on the massive Rancho de la Coyotada hacienda in the state of Durango. Villa came from a family of peasants and received just a scant education at a Catholic school. Like most children of his class and time, he knew mostly work, work, and more work. When his father died, Villa gave up all pretense of achieving an education. The oldest child in his family, he had to provide for his mother and siblings. He learned many skills, becoming a bricklayer, vaquero, butcher, sharecropper, and *arriero*. An American railroad company even hired him as foreman of a crew working on tracks in Mexico. None of these jobs lasted. He moved into banditry, adopting the name of an earlier bandit leader as his own— Francisco Villa.

Villa quickly rose to the top of *bandido* ranks in Durango, exhibiting leadership skills and making business connections with *hacendados* and affluent businessmen, who eagerly purchased the livestock and goods that Villa and his men had stolen. He was once arrested and impressed into Díaz's army rather than executed, Mexico's usual punishment for bandits. He absorbed much understanding about how the military functioned as well as the fundamentals of warfare strategy during his brief months as a soldier. He deserted and traveled to the state of Chihuahua, where he renewed his life as a bandit leader. He developed a friendship with Abraham González, a freethinking *hacendado*, who became Villa's political mentor. González convinced him to support Madero's revolution. Charismatic, intelligent if all but uneducated, fierce, fearless, and innovative, Villa became one of Madero's earliest and most effective military leaders.

When Pascual Orozco revolted against Madero in the north, Villa stepped forward to fight him. Villa again showed himself to be brilliant and fearless while establishing broad support for his leadership in northern Mexico. Villa was becoming a folk hero, and the ambitious Huerta determined that Villa needed to be eliminated. Huerta confronted Villa and accused him of stealing a horse. In anger, Villa slugged Huerta. Huerta had Villa arrested and ordered that he be shot by a firing squad for insubordination and thievery. Madero intervened to save Villa at the last moment, commuting his sentence to a prison term. At Belem Prison in Mexico City, Villa fell under the tutorship of a fellow inmate, a Zapatista, who not only helped Villa improve his reading and writing but also engaged him politically, expanding his revolutionary thinking. Transferred to another prison, Villa received further tutoring from an imprisoned Federal Army general. Villa escaped prison on Christmas Day in 1912 and crossed into the United States, eventually making his way to El Paso to bide his time until called to return to Mexico.

Huerta meanwhile was busy assembling a coup d'état as Madero continued to alienate much of Mexico with his bumbling government. The best thing for Mexico would have been for Madero to serve out his term, and for the country to select a new president in a fair, democratic election. Huerta wanted none of that. Neither did the United States, where business interests lobbied Republican president William Howard Taft's government to remove Madero. Taft's ambassador in Mexico City, Henry Lane Wilson, became Huerta's coconspirator. In many ways, Wilson was the primary architect of *La Decena Trágica*, the Ten Tragic Days, which unfolded in mid-February 1913.

At the end of *La Decena Trágica*, scores of Mexico City citizens lay dead, caught in the fighting between insurgents and troops loyal to Madero. Huerta, through multiple betrayals and with the help of Wilson's machinations, took charge of the country after forcing Madero to resign the presidency. Huerta promised Madero safe passage out of the country but never intended to honor the agreement. Instead he ordered Madero and his vice president, José María Pino Suárez, to be tortured and murdered. Huerta assumed the title of president a short time later, then began an extreme militarization of Mexico.

Old army cronies who had flourished in the days of the Porfiriato were now in charge of much of the government. The size of his Federal Army quadrupled as Huerta ordered the conscription of thousands of young men, though many deserted when they had the chance. Huerta was so hard-handed that he made Díaz seem like an open-minded compromiser. The sadism of the Huertistas was beyond compare, and blood flowed freely as Mexico entered its darkest period during the sixteen months that Huerta was in power.

More than forty years after his death from cirrhosis in El Paso, Huerta was still cursed as a jackal and usurper and, above all else, the betrayer of the revolution. Madero's reputation, on the other hand, had grown to be that of Mexico's greatest martyr. Villa, meanwhile, had become the stuff of mythology.

6.

By 1962, Green was back in the United States, where he considered what he should do with his future. Like countless other young men and women of the time, he set his eyes on the film industry. Just as he'd shown himself to be a precocious student of biology, he had been a movie buff for years already. Around the time he made his bird and mammal collection expedition to Mexico, he saw Vittorio De Sica's masterworks of neorealism, *Shoeshine* and *Bicycle Thieves*. The gritty portrayal of poverty in De Sica's work left a lasting impression on Green. "I liked things that looked like life," he said. "That's the way those people live." He also liked how some American movies, especially Jules Dassin's *The Naked City*, extended into neorealism, too. "I can't explain why, but it was my preference over science fiction and things like that, which didn't really interest me."[15]

Green faced a major obstacle in finding work as a filmmaker. The studios were cutting back in every way possible. Years later, Green remembered those days as a time when "you could have fired a cannon through Warner Bros. or Twentieth Century-Fox in the middle of the day and not hit anyone."[16] To even get inside the gate to talk to someone about a job, an aspiring industry worker needed a connection. Green's stepfather had died years earlier, and though his colleagues were still around, it never occurred to Green to approach them for a job. Instead, he set his focus on the booming medium of television, which seemed to have plenty of work available.

After kicking around for a while without success, Green remembered a friend from elementary school who had gone to work for David L. Wolper. Wolper had figured out how to assemble stock footage into commercially viable TV documentaries built on well-written teleplays. From that entry point, Wolper went on to direct and produce documentaries, including one that was nominated for an Academy Award. After winning an Emmy for a documentary based on Theodore H. White's *The Making of the President, 1960*, Wolper became the proverbial hot commodity in the business. As a result, Wolper Productions was hiring. With the entrée provided by his school chum, Green signed on to research story ideas. His job was to take a simple concept, usually expressed in a phrase, and develop it into a proposal that Wolper, a former ad salesman, could pitch to sponsors. Green soon learned how important writing was. It had to be "punchy, flashy" stuff for a Wolper documentary to attract the money necessary for a network broadcast. Through this work, Green began to learn the fundamentals of screenwriting. His Wolper job also gave him a foothold in the industry, which he would soon need to employ.

Wolper Productions' business would shoot up and then fall down, as was the case for most independent production companies. During one lull, Wolper temporarily laid off Green. Drawing on his experiences as a student abroad, his ability to speak multiple languages, and the connections he'd made working for Wolper, Green found work on international feature productions as a dialogue coach. It was the ideal job for a screenwriter in the making. Day after day, he read and reread pages of scripts, and as he did so, the underlying structure of a successful story revealed itself to him. Being on set to watch filming also helped him grasp what

Walon Green at work on a documentary in the late 1960s. Photo from the author's collection.

worked and what didn't work in a movie. Soon enough, the directors he worked with asked him to polish dialogue.

Green may have been something of a multilingual biology nerd who was mastering the nuances of screenplay composition, but he also was a rough-and-tumble guy who developed a passion for motorcycles. He fit right in with the high-testosterone L.A. culture of off-road racing at a time when it appealed to many Hollywood types. Green was a regular at a TT track off Mulholland, where he met Lee Marvin among dozens of other racers. Another person Green ran into there was Steve McQueen, who would stroll shirtless among the motorcycles while preparing for his own balls-to-the-wall time trials, never giving off the slightest hint that he was anything more than just another biker gearhead. McQueen had formed a racing team with brothers Dave and Bud Ekins—Bud Ekins doubled for McQueen in John Sturges's massive 1963 hit, *The Great Escape*, and performed the motorcycle jump over a towering barbed-wire fence that became the stuff of movie legend. Another team member was a tough Hollywood character named Cliff Coleman, who was just beginning his career as an assistant director, following in the footsteps of his father, AD and director Charles C. Coleman. In 1964, McQueen, the Ekins brothers, Cliff Coleman, and John Steen became the first Americans to compete in the International Six Days Trial (ISDT), now known as the International Six Days Enduro (ISDE). The ISDT was the oldest and most prestigious race on the Fédération Internationale de Motocyclisme calendar and featured the world's best off-road riders. Coleman rode especially well there and won an individual gold medal on his 500cc Triumph Trophy T100S/R.

Green never claimed championships on par with those won by McQueen, Coleman, or the Ekins brothers, but people in the off-road community accorded Green credit because of his gutsy determination. Green once rode a bike in the dirt from Ensenada south of Tijuana all the way down Baja California to La Paz, probably becoming the first person ever to do so. After returning to L.A., Green rode his battered Triumph Tiger Cub to Bud Ekins's shop, where Green was accorded something of a hero's return: *Jesus, this guy rode to La Paz!* Word spread about him. "I wasn't like a hotdog racer," Green said. "I rode the Big Bear run, and I finished fifty-seventh, but it was out of, like, six hundred bikes. The joke was, 'Well, Green's not very fast, but he'll *finish!*'"[17]

Green's girlfriend was into horseback riding, so the two of them frequented the river-bottom stables along Riverside Drive. There, he met and began to hang out with a bunch of guys who worked in movies as either stuntmen or wranglers. Some of them were pure outlaws. They performed stunts in movies when they had the chance, but they found other means for raising cash when Hollywood wasn't calling. In the mid-1960s, apartment complexes seemed to be sprouting up everywhere in the booming San Fernando Valley. At night, the outlaws from the stables stole air-conditioning units from the new apartment buildings and hauled them to places such as parched-but-booming Yuma, Arizona, where contractors lined up to buy equipment on the cheap, never asking questions about just where it came from.

Some of the outlaws went beyond mere building-site theft to violent crimes. In the mid-1960s, unemployment offices in California paid out cash to recipients, which tempted anyone with armed robbery on his mind. One of the stuntmen—a genuine badass who would drive to a roadhouse between Lancaster and Palmdale just to start brawls with Indians who hung out there—stuck up an unemployment office in Burbank. He shot and killed a security guard. Another stuntman, Jack Coffer, knew the killer from when they'd worked together on cattle ranches up north near Sonora. Coffer didn't like the man, whom he considered to be a dirtbag. Nevertheless, Coffer gave perjured testimony in the murder trial in an unsuccessful attempt to get his fellow stuntman acquitted. Green couldn't understand why Coffer would do such a thing. Coffer said, "Because he came down with me from Sonora, and when you side with a man, you stick with him." Green came to appreciate that one code the cowboys around the stables shared: *When you side with a man, you stick with him*—even the "bad fucking troublemakers."[18] Green began to think that these modern-day cowboys were not so different from the cowboys of the Old West, that harsh place where concepts such as right and wrong and institutions such as law enforcement meant little or were nonexistent. But *loyalty*—that had to be respected. Sam Peckinpah had been raised to respect that notion as well.

7.

On *Morituri*, the Brando picture on whose set Roy Sickner first met Green, Green began to come into his own as a writer, even if he received no screen credit for his scripting. The director was Austrian-born Bernhard Wicki, who later had a memorable cameo as a German doctor in the Wim Wenders/Sam Shepard collaboration *Paris, Texas*. The script for *Morituri* was terrible, which left Brando frustrated and desperate to make improvements. He called for change after change in the script, and because he was Brando, he could get whatever he wanted. The massive number of rewrites would have been problematic on a "normal" production, but *Morituri*'s cast included few English-speaking actors. Most were Germans, and a number of them spoke little to no English. They learned their lines by rote, working with the German-fluent Green. Every time Brando changed lines, Green had to teach the new ones to the Germans. Before long, Brando began asking Green to come up with the new lines himself. Brando liked what Green wrote. So did Wicki, who asked Green to take passes over whole sections of the screenplay as the production struggled to move forward at Catalina. Roy Sickner took notice.

The next year, as Sickner and Green worked on *Winter A-Go-Go*, Sickner made an attempt to interest the picture's producer, Reno Carell, in *The Wild Bunch*, with Sickner himself directing. Carell was barely into his midthirties but had already produced a film before *Winter A-Go-Go*. He owned a production company with William Wellman Jr., son of legendary director "Wild Bill" Wellman, but Carell and the younger Wellman's goals in the picture business fell far below the achievements of Wild Bill. They were interested in churning out fast-paced, cheap fluff for the burgeoning 1960s youth market. Carell seemed to be an odd match, at best, for *The Wild Bunch*.

Carell possessed the producer's greatest skill: He knew where to find cash—at least, he'd been able to go to the well a couple of times. Carell grew enthusiastic as Sickner described *The Wild Bunch*. Thinking he had a deal in the works, Sickner realized he needed money to kick off preproduction. He contacted a Chicago investment banker he knew through skiing connections, Anthony M. Ryerson, who had helped finance development at Squaw Valley. Ryerson gave Sickner several thousand dollars in exchange for points in the movie. Sickner used $1,500 of Ryerson's money to hire Green to write a treatment.

Buck Holland and his sister had already cobbled together some sort of treatment based on those liquor-fueled sessions with Lee Marvin at Chez Jay, but it was less than rudimentary, so vague on details that the characters lacked names. Sickner never bothered to show it to Green. Instead, Sickner arrived at Green's house, sat down before a small reel-to-reel tape recorder, and dictated a plot outline: Some guys rob a train depot in Texas, run across the border to Mexico with a posse chasing them, and meet some *bandidos* who hire them to steal guns from the U.S. Army. The American outlaws are successful in stealing the guns and take off, after collecting their money from the Mexicans. However, the *bandidos* planned a double-cross all along. They set off after the American outlaws with the intent of taking their money back. Finally, American outlaws, *bandidos*, and posse all get caught up in a big gunfight. The end. It wasn't much of a story. As had been true all along, the appeal came from stuntman Sickner's description of the action sequences he envisioned.

Sickner had envisioned his story taking place in Mexico during the 1870s or 1880s. Green, the student of Mexican history and culture, persuaded Sickner that the 1870s were somewhat boring in Mexico. Green thought it would be much more interesting to set the action along the Texas-Mexico border during the Mexican Revolution in the 1910s. At that time, *la frontera*, the border between Texas and Mexico, remained dominated by horse culture. However, it was being invaded by automobiles, electric lines, telephones, and what were, by the standard of the times, weapons of mass destruction: machine guns, hand grenades, bomb-dropping aircraft, and semiautomatic sidearms. Green wanted to include all of it. The story he envisioned concerned men caught up in this change, out of step with their times. Sickner quickly agreed. Green's imagination remained passionately fired by all those stories he'd heard from Ríos Zertuche and others in Mexico. Green was also influenced by Barbara Tuchman's *The Zimmerman Telegram*, a book detailing

Germany's meddling in the Mexican Revolution as Kaiser Wilhelm II sought global dominance for his country during the early years of World War I. To get a sense of what things looked like in Mexico during the revolution, Green watched and rewatched a documentary that turned up at L.A. art houses.

That film was *Memorias de un mexicano*, which actress, poet, and filmmaker Carmen Toscano had created using footage shot by her father, Salvador Toscano. The Mexican Revolution occurred just at the time that movies emerged as a major entertainment and news medium. American picture companies dispatched crank-turning cameramen south of the border to capture battle scenes and carnage to exhibit in storefront nickelodeons across the United States. Mexico had its own filmmakers, with Salvador Toscano ranking chief among them in the early days. He was Mexico's first filmmaker, shooting documentaries as early as 1896. Because of his high regard in Mexico, Salvador Toscano was accorded access to even Díaz. Salvador Toscano also shot footage of the other major players in the revolution: Madero, Villa, Zapata, Carranza, Obregón, Orozco, and Huerta. More important, he captured on film scenes of everyday life during revolutionary times, ranging from extravagant celebrations during the Porfiriato to scenes of bombarded buildings and rail lines as well as dead humans and horses lying in the streets.

Salvador Toscano ceased making films in the 1920s, and his work, which portrayed a distinctly Mexican point of view, was largely forgotten when Carmen Toscano began assembling it into *Memorias*. Her film appeared at the peak of the Golden Age of Mexican cinema, which ran roughly from the mid-1940s until the late 1950s. *Memorias* became a Cannes Film Festival entry, winning international acclaim. For Green, *Memorias* provided visual imagery to flesh out the stories he'd heard from Ríos Zertuche.

Green wrote his treatment for *The Wild Bunch*, and the plot never changed much from that point, though he and Peckinpah would both do extensive rewrites in the years to come. Green told me he did not have a precise date in mind for *The Wild Bunch*, just that it would take place after *La Decena Trágica* and before the despot Huerta's fall from power—sometime between February 19, 1913, and July 15, 1914. Pancho Villa, outraged by the murders of Madero and Abraham González, the governor of Chihuahua, began gathering forces to overthrow Huerta in March 1913. By that year's close, Villa had achieved spectacular victories in Mexico's northern states and had become the provisional governor of Chihuahua. He had also become a legend among the Mexican people of the north.

Though Villa never appears as a character in the story Green concocted, he is a strong unseen presence. It is likely, then, that Green's tale occurs at the end of 1913 or in the first few months of 1914.

Of the upper stretch of the Rio Grande in Texas, Jefferson Morgenthaler wrote: "For five centuries there have been many reasons to come here, but few reasons to linger."[19] This was especially true during the time of the revolution. Opportunists arrived by the hundreds hoping to make a quick score, but many other people fled the area because *la frontera* had developed into one of the most dangerous places on earth at the time of Green's tale. Law enforcement officers, soldiers, revolutionaries, and bandits were active on both sides of the river. Most were armed to the teeth. Few had any compunction about killing other human beings if the need arose. Ranching and rustling merged into a blur. Banks and railroads were fair game.

Green began his story with a gang of outlaws riding into a Texas border town situated not too far from the Rio Grande, maybe a town such as Uvalde, Del Rio, or Langtry. Ever since the Mexican-American War, the border between Mexico and Texas had been in contention. The U.S. government and most Americans believed the border was the Rio Grande. Most Mexicans thought the line lay much farther to the north, along the Nueces River through much of Texas. Or perhaps it is more accurate to say that Mexicans by and large believed the whole of Texas as well as enormous stretches of the American Southwest and California had been stolen from them by the United States as an invading power seventy years earlier. For many years, small towns in Texas north of the Rio Grande and west of San Antonio remained culturally Mexican. The advent of railroads brought an influx of white people to the area. Town names changed as an uneasy merging of cultures took place. Green selected just such a town in flux for the setting of the opening of his story.

Even the name of this fictional town is in transition. It was known as San Rafael in its earliest incarnation. With the arrival of the railroad and white Bible-thumping businessmen, the name is being changed to Starbuck. San Rafael/Starbuck straddles the tracks of a major railroad, undoubtedly based on the Southern Pacific and its line extending from San Antonio to El Paso and beyond. The outlaws are not green kids. They are well experienced at what they are doing. They are there to rob the railroad office. At the time, thousands of American soldiers were stationed in South Texas along the Rio Grande in reaction to the revolution and border violence. These troops were paid in cash shipped by railroad to military commanders. Also, railroad workers were paid in cash, so at any given time a railroad office might well have a lot of money. Moreover, the outlaws have been tipped off that an army payroll shipment is to arrive in the town. But it was a deliberately false tip. They've been set up. The railroad, alerted by an informant, has a company of armed bounty hunters awaiting the bandits' arrival. An ensuing shootout claims many casualties, including a number of gang members, as the robbers ride away. They disappear into Mexico, only to discover that their loot is not gold coins but instead nearly worthless steel washers. They have lost comrades and placed themselves at grave personal risk, all for nothing. Their future is uncertain. They are not young men, except for one new recruit, who comes from Mexico. The survivors, five gringos and one Mexican, move deeper into revolutionary Mexico to figure out what to do next.

They arrive at a town under the military control of one of Huerta's henchmen. The Huertista general, at the urging of his German advisers, entices the Americans to hijack a shipment of U.S. Army repeating rifles in exchange for gold. The gang agrees to do the general's bidding. They succeed in their hijack and hightail it back to Mexico, pursued by the bounty hunters as well as the U.S. Army cavalry. The Mexican member of the gang persuades the others to give up a case of rifles to people from his village. They turn out to be Villistas (followers of Villa) fighting the very Federal Army units commanded by the Huertista general who hired the wild bunch. The other gang members agree to give up the rifles in exchange for the Mexican's share of the gold. The wild bunch delivers the rifles to the general, case by case, cautiously. One case is missing; the gang lies about what happened to it, but the general knows the rifles were given to the villagers, and he blames the young Mexican member of the gang. The gringo members of the gang surrender their comrade to the general. While the general tortures the Mexican, a fiesta breaks out to celebrate the acquisition of the arms. The gringo members of the wild bunch now have enough gold to set them up for the rest of their lives. There is no reason to celebrate, however. They've sacrificed their colleague to a horrible death. They have an ethical obligation to attempt to save their friend. It means certain death for them, but they have a code of honor they must address. They are no different from Green's stuntman friend Jack Coffer, who stood up for his fellow stuntman during the murder trial. Now they have to stand up. A massive gunfight ends the story. All the members, except one old man, die in the carnage. The old man signs up with the Villistas.

As the treatment and then scripts underwent multiple revisions, first by Green, then, especially, by Peckinpah, the scope of the story would be considerably enlarged and refined. *The Wild Bunch* became a saga of men out of their time who face a fundamental ethical challenge. The men love each other in their own way and stand up for each other in the end. It would become a cautionary story about the dehumanizing effect of technology and the value of old codes of behavior versus what developed in the twentieth century. Much of this was still to be infused into the project, but Green provided a foundation that could carry additional weight. And more. It was Peckinpah who made the characters who inhabit *The Wild Bunch* so compelling. Still, it was Green who gave them their names, drawing mostly from people he knew in real life.

Green assigned the name of his stuntman friend Jack Coffer to the worst of the worst of the bounty hunters. The soulless railroad man who hired the bounty hunters in the first place wound up as Harrigan because railroad men "were often Irish. Harrigan was a hard-sounding Irish name that felt right for this kind of man." Green knew a family he described as being "real mill trash" with the last name of Gorch, so he gave that surname to two surly brothers who were members of the wild bunch. One he called Lyle; the other, Tector, after a guy Green once cleaned swimming pools with. Thornton, the former gang member who led the bounty killers, was named for a kid Green went to grade school with. He named the gang's second-in-command Dutch because it was a "warm and comfortable-sounding name, and I wanted to indicate something of those qualities in the man."[20]

For the leader of the gang, he created the name Pike Bishop. "Pike was a name I always wanted to use," Green said. "It's a kind of carnivorous fish, and it suggested someone who is tough and predatory." His last name, Bishop, carried no special meaning for Green. A half century after he wrote the treatment, I asked Green if he'd come up with Pike Bishop as a play on Bishop Pike, James A. Pike, the eccentric Episcopal coadjutor of California who appeared frequently on television in the mid-1960s to speak out against the war in Vietnam and racial prejudice. No, Green said, he'd given no thought to the cleric. If there was a connection of some sort, it was purely subconscious.[21]

Green showed the most naming creativity by calling his Huertista general Mapache. To many Anglos who read his treatment and subsequent screenplays, the name carried no particular significance. A few might have recognized it as the word for "raccoon" in Spanish, but Green knew from living in Mexico that the word *mapache* carried connotations

Mexican Revolution general Antonio Ríos Zertuche (center) circa 1910. Walon Green developed the character of Mapache based on stories he heard from Zertuche and other fighters in the revolution. Photo from the author's collection.

that went beyond a mere descriptor. Along the border, *el mapache* was considered an agent of evil. The word *mapache* itself seemed to have evolved from an ancient Aztec term for "thief." Green knew exactly what he was doing. He avoided stereotypical Mexican names and instead used one that suggested something sinister.

Green also infused his story with images he thought were meaningful and fresh, one being that of a Texas cowboy with a Colt Model 1911 .45-caliber automatic pistol in his holster instead of the standard six-shooter. "I really wrote the film because it was a film I wanted to see," he said. "I'd seen a lot of Westerns. They were usually heroic, some of them were very good. They played to these mythic characters." Green thought Westerns by and large were too heroic, too glamorous: "I'd read enough to know that Billy the Kid shot people in the back of the head while they were drinking coffee." Green wanted to recast the mythic, heroic cowboys of American Westerns on their ear. He gave them some of the characteristics and values of the stuntmen he knew, which stood at odds with those of the mythic heroes of most American Westerns. "I imagined that was what people in the early West were like." But it went beyond just the West. Green wrote *The Wild Bunch* "to show that the world is an immensely violent place." He later said, "I wrote it, thinking that I would like to see a Western that was as mean and ugly and brutal as the times, and the only nobility in men was their dedication to each other."[22]

8.

Roy Sickner was pleased with the work of the all-but-unknown writer he'd hired. He shared the twenty-eight-page treatment with his star, Lee Marvin. Sickner, Green, and Marvin met to hear Marvin pronounce his approval. It was more than that: Marvin loved it. He had suggestions, and while Marvin was no writer, he possessed a good sense of story and knew much about history, particularly military history. "I would go a little farther out with it," Marvin told Green. "Since you're setting it in a different era from most Westerns, why don't you *really* go there? Why don't you have these guys come into town looking like Pershing's troops along the border, you know, dressed as doughboys?"[23] Green ate up Marvin's idea. It made perfect sense, given that the American side of the border became highly militarized with all those thousands of U.S. soldiers stationed along the Rio Grande. It was reasonable that a group of uniformed, armed soldiers would arrive in town on horseback and proceed to the railroad office.

The more telling details Green could add, the more his story would shine with verisimilitude. The U.S. border with Mexico was among the deadliest regions on earth during the 1910s—the perfect setting for a picture that would at its foundation be an action-adventure epic. Gangs such as those formed by the vanquished cowhands from the T.O. Ranch were a serious liability for railroads and banks in the region; some of the gangs were made up of both gringos and *mexicanos*. The wild bunch of criminals Green developed was much like those real-life outlaw bands.[24]

Law enforcement on the Texas side of the river, composed by and large of bigoted, dishonest, and corrupt men, could be worse than the criminals themselves. Pascual Orozco met his demise in the Lone Star State at the hands of a posse led by Dave Allison, a onetime sheriff and Texas Ranger who was notorious for killing ethnic Mexicans simply because they were Mexicans. Allison believed that Orozco and his companions were *Mexican* horse thieves. *White* horse thieves would not have been shot outright. Allison only later learned that he'd killed one of the most important figures in the Mexican Revolution.

Sam Peckinpah once said the setting for *The Wild Bunch* was along the Rio Grande in Texas's Big Bend Country; during the Mexican Revolution, white Texans sometimes shot Mexicans walking along the opposite bank, just for sport. On occasion, Mexicans shot at Texans from the other side. Bob Keil, an American cavalry enlisted man from Pennsylvania, was stationed in the upper Big Bend and observed killings from both sides. He thought the Texans were the worst offenders, by a ratio of ten to one. Bad as violence was there during the 1910s, matters were even worse down the river in the counties known as the Valley. There, Texas Rangers and their allied posses murdered or uprooted thousands of ethnic Mexicans to acquire land for U.S. agricultural concerns. Even Walter Prescott Webb, a conservative defender of the Rangers, conceded that between five hundred and five thousand Tejanos died in the Valley carnage during the 1910s, "but the actual number can never be known." The existential sense of violence was overwhelming up and down the river.[25]

Green certainly wanted to capture this bloody atmosphere in the movie he was imagining, and Marvin's suggestions helped, especially his urging Green to have the gang show up in the border town as American soldiers. At this meeting, however, Marvin straightforwardly shared his concern about starring in the picture. He'd just finished production on a movie based on a novel by Frank O'Rourke, who was one of those guys banging away at typewriters in the mid-1960s to churn out three or four or more lightweight novels a year. In 1964, O'Rourke published a border yarn he called *A Mule for the Marquesa*. The film rights wound up in the hands of Columbia, where it was assigned to writer turned director and producer Richard Brooks. Brooks was a natural-born storyteller, though no one in the movie business liked him much—he seemed perpetually angry and was often abusive—but he was obsessed with making good movies, and for that he was respected. He transformed *A Mule for the Marquesa* into a screenplay called *The Professionals* and filmed it with a cast headed by Marvin, Burt Lancaster, and Claudia Cardinale, and with a strong supporting cast, including Robert Ryan. With dialogue edgy for the times, a few comic book elements, first-rate acting from seasoned pros, and crisp direction from Brooks, *The Professionals* had all the markings of a hit that would, once released, only elevate Marvin's standing in Hollywood.

Marvin's issue with *The Wild Bunch* was with its setting and period. *The Professionals* was a latter-day Western set in Mexico during the revolution, as was Sickner's *The Wild Bunch*. Marvin wanted to maintain his hard-earned spot on the A-list and feared it would be a bad career move for him to do two movies so similar so close together. He did not drop out of the project, but his concern was ominous.

Undeterred, Sickner moved forward. Using his Ryerson money, he paid Green to develop a full-fledged screenplay. Green wrote and rewrote the script for *The Wild Bunch* and returned to working for Wolper, assuming his work on the project was complete. Wolper was moving into feature films, so Green gave a copy of the *Wild Bunch* script to a Wolper associate, Ted Strauss, who filed it away, unread. A couple of years later, as the trades reported production was commencing on *The Wild Bunch*, a livid Wolper confronted Green. "I can't fucking believe it!" Wolper shouted. "You wrote a fucking movie for William Holden, you never told me about it!" Green explained that he wrote the film during the time he'd been laid off from Wolper. His boss would have none of it. He accused Green of writing it on Wolper's time: "You son of a bitch, I own it!" No, Green assured him, Wolper didn't. After Green told him that he'd actually submitted the screenplay to Strauss, Wolper summoned Strauss, who admitted he'd never gotten around to reading the Western Green had given him. Thus, the tempest died down. For now, Green put *The Wild Bunch* out of his mind and buckled down to work on Wolper projects, which led him to travel the globe as he produced and directed some of television's most respected and successful documentaries, including Jacques Cousteau and *National Geographic* specials.

9.

Producer Reno Carell moved on from *Winter A-Go-Go* to write, produce, and act in *A Swingin' Summer*, yet another beach movie. He notched a small claim to fame with this film by casting Raquel Welch, until then best known as a television weather girl, in her first featured role. Carell's films ended up in the black, but his production company still operated on the cheap. He ran the numbers on what it would cost to film *The Wild Bunch* and choked on the number. It was way out of his range. He told Sickner that he was passing.[26] So now Sickner had to begin shopping his film around town all over again.

He thought Green's script still needed work, so he turned his attention once again to an old friend, Sam Peckinpah, who had in just a couple of years gone from golden boy director to Peck's bad boy in the eyes of Hollywood power brokers following a couple of disastrous projects. They blacklisted Peckinpah, not for his politics—he was a lifelong Democrat—but for his independence and his refusal to kowtow to producers and executives who were wrong in the demands they made of him. However, his reputation as a writer remained intact, something that was not lost on producers and directors who needed script work done. Sickner dipped into Ryerson money yet again and hired Sam for rewrites. Peckinpah gladly accepted the work. Sam had forgotten his conversation about *The Wild Bunch* with Sickner on the set of the ill-fated *Major Dundee*, but Sam had heard Lee Marvin speak of Sickner's pet project. Peckinpah needed cash, but soon after he started reworking Sickner's Western, *The Wild Bunch* became something more to him than just a writing project—much, much more.

PART II

"Who the Hell Is They?"

1.

S am Peckinpah was a rarity, a Hollywood director known for Westerns who could actually claim to be a Westerner himself. He was an "old Californian," with both his mother's and his father's families landing in the Golden State as the fabled gold rush that began in 1849 reached its peak in the 1850s. They arrived as part of a seismic population shift for the North American continent as tens of thousands of white Protestants poured into an area that had largely been home only to American Indians and Californios. His mother's family, the Churches, and the Peckinpahs seemed to have been around Central California and the city of Fresno, where Sam was born as David Samuel Peckinpah on February 21, 1925, for as long as dirt.

The Churches were the more distinguished family when Sam drew his first breath; his grandfather, Denver Church, had once served in the U.S. House of Representatives. Whatever social stature Church achieved, he came by it honestly. He'd been born to extremely poor parents, both of whom died of tuberculosis when the future congressman was just a child. He was shuffled around to relatives, but for the most part, Denver Church made his way through a demanding world on his own from the time he was just a boy. By the time Sam was born, Church had left Congress and was an affluent lawyer, judge, and stockman in Fresno and Madera counties. Church ran a couple of hundred head of cattle on the four-thousand-acre Dunlap Ranch, named for the American Indian from whom Church purchased it.

David Peckinpah, Sam's father, worked on Denver's ranch as a young man. (He would leave to take a job driving the stagecoach running between the Madera County hamlets of North Fork and South Fork, near Shuteye Peak.) David caught the eye of Church's daughter, Fern, and with Church's enthusiastic approval, a romance developed between the two, leading to marriage. Church saw much to admire in the young David Peckinpah and helped him get an education. With his father-in-law's support, the onetime stagecoach driver became an attorney himself and entered Church's law practice. David came to be regarded around Fresno as the living, breathing embodiment of a character from a Horatio Alger story, being well respected by people from all social levels in the small city. Abraham Lincoln was his hero, and people around Central California could see at least a touch of the Great Emancipator in David Peckinpah.

David sometimes spoke in aphorisms, many of them rooted in the King James Version of the Bible, which he knew front to back. From the Gospel of Luke, he knew the parable of the Pharisee and the tax collector. In particular, these lines resonated with him: *I tell you, this man went down to his house justified rather than the other: for every one that exalteth himself shall be abased; and he that humbleth himself shall be exalted.* David drew from those words a maxim his son Sam associated with his father: *All I want is to enter my house justified.* Sam held complete respect for David and later rendered him into the character of Steve Judd in *Ride the High Country.* The high regard for his father remained even as Sam grew up to be a different sort of man from his father.

"My father, David E. Peckinpah," Sam once said, "and also my grandfather, Denver Church, and my brother, Denver C. Peckinpah—they were all superior court judges." He added, "They were the gunfighters. When I was a kid, I grew up with those people, including my uncle, Earl Church, sitting around the dining room table and talking about law and order, truth and justice, and the Bible, which was very big in our family. I suppose that I felt I was an outsider. And I started to question them. I'm still questioning."[1]

Denver Church and David Peckinpah may have been professional men, but they were deeply rooted in traditions of the West, in the land and its people, and never turned loose of those roots. Sam Peckinpah's anteced-ents included timbermen, miners, cowboys, and ranchers—the kinds of characters readers could have found in Western novels of the early twen-tieth century.

Sam's Church grandparents had wandered around states in the West as a young couple, ranging as far as Montana and the Dakotas. "My grandmother was one of the great ladies of the world," Sam said. "I was raving about Calamity Jane. She turned and told me that she was a dirty, drunken woman. And she smelled bad. And I said, 'Well, how do you know?' And she said, 'Because I saw her and talked to her. And your grandfather spent too much time with her!'"[2]

Sam was not above occasional self-mythologizing. At least once he said he was born on the side of Peckinpah Mountain in Madera County, where his grandfather had once operated a sawmill. The truth is that he came into this world in a hospital in Fresno, where his father was making a good living as an attorney. Eventually the family moved to a large, comfortable house in Clovis, a town that hugged the northeast city limit of Fresno. Though one municipality bled into the other with virtually no physical notice, the social chasm between them had always been substantial. During Sam's youth, Fresno, though segregated, was a multicultural city, largely blue-collar, with pockets of affluence and poverty, and where people knew "their place." Some Mexican American Fresnans would come to refer to the irrigation ditch that ran alongside McKinley Avenue as the Rio Grande: "Mexico" on one side, "America" on the other.[3]

Clovis was different territory. It was whiter, more affluent, and more exclusive than Fresno. It also embraced cowboy culture by hosting the Clovis Rodeo, one of the oldest and largest such events on the West Coast. At the time Sam was growing up, a white kid from Clovis might go through life unsullied by the kind of tough circumstances suffered by the hardworking but impoverished characters in Fresno whom William Saroyan wrote about. Sam never wanted for much in toys, clothes, and, later, automobiles. He took an earnest interest in reading and enjoyed movies and the radio dramas popular in the 1930s.

But the time Sam spent as a youth on his grandfather's ranch made more of an impression on him than anything he experienced in town. There he was exposed to the rigors of raising cattle but also to the wonders of nature and the freedom found in the wild. When he was an adult, it would seem to his friends that Peckinpah always seemed most at ease whenever he could escape the city for wide-open spaces or mountains. He could find both at the Dunlap Ranch. He was also introduced to ranch hands who came from a different era.

One was Bill Dillon, who was in his sixties when Sam knew him. That meant Dillon had been born in the 1870s, when outlaws still rode the owl-hoot trail and when battles between U.S. cavalry forces and Plains Indians still made the newspapers regularly. In the 1930s, Dillon ran the lower portion of the Dunlap Ranch. He stood well over six feet tall, wore overalls, and carried a double-action .45-caliber pistol in the bib, along with a large pocket watch. One day a mule kicked in him the chest, but the watch and the pistol shielded him somewhat. The blow knocked him off his feet. Dillon lifted himself off the ground, looked at the mule, and said, "Well, how'd you like to kiss my sister's black cat's ass?" Sam filed that line away in his memory, just as he did many other lines he'd heard growing up around men like Dillon, men who seemed to have outlived their times.[4]

Those men, as well as David Peckinpah and Denver Church, subscribed to what was known as the Code of the West. Diana Serra Cary, who, as I write, is the last surviving child star from the Silent Era, was the daughter of a real cowhand who began working on Broncho Billy Anderson pictures when moviemaking was in its infancy. (Anderson had been the star of the very first Western, *The Great Train Robbery*, then went to Central California in 1909, where he filmed dozens of shorts around Niles Canyon.) The movie industry never turned Cary's father's head away from his core beliefs. He was always a cowboy first and foremost, and he pledged himself to live by the code, whose primary tenet was honesty—keeping your word meant everything—followed by courage. There was no room for grumbling, nor for bellyaching about being tired. You sucked it up when you faced difficulty. Loyalty to a friend was paramount—no dry-gulching, no behind-the-back character assassination. A cowboy who followed the code was someone you'd "ride the river with."[5] As evidenced by Sam's later films, these were the

Sam Peckinpah and his big brother, Denver, circa 1930. Photo courtesy of Adra Brown.

ethics that he came to value the most. As he moved into adulthood, he would be outraged that so few twentieth-century people gave the Code of the West much credence. His fate was to wind up working in an industry in which riches and ego trumped almost everything else, and in whose boardrooms standards such as those embodied in the Code of the West were an anachronism.

Peckinpah also received daily exposure to the Bible. His mother converted to the "new religious movement" known as Christian Science, which embraced the belief that prayer and prayer alone cured sickness, and her family likewise joined the faith. Bible reading and spiritual discussions were a mainstay in the Peckinpah household. L. Q. Jones, who appeared in more Peckinpah movies than anyone else, would say that Sam's pictures were always religious at their foundation.[6] Peckinpah carried a Bible with him throughout his life.

Fern Church Peckinpah was a difficult woman, but she did instill in Sam an interest in creativity. She was widely known for her horticultural talents, and she was a skilled watercolorist: A painting of Fern's survives in the Peckinpah family—it depicts Fern herself riding a horse with a slain deer draped over the pommel.

2.

As an adolescent Peckinpah had a discipline problem. Even the stern David Peckinpah couldn't get his son to straighten up and fly right. In keeping with the practices of relatives from the Peckinpah side of the family, Sam began drinking regularly, which sent his teetotaler mother into fits of denial. He was seldom short of female attention, and his romantic conquests became legend among his male friends; they'd call him the make-out king. This was not lost on his father, who made Peckinpah sit through a statutory-rape trial so he could observe firsthand what happened to boys who went too far. The experience gave Sam nightmares.

School problems began to multiply, and his parents were at a loss as to what to do. He began high school in Fresno, where the faculty regarded him as juvenile delinquent. David and Fern transferred him to the suburban high school in Clovis, but even that failed to improve Sam's behavior. Finally, they packed him off to San Rafael Military Academy, in Marin County, two hundred miles from Fresno. San Rafael combined military discipline with all the trappings (swimming pool, tennis courts) of a high-end boarding school for boys of privilege. Peckinpah chafed at the strict rules, endless drilling, and martial orderliness of the place. He took every chance he could to escape to his favorite refuge, the local movie houses.

The darkened theater smelling of popcorn was familiar turf. Sam had haunted Fresno's moving-picture palaces from the time he was a boy. Like other kids of his generation, he watched mindless shoot-'em-up serials featuring the likes of Gene Autry and William "Hopalong Cassidy" Boyd. Westerns were starting to change, some of them morphing into big-budget movies aimed at grown-ups. In 1936, Paramount released Cecil B. DeMille's *The Plainsman*, a spectacle made up of almost completely fictionalized tales of George Armstrong Custer, Wild Bill Hickok, Buffalo Bill Cody, and Calamity Jane. Broad and splashy, it ultimately was no deeper than spit on a flat rock, yet people across the country lined up to watch it. It joined a short list of other major-studio Westerns released around that time that also proved successful, RKO's *Annie Oakley* and Paramount's *Wells Fargo* among them. These hits renewed producers' interest in Westerns. The year Sam turned fourteen, John Ford, who had been among the innovators who created the genre back in the early days of silent pictures, returned to the Western with a vengeance with a picture called *Stagecoach*. It changed everything.

People who sought out something more than simple entertainment at the flicks found plenty in *Stagecoach* to captivate them. Beyond that, it acted as a creative catalyst affecting filmmakers worldwide. Orson Welles, preparing to expand from the stage and radio to film, screened *Stagecoach* as many forty times, captivated by the seamless camera work and editing. Welles famously said his three big influences as a filmmaker were John Ford, John Ford, and John Ford. Welles said, "My style has nothing to do with his, but *Stagecoach* was my textbook."[7] Without *Stagecoach*, there would be no *Citizen Kane*, at least not as we know it. Ford's sophisticated use of camera angles, character point of view, scene lighting, and shot composition fired up Welles's imagination as he considered film possibilities.

Ford set *Stagecoach* in Monument Valley, located on the Navajo Nation not far from Four Corners. Most of the significant events related to non-Native migration into the West occurred in grassy country, places such as Abilene and Dodge City in western Kansas. Monument Valley was a far different locale. Nevertheless, with *Stagecoach*, Ford established it as the quintessential setting for the mythical West. A shot of those stunning sandstone buttes rising above the sunbaked Colorado Plateau was all it took to signal moviegoers that they were watching a Western.

Stagecoach also elevated John Wayne to major-star status, lifting him from B-movie obscurity. That in itself changed Westerns forever as the Duke came to epitomize the American cowboy. If *Stagecoach* made a star out of John Wayne, the film's MVP was a stuntman Wayne brought with him from Hollywood's Poverty Row to serve as his double as well as perform other stunts in the movie. Like earlier cowboy stars Hoot Gibson and Art Acord, Yakima Canutt was a Westerner with real ranch credentials. While still a teenager, he became a familiar contestant at major rodeos of the early 1900s: Cheyenne Frontier Days, Pendleton Round-Up,

Calgary Stampede. By the time he turned seventeen, he was recognized as a world-champion bronco rider. Soon he went to work in pictures, where he made a name as a stuntman.

Canutt performed stunt after stunt in *Stagecoach* that astonished audiences and went on to become legendary in moviemaking. All were innovative and convincing and raised the bar for stunts in any movie, especially cowboy pictures. By the time Peckinpah was directing pictures himself, stunt work had become something of an art itself, and first-rate stunts would become a hallmark of his films. *Stagecoach* was also different because of how it portrayed the cowboy hero. It narrowed the gap between good and bad, which opened a whole range of possibilities for future filmmakers such as Peckinpah.

Revisionist Western was a term that would not become in vogue for another thirty years or more, but John Wayne was convinced that he had just completed production on one when *Stagecoach* wrapped. "Let me explain something about my career," he said later. "They've never made a point of this, but I have tried never to play the pure hero. I have always been a character of some kind."[8] Even while working on Poverty Row serials, he attempted to avoid the white hat, white-gloved stereotypes established by Tom Mix, Buck Jones, and Tim McCoy. Those supermen on horseback never started a fight. They always waited for the other guy to throw the first punch, then fought in a way that Wayne described as "pure and clean," which Wayne wanted no part of. He eschewed fancy cowboy outfits worn by pure heroes. When it came to fighting, the characters he portrayed damned sure threw the first punch if they had a chance. If it helped win the fight, they'd hit a guy over the head with a chair. Wayne's antihero persona carried over to *Stagecoach*. As the Ringo Kid, Wayne was an outlaw whom audiences embraced, just as Claire Trevor won empathy for her portrayal of an unrepentant prostitute. *Stagecoach* proved moviegoers could care about less-than-wholesome characters, and set loose a stampede of Western movies with increasingly sophisticated characters and plotlines, all of which set the foundation for the classic movie Peckinpah would make thirty years later.

3.

At a movie house not far from San Rafael Academy, Peckinpah took in one of the Western art films that appeared in the wake of *Stagecoach*. Director Wild Bill Wellman based *The Ox-Bow Incident* on Walter Van Tilburg Clark's novel of the same title, itself a landmark of Western writing. *The Ox-Bow Incident* was by any measure a literary novel, not a pulp Western, and was built on the structure of a five-act classical tragedy. It concerned three men who are lynched for a murder that never actually occurred.

Wellman, like Ford, was a tough-guy director. Wellman had looked death in the face a number of times as a flying ace during World War I. He had downed six German aircraft and limped from having been shot down himself by antiaircraft fire. Foppish studio bosses and producers with good manicures and inflated egos posed no threat to him. While vacationing at Arrowhead Hot Springs in the early 1940s, Wellman was approached by a bottom-feeder producer who gave him a copy of *The Ox-Bow Incident*. Wellman read the book over the next couple of days. He returned to his work in Hollywood, but his thoughts kept turning to *The Ox-Bow Incident* and the tragic contours of the story. He acquired the film rights for the book and began to shop it to every studio for which he'd ever made a picture. All of them passed, considering such a dark story to be box-office poison. Finally, Wellman went to Twentieth Century-Fox and pitched *The Ox-Bow Incident* to mogul Darryl F. Zanuck, who agreed to read the book. A short time later, Zanuck offered Wellman a deal. "It won't make a dime," Zanuck said, "but I want my name on it."[9] The other execs at Fox thought Zanuck had lost his mind. Zanuck was convinced he was right and sent the picture into production.

Zanuck was right. *The Ox-Bow Incident*, released a year later, was no hit. It opened at theaters in 1943, a year when Hollywood mostly turned out escapist, feel-good fare for a nation at war. *The Ox-Bow Incident* hardly fit into that category. In addition to its somber theme, the movie pushed racial buttons in ways that were uncommon in American cinema. The most honorable and humane of all the characters is Sparks, a poor African American preacher, played by Harvard Law School graduate and Negro Actors Guild founder Leigh Whipper. The most educated and sophisticated character is a Mexican, Juan Martínez, played by Anthony Quinn, who had been born Antonio Rodolfo Quinn Oaxaca in Chihuahua during the Mexican Revolution; his grandfather was an Irish immigrant turned Villista. By comparison, the white characters come off as ignorant rubes. None of this was in keeping with what audiences expected from Hollywood movies. A young Harry Morgan, who costarred in *The Ox-Bow Incident* with Henry Fonda, saw the movie in a theater, where audience reaction to it was cool. As Morgan was leaving, Orson Welles stepped up to him and said, "They don't realize what they just saw."

But a teenage Sam Peckinpah, smarting from military-school regulations and hunkered down in a theater for refuge, understood exactly what he saw: a masterpiece of acting, writing, and, most of all, directing. When he returned to Fresno, he carried on about the picture to his younger, adopted sister, Fern Lea, describing to her tricks he'd noticed Wellman using to keep the film from getting sentimental, "too mushy and weepy eyed."[10] It was the first time he described directorial technique to anyone. When he watched *The Ox-Bow Incident*, he allowed his mind to slide inside a movie itself. It was a life-changing experience.

4.

There was no question that Peckinpah would join the military as soon as he graduated from San Rafael. He enlisted in the U.S. Marine Corps. By the time he shipped out, Japan had surrendered, so Peckinpah engaged in no combat. His orders took him to China, where he served with marine observers of the civil war between Maoists and KMT supporters of Chiang Kai-shek. He carried home with him tales of torture and public executions, including beheadings, all of which he viewed firsthand. He also witnessed the torture of Maoist prisoners and complained to his commanding officer. He received a stiff rebuke: The marines were there only to observe, not to intervene. Sam was infuriated by the officer's response.

Even if the marines were in China only as observers, they nonetheless faced danger. Peckinpah once rode on a train that came under fire from Communist insurgents. He huddled on the floor to protect himself as shots slammed into the passenger car. Everything seemed to move in slow motion. The attack was actually quite brief, but to Peckinpah it *felt* as if it lasted much longer. He filed away this event along with the images burned into his mind of the tortured Maoist prisoners. He would use them later once he started directing.

His service in the marines left Peckinpah conflicted. He bought into *semper fidelis*, but his experiences also challenged that concept of faithfulness. The Corps denied his request to muster out in China, where he had hoped to continue a romance with a young Communist woman he'd met. He seethed about this lost love for years. The Corps also exposed him to incompetent commanders as well as to corrupt marines who were black marketers. What he found in the United States upon his return disgusted him as well. The America he came back to was locked into Babbitry at its shallowest, something Peckinpah abhorred. Not much was

Sam Peckinpah as a student at Fresno State. Photo from the author's collection.

to be found in the way of values among the materialistic people living in the suburbs spreading like fungus in all parts of California.

Sam started classes at the "hometown Harvard," Fresno State, but he dashed any hopes his parents might have held that he'd enter the family business of practicing law when he discovered the college drama department. He threw himself into Fresno State's theater productions. He acted, directed, built sets, and worked on lighting and sound as he became a devotee of the works of America's best playwright, Tennessee Williams, and staged his plays. "I guess I've learned more from Williams than anyone," Peckinpah said.[11]

For one class assignment, Peckinpah cut *The Glass Menagerie* down to a one-act play. In doing so, he came to see how a story is built on a dramatic structure that is at once essential yet invisible, much like the studwork behind a Sheetrock wall. Peckinpah learned how to trim away everything except the essentials needed to keep the wall standing. He also learned that no matter how well an actor acts, how well a set is designed, how innovative and effective sound effects might be, or how well a production is staged, if the story is not there, everything else is for naught. It was true for dramas performed live in the theater and, Sam was starting to understand, for movies as well.

Around the time Peckinpah returned to the United States, he saw John Ford's *My Darling Clementine*. The film is a telling of the 1881 shoot-out in Tombstone when Wyatt Earp, his brothers, and Doc

Holliday faced down the Clanton family. From a historical perspective, the film was a farce, but deep down, Ford understood that audiences didn't want history lessons. They wanted drama, something meaningful to think about after they left the picture show. Ford delivered. He concerned himself with the essentials of morality, what is right, what is wrong. In the end, law trumped anarchy, as Ford believed it should. The message was not the point for Peckinpah. Instead, it was how Ford made *My Darling Clementine*. The story was lean and assembled with intricacy. Everything about the camera work was sublime. For the rest of his life, Peckinpah would proclaim *My Darling Clementine* to be Ford's best Western.

5.

The summer after his first year at Fresno State, Peckinpah traveled with friends to attend classes at the Universidad Nacional Autónoma de México. Peckinpah began his love affair with Mexico then. To get from the U.S. border to Mexico City, he had driven a jeep through the northern two-thirds of the country, taking in mountains and deserts, villages and cities, farms and ranches, and opulence and poverty. Visually, it all enticed him, and he liked the Mexican people he met along the way. Mexico was a religious nation, but the Catholicism practiced by most of its citizens was not as condemning of drinking and carousing as what Sam had experienced in the Protestant stronghold of Fresno—or what could be found in much of the rest of the United States in the late 1940s.

Attitudes toward liquor and sex were just part of the appeal of Mexico to Sam. With this trip to Mexico, he became a fan of what his friend Don Hyde would later describe as "hard Mexican music,"[12] that is, *la música* familiar to Mexicans living in the interior of the country, not sanitized and sweetened for export across the border. He heard mariachis in the plazas. He picked up on the artistry of solitary guitarists in cantinas and in brothel lobbies as they performed tunes that had been handed down for generations. On radios and record players, he heard the soaring vocals of José Alfredo Jiménez, Cuco Sánchez, and the Tres Gallos Mexicanos, Pedro Infante, Jorge Negrete, and Javier Solís. From this point on, he requested singers and guitarists to perform songs that had taken on special meaning to him from his time in Mexico. One was "Dos Arbolitos," which he likely heard first by way of a popular recording by Infante. Even more important was "Las Golondrinas" (sometimes simply called "La Golondrina"), Mexico's musical elegy of farewell.

Peckinpah's three-month stay in Mexico City occurred during the heyday of the Golden Age of Mexican cinema, which began in the mid-1930s, when Fernando de Fuentes released *El Prisionero Trece*, the first entry in his trilogy dealing with the Mexican Revolution. For the next twenty years, Mexican filmmakers turned out work that caught the world's attention. Emilio "El Indio" Fernández emerged as the most important Mexican director with such pictures as *Flor silvestre*, *María Candelaria*, *Enamorada*, and *La perla*. He owed much of his success to his longtime collaboration with Gabriel Figueroa, who came to be recognized as one of cinema's great cinematographers. Their work, along with that of other Mexican filmmakers active at the time, left a lasting impression on Peckinpah. Everything about Mexico impressed Sam. Like Walon Green, Peckinpah resolved to return whenever he could.

"In Mexico," Peckinpah once said, "it's all out front—the color, the life, the warmth. If a Mexican likes you, he'll touch you. It's direct. It's real. Whatever else it is, they don't confuse it with anything else . . . In Mexico, they don't worry so goddamn much about saving the human race or about the wheeling-dealing that's poisoning us. In Mexico, they don't forget to kiss each other and water the flowers."[13]

In years to come, people who knew and worked with Peckinpah came to realize that Sam saw Mexico as being what the American frontier must have been like back in the days when Billy the Kid and Doc Holliday—not to mention his own Church and Peckinpah relatives—roamed the West. "Everything important in my life has been linked to Mexico one way or another," he said. "The country has a special effect on me."[14] This became manifest when he directed his greatest movie there, *The Wild Bunch*, two decades later.

6.

Back at Fresno State, Peckinpah immersed himself deeply into the theater crowd. He married Marie Selland, the finest actress on campus and one of the first students to embrace a bohemian lifestyle. She was a bridge for Sam to a world of hip poetry recitals, avant-garde movies, and experimental theater and was about as far removed from the cowboyish Peckinpah clan as someone could be.

Peckinpah headed to L.A. after he graduated from Fresno State to work on a master's degree at USC. USC's film school had yet to blossom, and Peckinpah's focus remained on live theater, although his thesis was built around a videotaping of a Tennessee Williams play. After finishing grad school, Peckinpah worked as a live-theater director in Southern California and New Mexico. He became a father, and as his family grew, it became clear that he needed to take up a different kind of work to pay mounting bills. He found a job as a stagehand at an L.A. television station, and his life changed.

Peckinpah spent the 1950s working in the booming TV industry, save for a few short forays into big-screen projects. Most notable of the latter was his collaboration with director Don Siegel, a talented maverick who hated producers and studio executives; Peckinpah worked on two Siegel classics, *Riot in Cell Block 11* and *Invasion of the Body Snatchers*. Television became for Peckinpah film school on a fast track, as it did for dozens of other future moviemakers. The medium was a monster that required constant feeding, and opportunities aplenty presented themselves to young talents such as Sam. In rather short order, he learned just about everything that could be learned about making movies: scriptwriting, lighting, cinematography, sets, properties, film editing, coaxing performances from actors and actresses. Siegel recommended Sam as a writer to the producers of CBS's Western *Gunsmoke*, in its earliest days as a TV series—it originally was a radio drama. Peckinpah proved to be a success. Soon he garnered a reputation for being one of the best writers working in the new medium.

7.

In the midst of his success in television, Peckinpah had an opportunity to work on a major motion picture. Marlon Brando's Pennebaker Productions had been created in part to produce a Western for Paramount starring Brando. Pennebaker fumbled project after project and was years overdue in delivering the movie to the studio. Meanwhile, Charles Neider had transformed the Pat Garrett and Billy the Kid legend into the literary novel *The Authentic Death of Hendry Jones*. In Neider's telling, the action is moved from New Mexico to Carmel on the California coast, and Garrett becomes Sheriff Doc Baker. The Kid remains the Kid, although his "real" name is changed to Hendry Jones. Producer Frank Rosenberg optioned the film rights and hired Peckinpah to transform the novel into a screenplay.

Peckinpah had already tried his hand at scripting a movie. His partners in the *Rifleman* series had acquired the rights to a novel about Custer's bloody debacle at the Little Bighorn River. They hired Peckinpah to write the screenplay. He succeeded, and that script, ultimately known as *The Glory Guys*, was making the rounds in Hollywood. For Rosenberg, Sam wrote a highly polished adaptation of *The Authentic Death of Hendry Jones*, changing a name here and there (Baker became Dad Longworth) but otherwise remaining true to Neider's book.

Pleased with Peckinpah's work, Rosenberg rolled the dice and sent the screenplay to Brando. Pennebaker wasted little time buying it. Sam and the reigning king of cool in American cinema met daily for three weeks to discuss rewrites as well as the state of the American Western in general. Soon Brando hired Stanley Kubrick, who was still in his twenties, to direct. Kubrick was no fan of Peckinpah's script, and a short time later Brando fired Sam. Kubrick himself lasted only a short time as Brando's Western moved ahead in fits and starts. Finally, Brando decided to direct it himself, using a shooting script that sparked controversy for years over who exactly wrote what. Peckinpah claimed that few lines of dialogue from his script survived in the picture, eventually released as *One-Eyed Jacks*. *One-Eyed Jacks* developed a cult following, and it now stands as an important early revisionist Western. A bitter Peckinpah always considered it garbage.

8.

In 1958, ABC decided to cancel *Broken Arrow*, a Western series that attempted to deal sympathetically with American Indians based on a successful Delmer Daves feature film from earlier in the decade. Its producers offered Peckinpah, who was still stinging from the Brando debacle, the chance to direct the final episode. They had nothing to lose, given that the series was going away. For Peckinpah, who ached to direct, it was a once-in-a-lifetime chance. Everything was on the line. If he pulled it off, he would be on his way as a TV director. If he failed, he'd remain just a writer. Sam succeeded.

Peckinpah's reputation in TV stood at odds with the notoriety he later acquired as a film director who busted budgets and schedules alike. In television, he worked fast and economically, churning out thirty-minute episodes with the best of them. He cocreated the *Rifleman* series and wrote its pilot episode, "The Sharpshooter," which featured Dennis Hopper as the guest star. With *The Rifleman*'s success, Peckinpah continued his climb in the world of network television.

As Peckinpah worked on TV Westerns, extraordinary things were happening with Western big-screen offerings. Crusty director Sam Fuller had pioneered the psychological Western with his ultra-low-budget yet compelling *I Shot Jesse James*. Westerns that followed placed more emphasis on examining characters' motivations than on the shootin' and ridin' of Tom Mix Saturday-afternoon oaters.

A former New York stage actor turned Hollywood film director named Anthony Mann became one of the best directors creating this new kind of Western. *Winchester '73*, *The Naked Spur*, *Bend of the River*, *The Tin Star*, *The Man from Laramie*, *Man of the West*, and *The Furies*—all would come to be considered classics. The Western and Mann seemed to be an odd fit. Mann spent most of his childhood in San Diego but moved to New

York City when he was fourteen. He began acting in plays staged by the Young Men's Hebrew Society. From that point until he began directing movies, he had almost no exposure to cowboys or ranches. Yet he mastered the Western form. He once said that the Western's popularity among directors was because "it gives you more freedom of action, in landscape, in passion. It's a primitive form. It's not governed by rule; you can do anything with it. It has the essential pictorial qualities; has the guts of any character you want; the violence of anything you need; the sweep of anything you feel; the joy of sheer exercise, of outdoorness. It is legend—and legend makes the very best cinema. It excites the imagination more—it's something audiences love."[15] It was also something post–World War II film scholars loved.

Directors of Westerns, along with directors of American film noirs, became among the artists most applauded by the bold emerging critics writing for *Cahiers du cinéma*. The highbrow French movie magazine introduced the auteur theory of filmmaking in its first issue by publishing François Truffaut's "La politique des Auteurs." The theory held that though filmmaking is a collaborative endeavor, some directors are able to take creative control and imprint a recognizable look and feel on their movies, as well as deal with recurring themes. Andrew Sarris brought the auteur theory to America through the pages of the *Village Voice*. Auteurism gained traction with a growing number of serious students of film, even if some influential critics, notably Pauline Kael, dismissed it. By the time *The Wild Bunch* went into production in 1968, it was taught widely at American colleges, where film-studies courses were growing in popularity among baby-boomer students.

The American director who claimed the most attention from European critics subscribing to the theory was John Ford. However, Ford's Westerns never impressed Peckinpah as much as one by directed by George Stevens, who was receiving his own fair share of critical attention. Like Peckinpah and Delmer Daves, Stevens was a native Californian; like Don Siegel, he was a maverick. He brought to his pictures an outstanding sense of composition, a sophisticated understanding of lighting, and an ability to charm moving performances from actors. He often worked with incomplete scripts, believing that a picture would find itself during the filming or later in the cutting room. Heads of production, their eyes forever affixed upon each dollar spent on a movie, fell into fits of anxiety every time Stevens commanded a picture. Yet Stevens consistently earned the studios money. He was respected throughout the industry because of that. Western-film director Budd Boetticher, who would become a favorite of film scholars himself, once said Stevens was the smartest man in Hollywood.

Beginning in 1948, Stevens made six pictures of some gravity, some of them blockbusters, all of them Oscar favorites. He hit his peak with what came to be called his American Trilogy, *A Place in the Sun*, *Shane*, and *Giant*. From the day Peckinpah first saw *Shane* in 1953 until his death, he proclaimed it to be the best Western of them all.

There was much for Sam to admire about *Shane*. This big, bold, impeccably photographed movie was technically right in every way. The character Shane (Alan Ladd) is not unlike some of the old-timers Sam met as a boy on his grandfather's ranch—a gunfighter from a wilder era caught up in changing times. Shane tries to go straight by working as a hired hand for a homesteader (Van Heflin). The homesteader's young son, Joey (Brandon deWilde), develops a fascination with his dad's new worker, sensing something is different about Shane, just as Peckinpah knew something was different about the men at Dunlap Ranch. A cold-blooded cattle baron menaces the farmers in an attempt to uproot them from land he wants for grazing. His chief weapon is a pistolero, Jack Wilson (Jack Palance). Shane reverts to the old ways and kills Wilson and the cattle baron in a gunfight. Because Shane has embraced his killer ways again, he must leave the peaceful homesteaders of the valley. The movie ends as he rides away while Joey pleads for him to stay. Much of the action is seen through Joey's eyes, and the power of the movie concerns the life lessons the boy learns from his encounter with a man of the Old West, the kind of theme that appealed to Peckinpah.

Stevens broke new ground in *Shane* in how he portrayed violence. In one scene, cattle-boss henchman Chris Calloway (Ben Johnson) attempts to throw a "sody pop"–drinking Shane out of the town saloon because Shane is a sodbuster who "smells of pigs." Shane hits Calloway with a punch to the face, knocking him into the next room. As Calloway rises from the floor, he's in obvious pain, with his nose busted up and blood on his face. As the fight continues, Shane suffers abrasions of his own. Calloway gets the worst of it. His breathing grows heavier. His face swells. The message is clear. Fighting is never pretty. It hurts. Blood flows. This was not in keeping with how Westerns of the time portrayed violence.

In another fierce scene, a gunfight between Palance's Wilson and a farmer named Stonewall (Elisha Cook Jr.) comes closer to what really happened in Western duels than anything that had appeared in American movies before it. The confrontation occurs just after a thunderstorm, and mud and puddles pock the street, loose chickens peck for food, and skittish horses fidget at their posts. Wilson, high and dry on a board sidewalk, has the advantage; Stonewall is below him in the street, slipping around, doing his best to keep from toppling over into the mud. The two men are only a few feet apart when their pistols leave their holsters after some waving of the bloody shirt over the Civil War. There was no stepping off on a perfectly dry, dusty street, no time for the townspeople to flee to safety. When Wilson shoots Stonewall, it happens suddenly and surprisingly. Stonewall is dead before he falls. The impact knocks him backward into the fetid mud and water. Such is violent death—dirty and over in an instant. No breast clutching. No eyes cast heavenward. Just, *boom!* And it's over with a muddy splash. George Stevens had seen it happen in real life during the war in Europe. Now he had re-created it on the screen in Technicolor. He'd given Americans, comfortable in their theater seats, clutching their popcorn and sodas, a nasty taste of what death was really like.

To a young filmmaker with Peckinpah's sensibilities, Stevens achieved with *Shane* what every director should set out to accomplish: He pushed the boundaries. He didn't hold back. Hollywood convention might have called for Stevens to attach a sappy ending to his picture, but he avoided that. Shane lights out for whatever territory ahead might be waiting for him, breaking the heart of the kid who adores him. In Peckinpah's mind, Stevens succeeded where John Ford failed with *The Searchers*; Sam thought Ford should have pushed further in exploring disturbing aspects of Wayne's character.[16] With Howard Hawks's *Red River*, John Wayne had already shown he could be at his most effective playing a character who was at least partially sinister. Wayne's character from the novel upon which *The Searchers* was based had ridden with bushwhackers and committed atrocities during the Civil War. Rendered as Ethan Edwards in Ford's movie, the character is much cleaner, and that certainly had to frustrate Peckinpah. Why didn't Ford go deeper with it? Why did he make the ending so sentimental? To Peckinpah, a director should never play it safe.[17]

9.

Peckinpah certainly did not play it safe when Four Star Television allowed him to develop his own Western series. Company head Dick Powell had set Peckinpah up with an office and staff at the old Republic Studios property, now owned by Four Star. On this B-Western hallowed ground, Sam began work on a pilot concerning a drifting cowboy—not a "professional" gunfighter, but a *cowboy*—who moves from place to place, unfettered, accompanied only by his horse and his dog. His melancholy is not completely understood by anyone except the cowboy himself—and maybe even he doesn't fully comprehend it.

The cowboy, whom Peckinpah named Dave Blassingame, had little education. Like many Western heroes, he seems uncomfortable speaking, though Blassingame took the laconic to an extreme. Sam called his pilot "Trouble at Tres Cruces," and it was much darker than anything found on *Gunsmoke* or *Rawhide*. Four Star put the pilot into production, with Brian Keith starring. Keith and Peckinpah suited each other as creative partners in crime. They were both ex-marines, both independent souls ready to snap at the hand that feeds, and both heavy drinkers. Together, Peckinpah and Keith hammered out a plan for a series to grow out of "Trouble at Tres Cruces." But after the pilot aired, no advertisers approached Four Star about sponsoring a weekly show. Peckinpah was not ready to give up. He somehow got "Trouble at Tres Cruces" screened for David Levy, head of programming for NBC. Peckinpah told Levy about the way he and Brian Keith saw the series playing out. Levy was hooked. He maneuvered the project through the approval maze at NBC. Both the network and Four Star agreed to give Sam complete creative control of the thirteen episodes green-lighted for the series, which would be called *The Westerner*.

Once he had a show that was his, all his, Sam threw himself into it with total devotion, arriving at the Four Star studio early in the morning and working until deep into the night. He was willing to set aside everything else in his life—wife, family, friends, everything—to focus on the show. He smoked like a fiend, skipped meals and sleep, and at times drove himself to anxiety attacks. The series was *the thing* for him, just as later any movie he directed became *the thing*. He expected the same level of commitment from everyone else—and he especially had no time for grumbling. The constant stress of producing a weekly TV series took its toll on him. Still, he continued to push, push, and push. In the end, it paid off.

The Westerner debuted with a film-noir-like unity of look and feel running through it. The episodes explored themes such as disillusionment, betrayal (especially the cost of self betrayal), the failure of old modes of wrong and right, and a man wandering alone in the wilderness, like a twisted refugee from the Old Testament. Peckinpah set *The Westerner* in the harsh country along the Texas-Mexico border, a creative terrain to which he would return time and again.

Peckinpah was aided by a group of extraordinary actors and crew members who were beginning to coalesce around him, including Warren Oates, R. G. Armstrong, Slim Pickens, Katy Jurado, Robert Culp, cinematographer Lucien Ballard, and guitarist Julio Alejo Corona. Peckinpah had met Corona somewhere in Mexico, and he became Sam's constant traveling companion south of the border. Julito, as friends called the diminutive guitarist, earned his living playing for tips in cantinas, so he had an extensive repertoire committed to memory.[18] Later he would help create *The Wild Bunch*'s memorable soundtrack.

In 1960, *The Westerner* may have been artistically far above anything else on American TV. The dollars-and-cents realities of the television industry were never at bay, however. The series was up against ABC's *The Flintstones*, an animated, prehistoric reworking of *The Honeymooners*, and CBS's attempt at Kerouacian hipness, *Route 66*. *The Westerner* ran third in the ratings, and NBC canceled it.

However, through the Keith connection, *The Westerner* led to Peckinpah's directing his first big-screen effort, *The Deadly Companions*, in 1961, as well as to his second feature, *Ride the High Country*. Peckinpah emerged from *Ride the High Country* with a reputation as the up-and-coming successor to John Ford, both as a spinner of Old West mythology and as a master of screen artistry. The *Major Dundee* fiasco snuffed out that reputation in short order. Peckinpah made his mistakes on that film, but they hardly warranted the scorched-earth reaction that came from Jerry Bresler and Columbia. Bresler took the film away from Peckinpah during editing, then destroyed his cuts, thus ensuring that Sam's vision for the film never hit the screen. After that, Bresler took a primary position in Peckinpah's gallery of villains.

Peckinpah dusted himself off and moved on to *The Cincinnati Kid*, a high-stakes-poker tale set in New Orleans during the 1930s starring Steve McQueen. The script was written by Texas-born hipster hero Terry Southern and Ring Lardner Jr., who was making a return to screenwriting under his own name after his political blacklisting. Academy Award winner Paddy Chayefsky and the young playwright turned screenwriter Charles Eastman also performed uncredited work on *The Cincinnati Kid*. Peckinpah had ideas for the film that strayed from the script he'd been given. Sam had read much about 1930s social history, in particular the role labor unions played in combating economic inequality, and politically he came down on the side of the unions. Peckinpah's aim with *The Cincinnati Kid* was to create a gritty movie with battles between unions and strikebreakers as the backstory. He began filming in black-and-white.

Peckinpah's concept was certainly at odds with what the executives at production companies Filmways Pictures and Solar Productions and distributor MGM had in mind. Their goal was a lightweight color showcase for Hollywood's new king of cool, McQueen. Filmways' cofounder Martin Ransohoff said, "I wanted something that would be a licorice

Peckinpah first worked with Gordon Dawson, wardrobe supervisor, on *Major Dundee*. He would hold that same job on *The Wild Bunch*, although he took on more responsibilities as filming progressed. He also played a Pinkerton agent, as shown here. Photo by Bernie Abramson, courtesy of Jeff Slater.

stick, popcorn."[19] Peckinpah was not the right cook to rustle up popcorn. Ransohoff gave Peckinpah the hook less than a week after production began and replaced him with Norman Jewison, who whipped up the licorice stick Ransohoff craved. The parting with Peckinpah was rancorous. Ransohoff told *Variety* that he axed Sam for shooting an unauthorized nude scene between costar Rip Torn and an extra.

Ransohoff's allegation angered Peckinpah to no end, especially because Ransohoff had told Sam that he *wanted* racy scenes included in the picture. Ransohoff entered Peckinpah's villains' gallery alongside Bresler. Meanwhile Bresler, Ransohoff, and other executives who had felt Sam's insolent sting wasted little time warning their colleagues not to hire him. Their phone-call and cocktail-party damnations were effective in Hollywood, which in many ways is like a small town. The triumphs of *The Westerner* and *Ride the High Country* were forgotten. People in the business focused on the debacles of *Major Dundee* and *The Cincinnati Kid*. As he hit forty, Sam found himself a branded man, blacklisted as a director, not for any political reasons, but because he was just too difficult to work with. It would take a while for it to come around, but *The Wild Bunch* would be his redemption.

PART III

"We're Gonna Stick Together
Just Like It Used to Be"

1.

Licking his wounds, Peckinpah settled into Malibu, where he'd lived for the most part since he first found success in TV. With its craggy and steep hillsides, thick brush, and magnificent beach, it seemed far removed from downtown L.A., though it was just thirty miles away. The area had become a hideaway for movie people as far back as the 1920s. Sam and his first wife lived in a house in the Malibu Colony. After their divorce, he called a hotel near Paradise Cove home for a while. Then he bought a house at Point Dume, which became known to the Peckinpah clan as the Bird View House. When his winter-of-discontent period began following the *Cincinnati Kid* debacle, he sold it and moved to a place on Broad Beach at the mouth of Trancas Canyon. He may have moved in during a period of professional despair, but the Broad Beach house was where Peckinpah did some of his greatest work. He also enjoyed there some of the happiest moments of his relatively short time on earth, though they were often offset by his dark mood swings.

From his Broad Beach digs in Malibu, Sam sent out feelers to the television world and was open to writing assignments for the movies, but producers weren't exactly lining up outside his door. He certainly needed money. He had fathered three daughters and a son with Marie before they divorced. Family financial obligations were always a worry. He was never good with money. His makeup was that of a grasshopper, not an ant. If there was a dollar to be spent, he'd spend it.

Peckinpah had moved into the Broad Beach house with his second wife, Begoña Palacios, the actress and dancer from Mexico City whom he'd met while filming *Major Dundee*. Palacios was young, sixteen years Sam's junior. She already was a significant movie star in Mexico, but Bego, as their friends called her, spoke little English and never developed a Hollywood career. Before she married Peckinpah, Palacios had been acting in as many as four Mexican movies a year, but that number tailed off. After 1966, she made no pictures at all for three years. Both husband and wife were mired in career frustration. The bond between Sam and Bego was deep and intense—she clearly was the great love of his life—but sometimes the relationship grew fiery. She, like Sam, drank, and as the liquor flowed, disputes broke out and sometimes turned physical. One boozy night Sam sent her to the emergency room with an injured arm.[1] Ultimately, the problems between Sam and Bego outweighed whatever they held in common. Within two years during the period Sam lived at the mouth of Trancas Canyon, they married and divorced twice; several years later, they'd marry for a third time, then split up once more.

Offsetting the rancorous moments were cookouts with family and friends at the Broad Beach house. Peckinpah was a good cook and was especially adept at grilling in the backyard. His kids, who lived with their mother during the week, would be there, as would his friend Robert Culp, an actor who also was writing scripts under Sam's mentorship and who wanted to direct. Culp was divorced, too, and he'd pick up his own children to bring to the gatherings at Sam's place. Culp had first met Sam while working in television at Four Star, where Culp starred in one of the most artistically successful of the 1950s cowboy series, *Trackdown*. Later, Sam cast Culp as the lead in an episode of *The Westerner*, "Line Camp." Culp's career as a TV actor reached a stratospheric high around the time of the Broad Beach cookouts with the smash success of his newest series, *I Spy*, in which Culp starred with young stand-up comedian Bill Cosby. The groundbreaking show featured Bond-like spy capers but with a twist: The stars played espionage colleagues who were also close friends, one of them African American, the other white. No prime-time series before it had featured characters with this sort of interracial bond.

Another regular at the cookouts was writer Lee Pogostin, an out-of-towner who stopped in whenever he was in L.A. An East Coast guy, he had lied his way into the army at age fifteen to fight in World War II. After the war, he began writing radio dramas in New York before venturing into live-TV programs. He became one of TV's most respected writers and contributed to some of the new medium's classier fare, including adaptations of Somerset Maugham and Arthur Miller. Pogostin's original stories also won awards, and he made enough money from them to live in Spain and France. He jetted into L.A. when work required it, and while in town he inevitably made his way to Sam's place. He, Culp, and Peckinpah collaborated on a screenplay for the big screen, *Summer Soldiers*, which, despite their best efforts, never made it into production.

Sometimes Peckinpah's brother, Denny, now a powerful superior court judge back home in Fresno, might show up. Sam's sister, Fern Lea, and her beloved stockbroker husband, Walter Peter, seemed always to be at Trancas cookouts, as was Sam's *Westerner* collaborator Tom Gries. Gries was entering a period of career highs himself. A World War II action series he'd created, *The Rat Patrol*, was among the top thirty shows on network TV. He also had adapted "Line Camp" from *The Westerner* into a movie script called *Will Penny*, and it would shortly go into production with Gries directing and Charlton Heston in the title role.

Whenever he was in Los Angeles, a New Mexico cowboy turned painter and novelist named Max Evans showed up at Broad Beach as well. Evans was a tough D-Day vet who could outdrink even the hollowest of Hollywood hollow legs and pound the bejesus out of just about anybody when it came to a fistfight. When money grew tight, Evans wasn't above running a scam or two to pay the bills, but he also possessed great native intelligence, an interest in mysticism, and a wonderfully creative mind. He wrote novels and novellas that concerned the contemporary West and the clash of mid-twentieth-century sensibilities with traditional values. In this, he was akin to such writers as Edward Abbey, William Eastlake, and a young Larry McMurtry. *The Hi-Lo Country*, Evans's dark novel of fratricide during the 1940s in the ranch country of eastern New Mexico, was a favorite of Peckinpah's—Sam would try but ultimately fail to put it into production as a movie for decades.

Evans was exactly the kind of Western character whose company Peckinpah enjoyed most, a man of the earth who was tough and intelligent. One time in the mid-1960s the two of them fled L.A. in a battered Jeep pickup. Sam was behind the wheel, a man twitching with anxiety as he broke the speed limit to make green lights. Peckinpah spoke not a word until they hit the wide-open desert country north of Los Angeles, where Evans noticed a physical change come over his friend. "Son of a bitch, I feel better already," Sam said. "We're out of the shit, Max." The two amigos then howled like "drunk panthers." They met up with some rowdy buddies in Lone Pine, California's cowboy-movie capital, and then the whole crew rolled on toward the high Sierras. They spent two days soaking in hot springs and feasting on freshly roasted venison. At night, they listened to coyote songs as they sat around a bonfire. "I think we all felt an old, old loss," Evans said. All too soon, it was time to hit the concrete pavement and return to "the shit."[2]

The weekend cookouts at Sam's place at least offered some respite once he was back in the city, though Evans was always perplexed by just how Peckinpah could support all the people staying at his house. "Begoña's whole family, youngsters and all, moved up from Mexico to join them," Evans said. "Sam roasted a piglet every Saturday, and the party carried through till late Sunday night. His own children, and our children, and other people's children were all over the place."[3]

Another person who became a part of the Peckinpah scene around this time was a young, all-but-unknown magazine editor, Jim Silke. He and Sam had met shortly after the release of *Ride the High Country*. Silke was publishing a short-lived magazine called *Cinema*, and he approached Peckinpah for an interview. Sam agreed, but the process was so unnerving for Peckinpah that it almost didn't get done. Finally, he asked Silke to submit written questions. Sam answered while holed up in the privacy of his place on the coast using a Dictaphone and writing on paper in his all but indecipherable scrawl. The depth of the answers surprised Silke. Silke had asked Sam how he might have cast the role of a mountain man in A. B. Guthrie's *The Big Sky*. Peckinpah's spoken answer ran forty-five minutes.

Silke condensed the voluminous responses into what became the first major Peckinpah interview. Sam fed Silke some of his self-manufactured mythology—"[I] was born on the side of a mountain in Madera County thirty-seven years ago"—and at times provided not so much answers to specific questions but statements he wanted to make. Early on, Silke asked him about message films, which Peckinpah dismissed—"Message films per se I find are usually dull and better left to army, university, and industrial filmmakers"—but Silke persisted, asking him to name ten good message films. Peckinpah responded with his list of good movies, not message films, and there were twenty titles, not ten, in no particular order: *Rashomon, The Treasure of the Sierra Madre, La Strada, Hiroshima mon amour, Ace in the Hole, Odd Man Out, Hamlet, La Dolce Vita, On the Waterfront, Last Year at Marienbad, Pather Panchali (Song of the Little Road), Tobacco Road, A Place in the Sun, My Darling Clementine, Viva Zapata!, Shane, Forbidden Games, High Noon, The Breaking Point*, and *The Magician*.

"*The Treasure of the Sierra Madre* is possibly the finest motion picture ever made," Sam said. Peckinpah was forthright about himself—"I will steal from anything and everybody to make a better picture"—and about his industry—"The guilds while protecting their members have priced the picture business into Europe, etc."[4]

Silke did nothing to soften any of Peckinpah's responses and was unsure how Sam would react. The interview earned Silke Peckinpah's respect, and the young magazine editor gained entrance into the heart of the realm of Sam. Theirs quickly evolved into a *Mutt and Jeff* sort of friendship.

The two men seemed to be opposites. If Sam allowed his drinking to get out of control, Silke was an abstainer, always sipping at a cup of coffee rather than a highball glass. Peckinpah sometimes played free and easy with the truth, fibbing to cover his ass or otherwise suit his needs. Silke had the reputation of being scrupulously honest, and Sam came to rely on Silke as someone who would always speak the truth to him. In spite of their differences, as their friendship developed, no one was closer to Peckinpah than Silke.

Silke's training was as a graphic artist, and while he never gave that up, his interests more and more focused on writing. Peckinpah became his teacher and collaborator. They established a working routine that began with a drive to the Mayfair Market at Point Dume. There, Peckinpah would find meat to cook while Silke collected peanut butter, white bread, and coffee. Then they'd meet up at the freezer case for ice cream. Silke always opted for vanilla, and Peckinpah would give him hell for such a bland choice. Sam preferred some fancied-up flavor. Then they'd go to Peckinpah's place, put the coffee on to brew, and set about working on a script.

It was an intensely creative period for Peckinpah and the others, even if Sam suffered by not having a picture to direct. The people who gathered at his place in Malibu supported his efforts to expand American motion pictures beyond the limits imposed by the conventions of the period. One night, Peckinpah, Silke, and Lee Marvin attended a showing of *Lilies of the Field*. After leaving the theater, the tall Marvin folded himself into the small backseat of Silke's Mercedes and observed, "Well, there's another movie in which no one takes a shit."[5]

A half century later, as Jim Silke and I sat in the living room of his suburban Los Angeles home (drinking coffee, of course), he related that story to illustrate what Peckinpah, his friends, and some of his family, who organized themselves into a nonsensical group called the Green, were interested in achieving: the creation of pictures that broke through to a deeper realism than standard Hollywood fare such as *Lilies of the Field*. They wanted movies that were scrubbed clean of sentimentality and false credos. They wanted no more *Pillow Talk*, *Gidget*, or, heaven help us, *The Sound of Music*. They wanted films that were distinctly American movies yet with the gritty feel of a Fellini or a Kurosawa picture. They were not after message movies. Silke believed Peckinpah never shot a didactic foot of film in his life—in fact, Sam did have his didactic moments later on—but he certainly seemed to be the American director most suited to batter down Hollywood's ramparts of restraint. If only he could be in command of the director's chair once more.[6]

The tough circumstances Peckinpah faced during his exile seemed to bring out his best. "When he's down, all of a sudden, he's tough, really marvelous," Silke said. "He was really resilient. We produced like you couldn't believe. We were always working, and on spec. I was on call twenty-four hours a day."[7]

Dan Melnick was one of the brightest lights working in television during the 1960s. Born and reared in New York, he headed for Hollywood while he was still a teenager, where he quickly figured out how the TV business worked. He then jetted to the top. The whiz kid from New York soon became the youngest producer in the history of CBS Television, with a knack for being able to foresee what the next hot trend in TV would be months before other producers. Shortly thereafter, he was hired by ABC before moving back to New York as an independent producer. He had a taste for quality and with partner David Susskind brought works by Shakespeare and Arthur Miller to the idiot box.

Melnick had been impressed by Peckinpah's *Westerner* during its short run on NBC. When Melnick decided to create an adaptation of Katherine Anne Porter's "Noon Wine" for *ABC Stage 67*, a dramatic anthology series, he recruited Sam to command the project. As word of Peckinpah's involvement spread, Melnick's phone began to light up with calls cautioning him against using Sam. Peckinpah himself had said to him, "I've got to tell you something. I'm blacklisted, there's going to be a lot of pressure on you not to use me."[8] The youthful Melnick was full of moxie. He trusted his gut and his eyes. That people were attempting to dissuade him from using Peckinpah made him all the more determined to ensure Sam's success. Melnick stuck by his guns. Peckinpah threw himself into the project.

"Noon Wine" appeared in Porter's book *Pale Horse, Pale Rider*. Like much of Porter's work, it was set in her native Texas, in particular the Brush Country of South Texas, during the early 1900s. Porter populated her tale of obsession, homicide, and, ultimately, suicide with carefully developed characters who in ways presage those of Tennessee Williams. In theme, setting, and characters, "Noon Wine" was right up Sam's alley.

2.

N oon Wine" aired on *ABC Stage 67* in November 1966. It was far from a ratings jackpot, but the production caught Hollywood's attention. Instead of film, it was shot on videotape, a relatively cumbersome medium in the mid-1960s. Nevertheless, the camera work and the editing were impressive, especially by 1966 television standards. It suggested a whole new world of possibilities for TV. Award nominations duly came Peckinpah's way.

Peckinpah was able to draw out the best from his lead actors, Jason Robards and Olivia de Havilland. For key supporting roles as a deputy and a sheriff, he turned to two actors with whom he'd already worked, L. Q. Jones and Ben Johnson. Both were part of what was developing into Peckinpah's stock company, and both would have important parts three years later when *The Wild Bunch* went into production. One quality members of Peckinpah's stock company brought to his films was authenticity. The actors came from flyover country, remote towns in unfashionable places where survival was challenging. Jones and Johnson seemed as if they weren't acting at all in Sam pictures. They came across as real people doing what real people do.

Jones was born Justus Ellis McQueen Jr. He grew up in East Texas and Oklahoma, and like most young men of that time and place, he knew how to ride horses and was schooled in roping by an uncle who competed in rodeos. After serving in World War II, he enrolled at the University of Texas, where he became a cheerleader known as Dodo and roomed with fellow student Fess Parker, a history major who was acting in campus plays every chance he had. Through Parker, McQueen developed an interest in the stage, as did one of their friends, Morgan Woodward, who had shown up in Austin from West Texas. They came under the tutelage of Adolphe Menjou, the red-baiting actor who had joined the UT drama department as a guest artist.[9] Menjou connected Parker with his agent, and soon the future Davy Crockett was in Hollywood, working in pictures. The Menjou-Parker conduit provided access to the business for Dodo and Woodward as well. (Woodward became best known as the prison guard behind the mirror shades in *Cool Hand Luke* and for his many guest shots on *Gunsmoke*: He was "killed" by Matt Dillon more than any other actor.)

With Parker's encouragement and help, McQueen landed a role in the film version of the Leon Uris novel *Battle Cry*, a boot-camp-to-battlefield World War II marine saga that had become a bestseller. Raoul Walsh, who directed the picture, had hired the inexperienced McQueen over the objections of the Warner Bros. casting department. When push came to shove, Walsh declared he would walk from the picture if McQueen wasn't cast. The studio acceded—mogul Jack Warner owed Walsh many favors—and McQueen was in the picture, playing a character named L. Q. Jones. The picture was a hit, and McQueen received high marks for his performance. Advised that Justus McQueen was not an appropriate name for a movie actor, Dodo simply adopted his *Battle Cry* character's name. As L. Q. Jones, he began working for some of the business's best-known directors, include Westerns master Anthony Mann and Peckinpah's old mentor Don Siegel.

Tall and tan, with blondish-brown hair and a somewhat reedy voice, Jones was effective playing against type as a bad guy. He could appear innocent and devilish simultaneously and could convey messages with just a wicked smile that might otherwise have required page after page

L. Q. Jones in Mexico, 1968. Photo by Paul Harper, courtesy of Nick Redman and Jeff Slater.

of dialogue. Peckinpah used him as one of the demonic Hammond brothers in *Ride the High Country*. A bond was set between director and actor. For a time, they were close friends, but then the personal relationship soured. Still, Jones never turned down a chance to act for Peckinpah because Jones knew he'd be doing absolutely first-rate work with Sam at the wheel. "I wouldn't piss in Peckinpah's mouth if his brain was on fire," Jones once said. But if Sam called him to work on a picture, even if it was just to drag cables, Jones would be the first in line, simply because of the high quality of Peckinpah's movies.

Ben "Son" Johnson was a real cowboy who had come of age in the vast tallgrass-prairie country of Osage County, Oklahoma. The county corresponded to the boundaries of the Osage reservation and came to be known simply as "the Osage." In this ideal grazing country, its cattle ranches were measured by the tens of thousands of acres.

One of the biggest was the Chapman-Barnard, which covered up to a hundred thousand acres at times and was home to ten thousand head of cattle. Johnson's father, also named Ben Johnson, was the Chapman-Barnard foreman and was widely known and respected by cattlemen from South Texas to Montana and beyond for his understanding of the beef business. The elder Johnson was also regarded as one of the best riders to ever sit a horse. His feats on bucking broncs became the stuff of legend, but he was even more respected for his abilities as a steer roper. He competed at the great rodeos of the day—Cheyenne Frontier Days, Pendleton Round-Up, Calgary Stampede, the Dewey Roundup—and won many championships. He was a famous man in his time and place. He was *the* Ben Johnson, so much so that the younger Ben Johnson was never even accorded use of his own name in the county where he grew up. In the Osage, the future Academy Award winner was forever known as Son Johnson. Son had a lot to live up to.

From the moment of his birth, the younger Ben was nurtured to be a cowboy. When he hit his teenage years, Johnson was already one of the best hands on the Chapman-Barnard—which is to say he was one of the best in all of America. He was particularly adept at riding. At this, he was his father's equal, maybe even a little better. As long as he remained in the Osage, however, he'd always be in his father's shadow. His chance to escape came courtesy of tycoon Howard Hughes.

Howard Hawks was working for Hughes on Hughes's pet Billy the Kid project, *The Outlaw*, and traveled to the Chapman-Barnard to get horses that could be shipped by rail to Arizona for use in the film. A deal was struck, and Johnson was assigned by his father to wrangle the horses as they were sent to location in Tuba City and Yuma. The movie company paid Johnson $300 for his labors; at the time he was earning $30 a month as a Chapman-Barnard hand. Hawks, impressed by Johnson's skill in the saddle, offered him work in the movies, both as a wrangler and a stuntman. Son realized he could make a whole lot more money in Hollywood than he ever could in the Osage. "I wasn't very smart," Johnson said, "but I knew that was better than thirty dollars a month. And I didn't have to get up at two or three in the morning to start work."[10] Moreover, he'd be far removed from his father's controlling eye. He accepted Hawks's offer.

Johnson fell in with a group of stuntmen who hung out at Fat Jones Stables in North Hollywood. This outfit, which had been around since 1912, was the industry's leading supplier of horses as well as stagecoaches, wagons, chariots, and just about anything else that could be drawn by horses. Jones Stables was where movie companies went to round up stuntmen for pictures as well. The young, athletic Johnson soon had the reputation as being among the best at stunt work, right up there with Yakima Canutt. Johnson found himself working in all sorts of pictures. Wearing a mop-top wig and a loincloth, he even doubled for Johnny Weissmuller in *Tarzan* films.

After John Ford elevated Johnson from stuntman to actor in the 1948 picture *3 Godfathers*, Johnson discovered that many women found him attractive. Johnson was not one to say no to a pretty face, and he was rumored to have a legion of bedmates.[11] Harry Carey Jr. told me that friend Johnson's reputation as a lothario cost him a role in Hawks's classic *Red River* after Hawks became convinced that Johnson was sleeping with Hawks's socialite wife and fired him off the picture.[12] Otherwise, Johnson had a reputation around Hollywood as a straight shooter, even if he sometimes drank a little whiskey and got rowdy with the boys. At his core he was a cowboy with a strong work ethic who adhered to his values. Johnson broke with Ford after the director attempted to bully him on *Rio Grande*.

Johnson worked steadily as a supporting actor, slipping away to rope at rodeos whenever he had the chance. (In 1953, he was the sport's best team roper, winning a world championship.) He had parts in such films as *Shane* and *One-Eyed Jacks*; on the latter, he and his friend Slim Pickens, the former rodeo clown turned actor, provided significant help to first-time director Marlon Brando beyond their work in front of the camera. Johnson became a well-liked and valued presence on movie sets, where he had an uncanny way of absorbing shooting scripts.

Sometimes directors turned to him to cue lines, which he'd gladly do, all the while fiddling with a rope. From time to time, he came up with improvements on dialogue in scripts, though he did not, as he later claimed, write what became the shooting script for *One-Eyed Jacks*.[13]

His matinee idol looks dissolved into a cragginess that worked to his advantage as a character actor. He acted in so many Western shows that his became identified as one of the faces of the West. It's no surprise that Peckinpah wanted Johnson to act in his pictures. Sam recruited him first for *Major Dundee*, but nearly lost him during their first meeting. As Johnson watched, Sam went off on some hapless crew member and fired him on the spot, using every invective in the book. When Sam turned his attention back to Johnson, Son said he couldn't work for him. Why? Peckinpah wanted to know. Johnson explained that if Sam ever talked to him that way, he'd lay Peckinpah's bony ass out on the ground. "And then you'd run me out of the business," Johnson said, "and I ain't ready to leave."

Peckinpah smiled. "That's just why I want you to work for me."[14]

For the score for "Noon Wine," Dan Melnick had recruited Jerry Fielding, a composer who'd had success in television and in Las Vegas. Fielding would go on to become one of Peckinpah's most important

Real cowboy Ben Johnson (left) with Bo Hopkins and William Holden during the early days of filming *The Wild Bunch* in Parras de la Fuente, Coahuila, Mexico. Johnson would become the only person to win both an Academy Award and a world rodeo championship. Photo by Paul Harper, courtesy of Nick Redman and Jeff Slater.

collaborators, writing the score for *The Wild Bunch*, but at the time they met on "Noon Wine," Fielding was a little-known musician coming off his own blacklisting. Fielding was a bit older than Peckinpah, born in 1922 in Pittsburgh as Joshua Feldman. Fielding studied composition and arranging under Max Adkins, the leader of the pit orchestra at Pittsburgh's Stanley Theater, and joined the likes of Henry Mancini and Billy Strayhorn as Adkins acolytes. Fielding spent hours studying the elements and finer points of arranging in Adkins's basement office beneath the Stanley stage. Among other things, all of Adkins's pupils learned how to work fast.

All roads in the entertainment world seemed to lead to Hollywood in the 1940s, and Fielding wound up there. He found work as an arranger, but he was quietly making enemies by mouthing his progressive political opinions. Compounding matters was his insistence on breaking the race line by hiring African American musicians for his orchestra. By the early 1950s, he was on the radar of both the FBI and the House Un-American Activities Committee as a likely Communist. Investigators leaned on him for the names of subversives working in the entertainment industry. Fielding refused and, as a result, found himself on Hollywood's blacklist.

Fielding found a temporary home in Las Vegas, arranging scores for stage performances by big-name acts. Once political blacklisting began to ease in the early 1960s, the infamously caustic director Otto Preminger hired Fielding to score his film *Advise & Consent*. With that, Fielding made his return to Hollywood. Around this time, Fielding studied with Mario Castelnuovo-Tedesco, a classically trained composer of operas who had, during a few years in Hollywood, raised the bar for complex and sophisticated movie scores. Fielding learned a great deal from him, including how to compose for guitar, one of Castelnuovo-Tedesco's specialties. This skill was essential for Fielding to compose the *Wild Bunch* score a few years later.

Fielding still looked like a bomb-throwing commie when he and Peckinpah first met. Fielding was a skinny chain-smoker whose hair seemed to have never known a comb. He wore a scraggly beard at a time when few men save beatniks and proto-hippies did so. The musical Jew from Pittsburgh and the cowboy Christian Scientist from Fresno might have been an odd pairing, but the two men hit it off, both professionally and personally. With the success of "Noon Wine," Peckinpah was back. At least sort of.

3.

In the spring of 1967, Peckinpah began rewriting *The Wild Bunch* for Roy Sickner. Sam did not invite Silke or any of his other cohorts to collaborate with him. He seemed to want to do this himself. Walon Green had fashioned a Western with realistic main characters who were mean, nasty, brutal, and careless in violence. Peckinpah scholar Paul Seydor told me, "It freed Sam's imagination to release the romanticism and the mythologizing tendency that is as vital, if not more vital, a part of *The Wild Bunch* as the darker side."[15] The story grabbed Peckinpah. His friends knew how it could be once he sank his teeth into something. He might replay each scene a thousand times in his head. He didn't write down extensive notes about what he imagined, let alone create detailed storyboards in the manner of a Hitchcock. Nevertheless, the ideas were still there, stored away.[16] The screenplay drafts he created while in Sickner's employ show that from the very beginning he had in mind a film that would extend far beyond typical Western adventure fare. Peckinpah's interest in the Mexican Revolution was also growing. Around this time, he received an offer from Paramount producer Ted Richmond to write a Pancho Villa biopic. If the script turned out well, Sam might be invited to direct.

The screenplay was to be based on William Douglas Lansford's book *Pancho Villa*. Richmond had lined up Yul Brynner to star, never mind the improbability of a bald Russian playing the Mexican revolutionary. Brynner had established some credibility as an actor in Westerns with John Sturges's *The Magnificent Seven*, released in 1960. Derived from Kurosawa's *Seven Samurai*, *The Magnificent Seven* found popularity among young, white male moviegoers of the early 1960s, on whom the film's fundamental racism was lost. *The Magnificent Seven* was a tale of Mexican farmers, meek as Slowpoke Rodriquez from the Speedy

Gonzales cartoons, who resort to hiring white gunfighters from across the Rio Grande to protect them from a *jefe de los bandidos* (played by a Jew from Brooklyn) and his ruffians.

The Magnificent Seven had no basis in historical fact. The story of Dave Rudabaugh is instructive about how Mexican townspeople of the late 1800s dealt with bandits in real life. A thug active in Kansas and Texas during the 1870s and '80s, Rudabaugh eventually attempted to throw his weight around Parral, Chihuahua. For his trouble, he was shot and beheaded, his *cabeza* posted on a stake, which no doubt served as a warning to other gringo outlaws. *That* was the reality, but Sturges and his white screenwriters opted instead to concoct a fantasy of stereotypes.

Sam Peckinpah hated *The Magnificent Seven*, but his opinion was in the minority. The movie made money, which is what mattered to studio businessmen, with Brynner at the top of the credits playing a cowboy/gunfighter. To the mind of typical mid-1960s producers, Pancho Villa was just a step away from a Western character. Paramount selected Brynner to play the Mexican Revolution's Centaur of the North.

Villa's life and career had been intertwined with American filmmaking since the movies' earliest days. One of the most complicated political and military leaders of the twentieth century, Villa was on the cutting edge of many modern combat techniques, among them making sophisticated use of trains to transport troops at high speeds, dropping bombs from airplanes, and using telegraph and telephone in effective ways to boost transportation. He considered cinema to be an effective tool for propaganda years before the Soviets and the Nazis reached the same conclusion. To advance his cause during the campaign against Federal forces in Ojinaga, Villa signed a contract with the Mutual Film Corporation giving it exclusive rights to film the real-life battle for use in a fictional biopic released as *The Life of General Villa*. "The Battle of Ojinaga came to be known as a battle to be filmed," said documentary filmmaker Gregorio Rocha. "Cinema was changing the course of history."[17]

The movie, with its intense scenes of warfare, helped cement Villa as a household name in the United States. He'd been a popular subject in American newspapers since the outbreak of the Mexican Revolution. Depending on the political leanings of the newspapers, he was portrayed either as a murdering rapist or as a brave, skilled, and just military man who was somehow "above the law," in the words of Mexican film historian and author Margarita de Orellana.[18] In fact he was a complex man with a Byzantine history (sorted out at last by the Austro-Mexican historian Friedrich Katz in his essential Villa biography published in the 1990s).

Villa as a character returned to American cinema screens in 1917 when Wallace Beery portrayed him in the *Patria* serial and in 1918 when George Humbert played him in the Pershing biopic *Why America Will Win*. After that, Villa disappeared from American movies for nearly two decades. During this time, Villa was officially villainized in Mexico—at least, in official Mexico during the regimes of Carranza, Obregón, and el Jefe Máximo, Plutarco Elías Calles. Nevertheless, Villa remained a powerful folk hero among many Mexicans and Mexican Americans, celebrated in stories and songs, and his reputation grew following his assassination in 1923.

In 1934, Villa returned to American movie theaters. Wallace Beery reprised his role as Pancho Villa in MGM's *Viva Villa!* This well-acted, well-constructed picture was also problematic in the extreme. Beery's Villa ran counter to the real man. The revolutionary leader was rendered as a womanizing buffoon constantly fussing with sore feet; MGM's poster for *Viva Villa!* portrayed him as a cartoon character, and Mexican stereotypes poured off the screen. The movie made money and set the popular image of Villa in the United States for the next twenty-five years.

Bill Lansford hated *Viva Villa!* Lansford was a Mexican American with an outsize life. He told me his father was a white Texas cowboy who impregnated his Mexican mother, then abandoned her before Lansford was born. Lansford grew up in an East Los Angeles barrio speaking both Spanish and English. He enlisted in the Marine Corps when he was eighteen and served through the totality of World War II, most of it in the Pacific theater. He was part of the Fifth Marine Division that hit Iwo Jima in February 1945 and suffered more than eight thousand casualties over five weeks. After the war, Lansford developed a lifelong passion for ensuring that the sacrifice of the marines on Iwo Jima would be remembered.

His passions also extended to correcting the image of Pancho Villa in what he referred to as "gringodom." Lansford became a successful TV writer, eventually churning out scripts for *Bonanza* and *Wagon Train*. Villa's story continued to haunt him. Lansford believed *Viva Villa!* was an insult to all Mexican people, lamenting that it presented Villa as "an apelike, greasy (albeit quite loveable) *peón* whose perpetually 'sandled' feet couldn't bear shoes, and whose answer to life was instant death . . . Every time I think of Wallace Beery groaning *car-r-ramba!* and massaging his feet in the *Palacio Nacional*, I groan, too."[19]

In his younger years, Lansford had traveled in Mexico to visit relatives, many of whom had lived through the revolution. He heard many stories told about Villa, none of them in keeping with Beery's greasy, sore-footed *peón*. He began researching both Spanish and English texts. He made return trips to Mexico, traveled trails Villa once rode, visiting the sites of his triumphs and defeats. He talked to many survivors of Villa's fabled División del Norte. Lansford also spent hours interviewing Villa's widow about her life with the *guerrillero*.

"I didn't start out to make Villa a saint or a devil," Lansford said in 1965. "Like so many great men, Villa wasn't always right, yet he was less often wrong, or he couldn't have survived. He was impulsive. He was a bloody savage, for the Gordian knots he cut through were often of flesh and bone. He was also incredibly tender, and there are more people still alive who bless him than curse him. He was a thief, a murderer, a fool, a sentimentalist, and, quite incidentally, a genius and a leader of unimpeachable idealism."[20]

When it came time to write his book about Villa, Lansford decided to write a nonfiction novel, a form that a number of writers attempted during the 1960s, including Norman Mailer and Truman Capote. Lansford felt the story merited more than a well-footnoted but dry history tome. He wanted to make Villa's story come alive. "But let me set this straight right now," he said, "the book, the facts, the scenery, and the characters are essentially correct—and most particularly in cases where my version varies from the popular or accepted 'fact.'"[21]

Lansford's *Pancho Villa* found a ready audience when it appeared in 1965. The smell of revolution hung in the air in the United States itself as America's war in Vietnam was reaching its peak, with the military drawing most of its troops through a corrupt and unpopular draft system. Relatively unrestrained television news organizations broadcast images of dead Vietnamese, of American soldiers and marines burning the homes of Vietnamese farmers, and of caskets containing the remains of dead U.S. combatants being unloaded from cargo planes. Beyond the war in Vietnam, violent crime in the United States was on an uptick. Likewise, drug use was on the increase. Raucous forms of music challenged the old standards as young people began to ignore long-held sexual mores, not to mention standards of attire and behavior. Young African Americans in cities, frustrated by the lack of progress to protect the civil rights of all citizens and by the wrongs perpetuated on their communities by the police, took to the streets in protest. The Watts riots, which occurred during the summer of 1965, were extraordinarily destructive. The TV images of blood in the streets of L.A. proved that even the dreamland of Southern California was not immune from the nation's troubles. Around this time the Brown Power movement began to coalesce with the League of United Latin American Citizens' activities in Texas and the United Farm Workers strikes, under the leadership of Cesar Chavez, in California. More and more young Mexican Americans were determined to end the discrimination and violence suffered by their forebears. The time was indeed right for a book about the charismatic revolutionary Pancho Villa that would be free of the clichés and capture the heart of the man.

Officials at Paramount believed that it was time to bring Villa back to the big screen as well. Sam Peckinpah, resurrected by "Noon Wine," seemed to be the ideal person to write the screenplay. Lansford already was on board with Paramount, having written a treatment. Paramount set both him and Sam up in offices on the studio lot, though they were far from luxurious. James Coburn, who'd acted in *Major Dundee*, paid Peckinpah a visit at Sam's cramped writing space. Coburn felt sorry for his old director. He remembered how Peckinpah had lorded over *Major Dundee*'s production, a general in command of his troops. Now he

Sam Peckinpah in 1968. Photo by Paul Harper, courtesy of Nick Redman and Jeff Slater.

seemed reduced to groveling for the Paramount brass just to get back in the door.

It was anything but a humiliating experience for Peckinpah. Instead, it was as if he'd enrolled in a graduate-degree program in the Mexican Revolution. He was reading everything he could about it, exhausting Paramount's substantial research department as well as ordering additional books from nearby university libraries. One thing that Paramount wanted in the script was the development of a fictional character, a gringo mercenary well acquainted with the twentieth-century technologies of war. Peckinpah's fascination with gringos caught up in the revolution grew as he built a script. He was especially affected by the photographs he saw in books and ancient yellowed newspapers.

Later in the spring of 1967, Peckinpah submitted his script. It certainly needed more work, but it had powerful elements, not the least of which was the character of Pancho Villa as both an inspiring revolutionary leader as well as a man with a violent temper and other significant flaws. Brynner, ever careful to protect his screen image, hated the screenplay, which included whole segments written in Spanish. What was he supposed to do with *that*? No audience would sit through so much border lingo. Brynner told producer Ted Richmond that Peckinpah didn't understand Mexico and wanted him off the picture. Suddenly Peckinpah, the creator of the lauded "Noon Wine," found himself back in *Cincinnati Kid* territory, fired.

Lansford went to the Paramount writers' building, where he learned that he, too, had been given his walking papers, allegedly for threatening to punch out Richmond. He was told to clear out his desk, then leave, after which he'd be barred from returning to the Paramount lot. He gathered his things, but before he departed, he noticed a light coming from Sam's office down the hall. When Lansford stuck his head in the door, he saw Peckinpah packing up his own gear. When Lansford asked Sam what was going on, Peckinpah said he, too, had been accused of threatening to dot Richmond's eyes. Shit-canned. Barred from the lot. Just like Lansford.

Peckinpah said to Lansford, "Let's celebrate!" and then produced a bottle of whiskey, seal intact, from a bottom drawer. Lansford took him up on the offer, and the two ex-marines closed the door and drank and talked until the wee hours of the next morning. As the last drops of the whiskey disappeared and it was time to begin their banishment from Paramount, Peckinpah said, "I don't give a shit. I'm going to go make a movie called *The Wild Bunch*."[22] Changes in Hollywood and in American culture would give him that chance.

4.

It wasn't simple. Peckinpah moved around his Malibu digs as a broken man. He was still married to Begoña Palacios, and she became alarmed as she witnessed his deepening despair. "I'll never get to make another film," he said. "They're never going to let me direct again."[23]

Neither Bego nor Sam could know that events were occurring in New York, Burbank, and elsewhere that would prove Peckinpah wrong. Four months after Peckinpah was fired off *Villa Rides*, Warner Bros. released *Bonnie and Clyde*, an Arthur Penn film starring Hollywood fashion plates Warren Beatty and Faye Dunaway. Penn crafted a superb criminal fantasy about Clyde Barrow and Bonnie Parker, who in real life were ignorant, small, ugly, and only marginally successful outlaws. Penn made them young and beautiful on-screen, and though the picture was set in the 1930s, they seemed emblematic of the disaffected youth of the 1960s. They were violent. Penn made pioneering use of slow-motion to tell their story in film, but it was the savage gun battles that created the most controversy. Blood flowed in *Bonnie and Clyde*, much more so than in any mainstream American movie before it, thanks to Penn's sophisticated use of blood squibs.

Squibs were miniature explosive devices that originated in the coal mining industry. They resembled nothing so much as tiny sticks of dynamite and were discharged electrically by wires running under clothing. By the mid-1950s, filmmakers began experimenting with them as a way to simulate a bullet striking a human being. Prior to squibs, the best that could be done was to use a series of film edits to the film to show a gunshot followed by a shot of an actor with blood smeared on his wardrobe. By taping a wired squib to an actor's body with a small container (condoms were used early on) of stage blood adhered over it, all of it hidden under a shirt, a special effects person could trip the switch to discharge the explosive, producing a bullet-hole-like tear in the shirt and breaking the container to cause an immediate flow of blood.

Bonnie and Clyde rattled the cage across America, with many mainstream reviewers condemning it for its violence and preachers damning it from church pulpits. It became a financial success with its stick-it-to-the-establishment message of rebellious love. Hollywood took note. A movie that pushed the limits in sex and violence could put baby-boomer asses in cinema seats. It kicked open the door for directors such as Peckinpah to explore risqué topics in an adult, artful way.

A film such as *Bonnie and Clyde* was too much for an old-time mogul such as Jack Warner, who demanded to know what the fuck he'd just seen when the movie was previewed for him. Beatty, who produced *Bonnie and Clyde* in addition to starring in it, was fast on his feet. He explained the film was an homage to the great Warner Bros. gangster films of the 1930s. Warner nodded, then said, "What the fuck is an homage?"[24] He didn't need to figure it out. He wouldn't be in charge of the studio that bore his name for much longer.

Warner and his brothers had pioneered the business end of moviemaking for what seemed like forever, getting their start during the days of nickelodeons. Over the years, as he rose in prominence, Jack Warner had established a reputation as something of a brutal clown. He told the worst jokes in town, squeezed his brothers out of the family business, was ruthless in his dealings with unions, underpaid his executives, took the lead in advancing cinema technology, recruited the best stars, sometimes seemed more interested in playing tennis than running a major studio, made stupid business decisions, and made brilliant business decisions. It was challenging to find a bigger mess of contradictions and complexities anywhere in Los Angeles. Sometimes Warner Bros. found itself operating in fire-sale mode.

During a period of financial struggle in the 1950s, Warner ordered the sale of all his studio's pre-1949 output (some 750 sound movies), at cheap prices, to a company called Associated Artists Productions Corp. This brought Warner into contact with the founder of Associated Artists, a onetime tire dealer named Eliot Hyman. After World War II, Hyman came to understand that the burgeoning TV industry needed content, and he knew that the financially struggling studios were sitting on tons of it in their back catalogs. He put together companies such as Associated Artists to acquire movies and sell them to television. Eventually he went into production himself.

Hyman's financing came from shady companies, some chartered in the Bahamas, and his colleagues at Associated Artists included the likes of three-hundred-pound Lou "the Moose" Chesler, a Florida real estate developer who was connected to Meyer Lansky's criminal empire. Hyman's associates included Charlie Allen, another figure with organized crime ties, and a Russian-born Boston banker named Serge Semenenko, who shunned publicity but who, behind the scenes, had become the "Medici of the movies," in the words of *Variety*.[25] Allen, meanwhile, was "the godfather of Hollywood."[26] Though their names were scarcely known to the outside world, no one exercised more power in the American movie industry of the 1960s than the secretive Semenenko and Allen. Warner Bros. was among their clients.

As Warner Bros' fortunes floundered during the mid-1960s, Semenenko and Allen decided that Jack Warner, now in his midseventies, was too old to run the studio founded by his family. Wielding the Warner Bros. notes they held, Semenenko and Allen informed Warner that it was time for him to sell his controlling interest in the studio. Warner, an egotist who liked to throw his power around, knew he could not say no to the two moneymen. He asked only that the deal include a proviso that the company would always bear the Warner name. Semenenko and Allen agreed. They paid Warner $32 million for his percentage of the business, but that was just a small part of the package. The studio had liabilities of nearly $60 million that had to be retired. Plus, another 16 million shares of stock were outstanding, which had to be acquired. Assuming control of Warner Bros. would be a much smaller company called Seven Arts Productions, which Eliot Hyman had created in 1960.

During its brief life, Seven Arts had underwritten an impressive series of Broadway plays (*The Night of the Iguana*, *Funny Girl*, and *The Owl and the Pussycat*) and provided financial backing for the movies *The Misfits*, *Gigot*, *Lolita*, *Is Paris Burning?*, and *What Ever Happened to Baby Jane?* Hyman oversaw the production of intelligent, well-made pictures, and his best producer turned out to be his own son, Kenneth.

Charles Feldman was a young, savvy publicist working at Seven Arts whose range of responsibilities expanded when he relocated from New York to California when he was made a vice president of the newly created Warner Bros.-Seven Arts. He later reported that Hyman and the moneymen backing him had no intention of making Warner Bros.-Seven Arts a permanent company. The idea was to cash out by selling out to a revenue-rich conglomerate looking to diversify its holdings, and to do so as quickly as possible. And it would do so.

5.

Warner Bros.-Seven Arts under the helm of Hyman would last less than two years before it was acquired by a company best known for its parking garages and price-fixing scandals. During that brief existence, Warner Bros.-Seven Arts put its imprint on around three dozen movies, including *Cool Hand Luke*; *Wait Until Dark*; *Petulia*; *The Heart Is a Lonely Hunter*; *I Love You, Alice B. Toklas*; *Rachel, Rachel*; *Finian's Rainbow*; *Bullitt*; *The Learning Tree*; and *The Rain People*. And, most important, *The Wild Bunch*.

Hyman wasted little time appointing his son, Kenneth, as head of production for the new Warner Bros.-Seven Arts. Ken Hyman left the heavy corporate finance matters in the hands of his father and focused on producing pictures. "I wasn't a deal maker," he said. "I was a hands-on producer, I was a picture maker, and I believed in doing everything I could to support the director, to allow him to make the movie he wanted to make." Once he settled in, he remembered meeting Sam Peckinpah at the Cannes Film Festival in 1965 after the premiere of Sidney Lumet's *The Hill*, which Hyman had produced. Peckinpah had shuffled up to him and said in voice so quiet that Hyman could barely hear him, "That's a hell of a picture you made." Hyman thanked him and asked his name, and the two men, both ex-marines, talked amicably for a while. Hyman left the conversation impressed by his new acquaintance.[27]

When Hyman returned to his office, he ordered a screening of *Ride the High Country*. Based on it, he began thinking of Peckinpah as a director he'd like to work with. Now, as production head for the new company, he wasted little time recruiting Sam. He dispatched producer Phil Feldman to Malibu with instructions to discuss with Sam directing *The Diamond Story*, a big-budget caper movie set in Africa.

Phil Feldman was for a time one of the shrewdest producers in what would eventually be called the New Hollywood or the American New Wave, a period of extraordinary creativity in American cinema roughly bracketed by the release of *Bonnie and Clyde* in 1967 and *Heaven's Gate* in 1980. A Boston native, Feldman was no one's uneducated fool. He held degrees from both Harvard and Georgetown, then went on to get graduate degrees from Harvard Law *and* the Harvard School of Business. As an army captain during World War II, he worked as a code breaker in a military intelligence unit. Afterward, he worked in retail and practiced law before heading west to become legal counsel for the Famous Artists Corp. talent agency. Famous Artists represented Francis Ford Coppola, and through Feldman's connection with the company, the budding director and the tough minded attorney met. Later, after stops at Fox and at Seven Arts as an executive, Feldman broke out as a producer with Coppola's *You're a Big Boy Now*, an early New Hollywood film, right down to its Lovin' Spoonful soundtrack. *You're a Big Boy Now* was also one of the final films released by Seven Arts before the merger with Warner Bros. Feldman was something of a provocateur as a producer, loving nothing more than to rankle censors and test boundaries. He seemed like an ideal producer to work with Peckinpah, but Sam nearly ran Feldman off at their first meeting.

Still smarting from his experience at Paramount on *Villa Rides*, Sam didn't trust Feldman's offer to let him direct *The Diamond Story*. To him, it was just another carrot dangled in front of him to get him to rewrite a screenplay. Feldman argued that the offer was legitimate, and he asked Peckinpah to travel with him to check out rain forest locations in Mexico that might substitute for Africa. "I guess I gotta take a chance," Sam told him, "because I don't think anybody's going to let me direct again anyway . . . What the hell?"[28] As he packed his bags for Mexico, Peckinpah tucked in a copy of the *Wild Bunch* script.

Peckinpah had long ago finished the rewrites that project owner Roy Sickner had commissioned from him. After that, even with Lee Marvin's name still attached to it, *The Wild Bunch* was going nowhere in Hollywood. Yet this story of aging Southwestern outlaws caught up in the fervor of the Mexican Revolution had bitten deeply into Peckinpah's psyche. In San Blas in the state of Nayarit, about at the halfway point of Mexico's west coast, Peckinpah and Feldman found themselves trapped in a hotel by torrential rainfall from a tropical depression. While waiting for the weather to clear up, and with nothing better to do,

Peckinpah gave Feldman the *Wild Bunch* script to read. Sam's timing couldn't have been better.

It seemed everyone in Hollywood was talking about a screenplay making the rounds by a human writing machine named William Goldman; he wrote so fast that he'd once spat out an entire publishable novel in a week. Goldman had learned about Old West outlaws Butch Cassidy and the Sundance Kid and their Hole-in-the-Wall Gang, which was sometimes referred to as the Wild Bunch. Goldman developed a fascination with their tale, enough so that when he churned out another quickie novel, *No Way to Treat a Lady*, he published it using the Sundance Kid's real name, Harry Longabaugh, as a nom de plume. Movies about Western figures such as Billy the Kid, Wyatt Earp, Buffalo Bill, and Wild Bill Hickok had been done to death. Goldman had discovered fresh cinematic turf with Butch and Sundance, a compelling story about outlaws at the end of the West. The two outlaws had never been the subject of a major motion picture.

The writing in the "Harry Longabaugh" novel struck movie star Cliff Robertson's fancy, and he hired Goldman to adapt the sci-fi novel *Flowers for Algernon* into a screenplay. Goldman, who could not even drive, was an odd figure in Hollywood, but he showed a knack for screenwriting and soon worked on other successful adaptations. Then he set out to write an original screenplay based on his Old West outlaw research. When his agent began pushing *Butch Cassidy and the Sundance Kid* to studio and production company execs, a buzz began around it quite unlike any surrounding a previous script. Most of the talk was laudatory in the extreme, with some people in the business calling it the best screenplay ever written. Part of this had to do with an old Hollywood principle: The more something costs, the better it has to be. Goldman's agent set the fee for *Butch Cassidy and the Sundance Kid* at $400,000 plus a percentage of the picture's gross. No screenwriter in Hollywood history had ever received that kind of money. Tongues around town flapped. And flapped. And flapped.

There were naysayers. One was George Stevens, whose last picture, *The Greatest Story Ever Told*, a biblical epic, was flat and boring, a far cry from *Shane* or *The Diary of Anne Frank*. After he read the *Butch Cassidy and the Sundance Kid* screenplay, he told Peckinpah's associate Jim Silke that it was ridiculous, with calls for shots that made no sense. "I'd rather make the kinds of movies your friend Mr. Peckinpah has been making," Stevens said to Silke. Silke himself thought *Butch Cassidy and the Sundance Kid* was not so much a great screenplay as it was a cleverly done job application to establish a name for Goldman among the industry's deci-sion makers.[29]

Goldman's script was just the sort of "licorice stick, popcorn" that Marty Ransohoff had desired for *The Cincinnati Kid*. It was well constructed, intricately paced, and studded with clever passages of dialogue. At times, it was quite funny. He'd written a glossy vehicle ideal for glamorous stars with perfect teeth and just the right tan. The *Butch Cassidy and the Sundance Kid* script had no more depth to it than a graham cracker. As Lee Marvin might have assessed it, it was a script for yet "another movie in which no one takes a shit."

Feldman had already read *Butch Cassidy and the Sundance Kid* when Sam gave him a copy of *The Wild Bunch* that rainy day in Mexico. Because of that, the gang name *the wild bunch* resonated with him. Feldman had in fact encouraged Ken Hyman to buy *Butch Cassidy and the Sundance Kid*. The studio's moneymen thought Goldman's price was outrageous and convinced Hyman to pass. (Darryl Zanuck at Twentieth Century-Fox was the last of the old-time moguls still in power, and he'd put his son, Richard, in charge of production. Richard Zanuck, on his way to becoming one of the most important players in the New Hollywood, acquired *Butch Cassidy and the Sundance Kid*.)

As he read through the pages of Green and Peckinpah's script, Feld-man's interest perked up. The *Wild Bunch* story paralleled *Butch Cassidy and the Sundance Kid* in some ways, and it seemed to bear kinship with a series of other American Westerns set in Mexico, all of which had been financially successful, starting with Robert Aldrich's *Vera Cruz* back in 1954 and continuing with *The Magnificent Seven* and *The Professionals*. And parts of the script were very much like *The Treasure of the Sierra Madre*. Perhaps even more important, *The Wild Bunch* had elements similar to two down-and-dirty Westerns that had stunned the American cinema world when they became surprise smashes in 1967. Who could have predicted that genre-changing cowboy shows could have emanated from Italy, of all places?

Director Sergio Leone's *Per un pugno di dollari* and *Per qualche dollaro in più* (released in the United States as *For a Fistful of Dollars* and *For a Few Dollars More*) were produced by Italian companies that drew funding from around Europe, were shot in Spain, and featured casts made up of Italian and German actors, with the odd Frenchman, Spaniard, and American thrown into the mix. They starred an American, Clint East-wood, who at the time was the second lead of a black-and-white Western series broadcast on CBS, *Rawhide*, which was most distinguished for its

Wild Bunch producer Phil Feldman in Mexico. Photo by Paul Harper, courtesy of Nick Redman and Jeff Slater.

rousing theme song. The first of Leone's Western series, *For a Fistful of Dollars*, was shot while *Rawhide* was on hiatus and Eastwood was contractually free to work outside the United States. The pay wasn't much, but Eastwood figured he'd get a free trip to Spain and, mostly because he'd never visited Spain, he signed on. He wasn't expecting much in the way of quality from the movie, but he figured it would never show up in the U.S. market, so he wasn't much concerned about it hurting his career.

Leone's was a goofy operation by American studio standards, with everything done on the cheap. Leone, however, was a cinematic virtuoso, with a wonderful eye for composition, and he shared the sensibilities of the exciting Italian and French directors who had emerged after World War II. Like many Europeans, he was totally absorbed by the mythology of the American West. His work in Italian peplum movies such as *The Colossus of Rhodes* revealed nothing of the genius he exhibited when he began making what would come to be called spaghetti Westerns. Drawing on a variety of influences, everything from John Ford pictures to Fellini art films to the open-air puppet theaters near Rome's Piazzale Garibaldi that fascinated him when he was a boy, Leone's Westerns were gritty, dusty, muddy, absurd, hyperrealistic, sometimes silly, sometimes profound—and they were completely fresh takes on the hoary Western genre. He more or less created the existential Western hero, as played by Eastwood. Nothing was sacred in the films; they certainly were the kinds of movie in which someone would take a shit.

The scores composed by Ennio Morricone were purely original, so much so that they could at times draw attention away from what was visually occurring on the screen to the music. If conventional thinking held that the score should sit below the story as a foundational element, Morricone's rode on top. Morricone was the spiritual brother of American composer Leroy Anderson in that Morricone loved intriguing combinations of exotic instruments—electric surf guitar set against traditional Spanish guitar, tin whistle against tubular bells, Jew's harp against timpani. He also employed elements that were not even musical: vocals akin to soldiers counting cadence, the squawk made by a Twin Reverb amplifier when kicked.

For a Fistful of Dollars cost about $200,000. Italian film distributors, who saw a preview, thought it terrible, so it was shuffled off to a solitary movie house. It opened in Florence during a stifling hot day in August 1964, the worst possible time of year to premiere a picture in Italy. Against all odds, it became a massive hit.

Dubbed into different languages, it was shipped off to other countries, first Greece, then West Germany, Spain, Japan, France, Argentina, Sweden, Portugal, and others through 1965 and '66. An absolute phenomenon in these other countries as well, this prompted United Artists to acquire rights for an American release.

When it appeared in U.S. theaters in January 1967, American critics were negative. Movie fans in the United States ignored the reviews, and *A Fistful of Dollars* became a hit, earning millions of dollars at the box office. Later in 1967, United Artists released *For a Few Dollars More* in America. Leone's budget on the follow-up had been three times that of his first Western, but the investment was worth it. In the United States alone, it did five times the business of *A Fistful of Dollars*. Within a few months, Eastwood was a superstar, leaving *Rawhide* far behind. As Phil Feldman was reading *The Wild Bunch* in Mexico, Leone's third entry in what United Artists promoted as "the Man with No Name" series had been released in Europe. The big-budget Civil War epic was called *Il buono, il brutto, il cattivo*, again starring Eastwood, and was another blockbuster. The picture was set to be released in the United States as *The Good, the Bad, and the Ugly* just before New Year's Day 1968, and every indication was that it would make even more money than the first two. (It would, earning $25.1 million against a cost of $1.2 million.)[30]

The first two Leone Westerns took place in imaginary settings along the Mexico-U.S. border and in New Mexico. Leone used desert settings in Andalusia and elsewhere in Spain to double for northern Mexico and the American Southwest and outfitted many of the characters with sombreros, silver conch belts, and ponchos. Many of the Spanish buildings he filmed were constructed of adobe. That such motifs played so well to American audiences was appreciated by Feldman and other Hollywood executives—not to mention that the Leone films played well to baby boomers, the cash cow that all of Hollywood wanted to tap into. Feldman had to see that the *Wild Bunch* script had much in common with elements of what Leone was doing.

Feldman pronounced *The Wild Bunch* "a gasser."[31] He now envisioned a multipicture deal for Sam at Warner Bros.-Seven Arts. Both he and Peckinpah understood that the *Wild Bunch* script needed more work, and Feldman asked Sam to do the writing. Peckinpah agreed. "Of all the projects I have worked on," Sam wrote to studio boss Ken Hyman, "this is the closest to me and as you already know, there is no other place in the world I would rather do it than here."[32] Hyman, too, came to love the project.

Shortly after Peckinpah and Feldman returned from Mexico, the deal was struck: The Marlboro Man Roy Sickner and his investors were paid $28,000 for the rights to *The Wild Bunch*. Peckinpah would get $72,000 for further rewrites, plus another $100,000 for directing the picture. To no one's surprise, Peckinpah's signature on the contract hardly had time to dry before the Internal Revenue Service swooped in to place a levy on Sam's salary. He owed $3,092.54 in back taxes, roughly the equivalent of $19,500 in late-2010s dollars. The IRS seizure of his money might have meant getting by on cheap beer and peanut butter for a week or two in October 1967. After that, Peckinpah could walk around with more money in his pocket than he'd had in years.[33] Sam set about completely reworking the characters, adding distinctive dialogue (some of it from the old-time Westerners he had been around as a kid), and adding new scenes here and there.

For half the asking cost of the screenplay for *Butch Cassidy and the Sundance Kid*, Warner Bros.-Seven Arts now owned *The Wild Bunch* and had a director in place. The race was now on for *The Wild Bunch* to hit theaters ahead of *Butch Cassidy and the Sundance Kid*. What had begun as a nugget of an idea that Sickner had kicked around with his stuntmen buddies on the set of a Yul Brynner costumer four years earlier was headed toward production at one of the great studios in Hollywood history, with the once-vanquished outlaw Sam Peckinpah at the helm.

6.

Peckinpah settled back in at Malibu to perform further work on the *Wild Bunch* script while also prepping to film *The Diamond Story*. The *Diamond Story* had little promise to it other than it was an action-adventure project that could make Warner Bros.-Seven Arts some money, with nothing about it that captured much of Peckinpah's artistic fancy, let alone his heart. It was just as well, then, that the *Diamond Story* project fell apart, and Phil Feldman moved *The Wild Bunch* into the first slot in the rotation of films he and Peckinpah had discussed making together.

Much still needed to be done to fully flesh out the characters in *The Wild Bunch*. Sam added new characters and new scenes to achieve the depth he desired for the picture. He mostly worked alone. His writing partner, Jim Silke, who had been all but surgically attached to Peckinpah since the shooting of *Major Dundee*, was feeling deflated beneath the weight of all-Sam-all-the-time and was attempting to recover his bearings when Peckinpah shoved one of the rewrites of *The Wild Bunch* into Jim's hands and asked him to read it. Silke was so worn-out that he only glanced at the cover sheet. Soon Peckinpah called wanting to know what Silke thought of the latest version of the script. Before Silke could say much, Peckinpah interjected that Lee Marvin had loved it, particularly the addition of a character named Crazy Lee. Did Silke like what Sam had done with Crazy Lee? "It's great," Silke said. Something about his voice betrayed him. After a strained silence, Peckinpah growled, "You son of a bitch. You haven't read it. You lied to me!" Sam slammed down the phone. It was the first and only time Silke had lied to Sam. As a consequence, Silke was banished from the Peckinpah realm for months.[34]

As Sam shut the door on Silke, he opened another. Syd Field was a Hollywood kid—his uncle Sol headed the camera department at Fox—who wound up enrolled at the University of California in 1959. Syd had the good fortune to arrive when the university had recruited the esteemed French film director Jean Renoir as artist-in-residence. Renoir opted to premiere his new stage play, *Carola*, at Berkeley. Field auditioned, and Renoir cast him in one of the lead roles, much to Field's delight. The title part went to Deneen Peckinpah, daughter of Sam's big brother, Denny. Through theater rehearsals, Field and Deneen became friends.[35]

After college, Field was hired by Wolper Productions and worked on several shows with Walon Green. Then, in 1962, *Film Quarterly* assigned Field to write a comparison/contrast piece about Sam's *Ride the High Country* and *Lonely Are the Brave*, a stunning black-and-white contemporary Western starring Kirk Douglas in what Douglas always claimed was the best movie of his career.[36] *Lonely Are the Brave* had been written by Dalton Trumbo, who based it on what was Edward Abbey's best novel, *The Brave Cowboy*. Good as *Lonely Are the Brave* was, Field found *Ride the High Country* to be superior: "It had a strong subject and a great style and was done with such color and humor that I was totally taken in by it. I loved it."[37] The last name of the director caught his attention. It was the same as that of his acting buddy at Berkeley.

Shortly after Field filed his piece with *Film Quarterly*, he received a phone call from Deneen, who'd shown up in L.A. to pursue an acting career. Field had not seen her since college and agreed to meet her to catch up. Over lunch a few days later, he asked her if she was related to the Peckinpah who was a film director. Deneen told him that Sam was indeed her uncle, and that she was staying at his house in Malibu. After Field expressed his admiration for Peckinpah's work, Deneen invited him to Sam's place for dinner.[38] Field had heard horror stories about Sam that had made the rounds in Hollywood. Over dinner a few nights later, Field discovered that Sam was anything but a drunken monster: "I found he reminded me a little of my uncle Sol—tough and honest, with a keen sensibility and understanding."[39] Peckinpah told Field that he'd been hired by Warner Bros.-Seven Arts to write and direct *The Wild Bunch*. As a result, he was limiting himself to just two beers a day and no liquor—a major sacrifice. He was focused on the script. "I wrote it as something I'd want to see from the story I was given," Peckinpah said.[40]

Field became a regular at Sam's place. Field once confessed to Peckinpah that he had discovered some writings about a group of latter-day Western outlaws who were known as the Hole-in-the-Wall Gang and were led by these characters named Butch Cassidy and the Sundance Kid. Field thought he could try his hand at writing a screenplay about them.

Then he learned that William Goldman had already beat him to the punch. Field felt dejected, but Sam told him that kind of thing happened in the movie business all the time. Sam added that Field should hang on to his Cassidy material—maybe he could find a way to use it down the road. Sam confessed his own biggest fear was not being able to work. Field saw clearly that directing movies was Peckinpah's life—everything else was secondary.

One afternoon, after Peckinpah had finished his day's work on the *Wild Bunch* script, Field asked Sam how he structured his stories. After giving it some thought, Peckinpah said he liked to hang his stories around a centerpiece. He would build the action up to that centerpiece, which occurred around midpoint of the story, "then let everything else be the result of that event."[41] Peckinpah put a copy of the shooting script for *Major Dundee* in Field's hands and told him to read it. In this revelatory experience, for the first time the nuts and bolts of how a screenplay worked became clear to Field. "I think that if there is any one script that taught me more than any other about the art and craft of creating a screenplay, it was *Major Dundee*," Field said years later after he'd written a bestselling text on screenwriting and had become Hollywood's best-known, if also controversial, script guru.

Finally, Peckinpah invited Field to read Sam's latest draft of *The Wild Bunch*. It was a busy time for Sam. With Warner Bros.-Seven Arts green-lighting the picture for production, Peckinpah was tending to the myriad necessary details before filming. He was working his way through the final drafts of the script. The day Field arrived to pick up a copy of *The Wild Bunch*, Sam was late, tied up at a meeting with the picture's art director. When Sam finally arrived, he handed Field a crisp copy of the script. Field took it home and read it in one sitting. "I can still recall that first reading of *The Wild Bunch*, and how emotionally drained I felt by the vibrancy of the experience," Field said.[42]

A few days later, beers in hand, Peckinpah and Field sat on Sam's porch and looked out at the Pacific while discussing *The Wild Bunch*. Peckinpah told him that, ultimately, he was trying to tell a simple story about what happens when killers go to Mexico. Ironically, the effect on the viewers of this story would be anything but simple. Like the great Greek and Shakespearean dramas, this story was cathartic. "The strange thing," Peckinpah said, "is that you feel a great sense of loss when these killers reach the end of the line." Field understood exactly what Peckinpah meant.[43]

Not everyone agreed with Field's excitement about *The Wild Bunch*. One "gray, empty morning," Peckinpah gave the script to his good friend Robert Culp, who, like Field, sat down and read it straight through. "I groaned with each foolish page," said Culp, "to think he had to go and do this nonsense for all those bleak months in Mexico." To Culp, the story was so simple that it didn't even matter if it held together. It involved just "witless, limited men." Besides, this kind of story had been done to death. "On four occasions that I can think of, it was called, in English, something with *Magnificent Seven* in the title. The Mirisch Company has made it into a sort of conglomerate unto itself."[44]

Culp considered himself to be not unlike many other young Americans who stood at the cusp of revolution as the pivotal year 1968 approached. Culp felt that his friend should be given a chance to do some kind of artistic work engaged with the fervor going on in the streets, whether it be, say, the "hippie riots" along Sunset Boulevard or the demonstrations associated with the United Farm Workers' Delano grape strike—anything but making another "dumb Western flick" down in Mexico, far removed from everything happening in the United States. Later, after he saw the film, Culp would have a different opinion entirely as he realized his buddy Sam had "created a tragedy and put it up on the screen, which is important in its way, in its very rude, empirical way, as any single work by Sophocles."[45] But at the time, the *Wild Bunch* screenplay seemed to Culp like nothing more than a blueprint for yet another cowboy picture set in Mexico.

But much work remained before this Sophocles-on-the-screen could make it into theaters.

7.

Field may have marveled at Sam the Teacher, but the darker elements of Peckinpah's soul were hardly at rest.

David Peckinpah was Denver Peckinpah's son (named for Sam and Denny's dad), and David's relationship with Uncle Sam had its troubling elements. Jason Culp, Robert's son, thought Sam was unduly harsh at times on his own children during those otherwise idyllic cookouts at Broad Beach.[46] If anything, Sam was even harsher on his nephew. A little more than two years earlier, when David was fourteen, he defeated his uncle in a game of poker. Throughout his life, Sam was known as a particularly bad loser, and he certainly was this day. He reacted by backhanding David with enough force to split his lip. An outraged Walter Peter, who witnessed the scene, sprang into action, scooping up the much smaller Sam and carrying his squirming brother-in-law onto the beach and hurling him into the Pacific. Peckinpah emerged slowly from the water like some broken creature from the black lagoon, then trudged inside to change clothes, cursing the whole time. He never once apologized to his nephew or to anyone else for his behavior that night.

In late 1967, the *Wild Bunch* script in tow, Sam traveled to a small ranch, the Lazy SP ("lazy Sam Peckinpah"), that he owned outside Ely, Nevada, in the company of his brother, Denver, Walter Peter, and other male relatives and friends from Bass Lake, Fresno, and L.A. Sam's nephew David was among the group, which styled itself as the Walker River Boys. "The boys" made their way to Nevada each fall to hunt deer, drink, and carouse at Ely's whorehouses.

These were rambunctious trips. One time, at a roadhouse in the big empty between Ely and Baker, Nevada, Peckinpah matter-of-factly ordered David to fetch a pistol from the truck so Sam could shoot the roadhouse cook for refusing to fry onions with the hash browns. Denver talked Sam out of it, though he agreed that hash browns without onions was a crime, at least by Fresno standards. "A capital offense," David later observed. Years afterward, he'd marvel that both his dad and his uncle died in bed with their boots off.

Over poker on this particular trip, it occurred to Sam that David was newly turned sixteen, time for a boy to become a man by Peckinpah family standards. He asked if David had lost his virginity yet. David fessed up that he hadn't. "Tonight's the night," Sam responded. He folded a piece of bread and some bacon he'd intended to eat into a napkin and jammed it into the pocket of his Levi's. Then the two of them loaded up in Sam's four-wheel-drive pickup and headed off toward Ely, David driving while Sam chain smoked and pontificated about women, the gist of which went that whores were the only women a man could trust. Among other things, prostitutes were checked by doctors regularly. You didn't have to worry about picking up gonorrhea from them. And if you did pick up a dose of the clap, it was no big deal. "I've had it so many times," Sam said, "I don't get shots anymore. I just lay my cock in a saucer of penicillin, and it laps it up."[47]

In Ely, Sam and David checked in at the Nevada Hotel. Then Sam insisted David sample talent at all three of the town's high street whorehouses. Then do it again, such a level of performance being possible for most sixteen-year-old guys. As David did his business with the prostitutes, Sam occupied by himself by drinking and chain-smoking Pall Malls.

They departed the last brothel stop, David's virginity well erased by the six rounds with the prostitutes, but Sam walked just a short distance before he passed out on his feet and fell to the snowy sidewalk. David attempted to tote Sam, who was now deadweight, on his shoulder, back to the Nevada Hotel but couldn't make it. A man driving a truck pulled over and offered David a ride. With a one-two-three-*heave*, they tossed Sam's inert form into the back of the truck, which was loaded with spools of wire. Then the man drove David to the hotel, where he dragged Sam to a room. Peckinpah came around the next morning, his ribs bruised and tender. He had no memory of the spools of wire in the back of the truck and figured someone had beaten him up. He found the bacon and bread in his Levi's and wolfed it down while sipping whiskey to fire up the day. Then he offered David some writerly advice: "You should take notes, write it down so you don't forget."[48]

When they made it back to the Lazy SP, Denver Peckinpah was waiting for them, Johnny Cash on the stereo, a pot of Denver's famous beans on the stove. "Did you get it done?" Denver asked his son. David said yes, and Denver dished up some beans and poured a glass of whiskey for his son as congratulations. Such was the way of the Peckinpah men.[49]

8.

O nce Sam returned to L.A. from Nevada, it seemed as if the project into which he had been investing so much of his heart and soul might collapse. Lee Marvin, who had been so intricately involved with *The Wild Bunch* all the way back to those boozy nights at Chez Jay, was off the picture. Marvin's concerns that his role as Fardan in *The Professionals* was too similar to that of Pike Bishop in *The Wild Bunch* had never abated. If anything, he grew even more worried. He simply did not want to get typecast as a grizzled American hero caught up in the Mexican Revolution.

Marvin's power agent, Meyer Mishkin, never liked the idea of his client appearing in *The Wild Bunch*. Now Mishkin had worked out an astonishing deal, at least by 1967–68 standards: Paramount would pay Marvin $1 million to star in its adaptation of Lerner and Loewe's lame Western-themed Broadway musical, *Paint Your Wagon*. The studio offered a similar costarring deal to Clint Eastwood, now hugely bankable because of the success of the Leone Westerns. A million dollars was enough in the late 1960s to set someone up for life. Not surprisingly, both Eastwood and Marvin said yes, and Marvin pulled out of *The Wild Bunch*. That could have been the death knell for the picture, but the Warner Bros.-Seven Arts brass decided to move forward with the movie, even without Marvin's star power.

Now Warners searched for a replacement Pike Bishop. Nothing was more important for the success of *The Wild Bunch* than matching the right actor with the right character. Peckinpah and Feldman would devote considerable time and effort to make the perfect choices. Marvin's departure would be one of the best things to happen to the movie. Marvin had limited range as an actor, but within that range he was one of the most effective film actors ever. The role of Pike Bishop had become vastly more complex with Peckinpah's rewrites. Bishop was a criminal so successful that the railroad was spending a lot of money to have him tracked down and eliminated. He would show great skill in organizing the bunch's final mission, the train robbery. He was also flawed and had led his gang into an ambush during the movie's opening scenes; he totally missed that he was being set up. He would give a speech about the need for men to stick with their comrades, yet he abandoned Crazy Lee to certain death in the opening robbery, hardly giving the matter any thought. Earlier, he had misjudged the threat from Pinkerton agents while drinking and carousing with whores. When the Pinkertons arrived, he fled instead of fighting, leaving his close companion Deke Thornton to be captured while saving his own hide. He'd often speak in platitudes, though he sometimes failed to live up to them with his actions. He redeems himself, though, when he leads the survivors of his gang in a final heroic act, exhibiting great courage and grace in the face of annihilation.

In the film's first thirty minutes, most aspects of Pike's character have to emerge as he leads the bunch to town for the railroad-office robbery, directs their escape against tremendous odds (bounty hunters on rooftops attempting to kill them), shoots an injured member of the gang to put him out of his misery, escapes with the surviving bunch to Mexico, and, ultimately, realizes he's been set up all along. It's a heavy burden. Many good men have died. When the Gorch brothers challenge his leadership, he stands up to them: "If you two boys don't like equal shares, why in the hell don't you just take all of it? . . . Well, why don't you answer me, you damn yellow-livered trash? I don't know a damn thing except I either lead or end it right now." The Gorches back down. It would take a skilled actor indeed to pull off the role of Pike.

Feldman and Peckinpah kicked around the names of many actors as a replacement for Marvin. One intriguing possibility was Robert Mitchum. Another was Sterling Hayden, who had starred with Joan Crawford in Nicholas Ray's deliciously freaky cowboy flick *Johnny Guitar*. Tried-and-true box office draws were sent copies of the script: Burt Lancaster, James Stewart (who had played all of those bad good guy/good bad guy characters in Anthony Mann's Westerns), Charlton Heston, and Gregory Peck (who had already starred in such significant Westerns as *Duel in the Sun*, *The Gunfighter*, and *The Big Country*). They even considered Paladin from TV's *Have Gun—Will Travel*, Richard Boone, who would have been popular with baby boomers.

In the end, Feldman and Peckinpah went with William Holden. There could not have been a better matching of character and actor. Holden was a first-rate actor but also a deeply troubled man, a real-life killer himself. He was on a conditional suspended sentence for manslaughter when he signed with Warner Bros.-Seven Arts. He had a full reservoir of internal turmoil to draw upon as he created Pike Bishop.

9.

In the spring of 1955, a Hollywood film troupe encamped in Hutchinson, Kansas, to shoot scenes for the screen adaptation of William Inge's play *Picnic*, with William Holden as the star. Holden was Hollywood gold at the time—given the way his career had developed, it seemed apt that he'd made a name for himself in pictures in a movie called *Golden Boy*. Athletic and handsome, he had a face the camera loved and a distinctive voice. He'd made a lot of money for both Paramount and Columbia, enough so that he was one of the few people in pictures who could tell Harry Cohn to go fuck himself and get away with it.

Yet for a man who seemed to have it all, he also had a self-destructive aspect that befuddled those who knew him. After shooting in Hutchinson wrapped late one afternoon, Holden invited several members of the cast to join him for drinks in his tenth-floor suite at Hutchinson's landmark Baker Hotel. As usual, Holden drank hard and fast, opting for his favorite, martinis mixed extra strong. Then, after arguing with the picture's publicist, he opened the floor-to-ceiling window and stepped out onto its ledge and walked on it—on his hands. The people in the suite were aghast, but Holden had just begun. He lowered himself over the side of the ledge, clinging to it with only his fingers. Finally, he climbed back inside the suite. Within hours, stories began to filter back to the West Coast about the crazy stunt Bill Holden had pulled in Kansas. No one who knew him well was surprised.

A part of Holden's makeup had always been puzzling, going all the way back to his childhood in Southern California. He had been born as William Beedle in Illinois in 1918, the son of a chemist, but the family moved to Monrovia, California, when he was five. Eventually the Beedles relocated to nearby South Pasadena, then an enclave of conservative Republican politics and Protestant Christianity. In South Pasadena, some things were respectable, others not. Living a life on the straight and narrow while making a lot of money in business was acceptable. Drinking heavily, sleeping around, and forging a career in motion pictures was not. Beedle, who from an early age enjoyed the applause he received in school plays, grew up conflicted. To the end of his days, a part of him believed he had let his family down by not following his dad into the chemical industry, never mind the acclaim and riches he eventually received as Academy Award winner William Holden.

Around the time his father fell ill from overexposure to chemicals, Beedle began engaging in daredevil stunts that became the stuff of legend in his hometown. He was forever leaping off garages and houses, sometimes using an umbrella as a makeshift parachute. He walked on telephone lines as if they were tightropes. Most ominous, he began hand-walking the railings of the Colorado Street Bridge[50] spanning the Arroyo Seco in next-door Pasadena. With its stunning beaux arts arches and distinctive light standards, the fifteen-hundred-foot-long bridge, built in 1912, was and remains a stunning work of architecture and design. By the time of Beedle's youth, it had developed a notorious reputation as Pasadena's suicide bridge. Dozens of distraught people leaped from it to their deaths on the arroyo rocks 150 feet below, seventy-nine in the 1930s. That same decade, young Bill Beedle was gleefully tempting death by hand-walking on those very same bridge railings. One day he raised the risk factor even higher: He rode a bicycle on the suicide bridge balustrades. His daredevil activities won him much attention from friends, but his younger brother knew that was not why Bill did it. "He did all the foolhardy things he did not so much to attract attention as to prove that he could do them, not to others but to himself," Richard Beedle said. "He accepted all challenges on a personal basis. He was a real competitor because he competed with himself."[51]

As a teenager, Beedle took up surfing, raced cars on the Murco Dry Lake bed, sped around town on a motorcycle, and escaped to the Mojave Desert or the San Gabriel Mountains whenever he could to get away from the monotony of South Pasadena life. Beedle also became a successful athlete, but not on the football field or basketball court, his father having admonished him against contact sports. Beedle's sport was gymnastics, not surprising given his proclivity toward walking on his hands.

Holden barely graduated from high school because of his low grades. Unable to gain admittance to a prestige university, he enrolled at Pasadena Junior College, which would be one of the best things to happen

William Holden never completely gave up his daredevil ways. Here he tightrope-walks a support cable for the bridge blown up for *The Wild Bunch*'s centerpiece explosion—and does so in full Pike Bishop costume, including boots with riding heels and spurs. Photo by Paul Harper, courtesy of Nick Redman and Jeff Slater.

to him. Through a connection he made there, he was invited to provide narration for a play staged at the experimental Playbox Theater. He agreed. Then one of the actors in the play had to drop out, and the part was offered to Beedle. "Why not?" Beedle said. So, on opening night, twenty-year-old Bill Beedle, with little experience beyond public school dramatic productions, played a stooped eighty-year-old man with a flowing white beard.

Milt Lewis, Paramount's talent scout, was in the audience at the Playbox. He was impressed by the actor playing the old man, and after the final curtain, Lewis made his way backstage to give his card to Beedle. Two days later, Beedle rode his motorcycle from South Pasadena to the Paramount lot on Marathon Street in L.A. The studio hired him and changed his name to William Holden, then entered into a long term contract to share Holden's services with Columbia.

Columbia was in preproduction for the film version of Clifford Odets's hit Broadway play *Golden Boy*, whose main character, Joe Bonaparte, was a youth torn between his dream of becoming a concert violinist and a boxing career. Studio boss Cohn and director Rouben Mamoulian agreed to use an unknown as the lead and hyped up the search for Columbia's Joe Bonaparte as prerelease publicity for the film. The nod went to Holden, despite his paucity of acting experience. It was a torturous experience for Holden. Not only did he have to learn the ropes of performing as a big-league actor, he had the additional burden of mimicking the skills of both a violinist and a boxer convincingly. (He studied with a violinist named Julian Brodetsky and a boxer named Cannonball Green.) The brutal days of work ran from six in the morning until after midnight. But with the nurturing support of costar Barbara Stanwyck, he made his way through the shoot.

Neither the film nor Holden's performance were particularly memorable. Still, it was the pivotal event in his career. He came out of it with an appreciation of what acting entailed and plunged forward in his new vocation. His heroes in the film industry became Fredric March and Spencer Tracy: "They're real *actors*," Holden said at the time, "not just movie stars."[52] Within a few years, Holden expanded his list of favorites to include Joel McCrea and Gary Cooper. Holden wanted to be a real *actor* like those four masters. It was hard work, something that might have appealed to the sort of Midwestern ethics the Beedle family embraced.

However, never mind his hard work, Holden discovered that as a contract actor he would seldom be given projects that demanded much in the way of acting skills. He came to understand that he was essentially a factory laborer, paid to come in, knock out a job, then move on to the next project. Early on, he started panicking before each day's shooting began. He learned this was not uncommon for Hollywood actors, and that many used alcohol to calm their nerves. Holden began downing a couple of shots of whiskey before his daily schedule, taking care to brush his teeth before he came into contact with anyone on the set. It worked. Liquor became a constant in both his professional and private life. It helped him soothe the uneasiness he felt as a star, but never eliminated it. He'd see his name on a cinema marquee while walking with a friend and say that he was not William Holden, movie star—he was just Bill Beedle from South Pasadena, California. Then he'd head toward the closest cocktail lounge.

Booze also helped him round off the painful corners of the guilt he always carried with him because he'd failed to follow his father into the chemical business. His drinking grew worse during World War II. Holden enlisted in the U.S. Army, the first married Hollywood star to volunteer for the war effort. After OCS, he received orders to work in the army's PR efforts. Meanwhile, his brother Bob became a navy pilot. In 1944, Bob was shot down over the South Pacific while Holden was tucked away at a safe post in Fort Worth. Once he received the news, Holden locked himself in his room to grieve and blame himself—believing that he, as the oldest son, should have been the one to meet death in combat, not his kid brother. As he mourned, he had a bottle in the room to comfort him.

At the end of the war, Holden toyed with the idea of giving up acting and actually going to work for his dad at the chemical company. It was a fleeting notion. Holden looked different now, more mature, and Harry Cohn thought that would only enhance his appeal to moviegoers, which would land him bigger and better roles. Holden needed a steady income. He had married a woman from the Philippines, Ardis Ankerson, who'd acted in movies under the stage name Brenda Marshall. They now had three children, so Holden had responsibilities—no more auto racing on dry lake beds or zipping through L.A. traffic on a motorcycle. He settled his family into a large house on Sancola Avenue in the San Fernando Valley, away from the trendy social life found in Beverly Hills and Bel-Air.

As he focused on his job in the movies, he churned out picture after picture, sometimes as many as four in a year. Westerns made their way into the rotation. He'd shot his first before the war, *Arizona*. Now came such titles as *The Man from Colorado*, *Streets of Laredo*, and *Escape from Fort Bravo*, a couple of them costarring his friend and sometimes rival

Glenn Ford. None was particularly memorable, but they showcased his athletic grace, and he looked terrific on horseback. He proved to be much more of a natural horseman than John Wayne ever was.

But most of Holden's postwar work was glossy, melodramatic junk. Every so often, just the right movie came along, and he was able to show his stuff as an actor. He proved he had great depth in such pictures as *The Dark Past, Sunset Boulevard, Stalag 17, Executive Suite, Picnic,* and *The Bridge on the River Kwai.* They elevated him to the highest rung of Hollywood stardom by the time he agreed to play Major Henry Kendall in John Ford's *The Horse Soldiers.* His costar John Wayne might have received first billing, but each actor received the same salary, $250,000, top pay for actors in the 1950s.

Holden's success did little, if anything, to stave off the conflicts in his life, which grew even more profound as his drinking worsened. He grew distant from his wife and children as he engaged in the hidebound tradition of leading men bedding their leading ladies. In 1954, he'd starred in Billy Wilder's smash *Sabrina,* with the exotically featured Belgium-born actress Audrey Hepburn in the title role. They fell in love during the filming, even though they both were already married. The relationship went nowhere, but he could not turn loose what might have been. Years afterward, when he would lower his guard, Holden would confess to buddies that Hepburn was the great love of his life.

From the peak it hit around the time of *The Horse Soldiers,* Holden's career began to slide. He and his agent made bad choice after bad choice for movies for him to appear in. Moreover, he and his contemporaries who'd been stars in the Old Hollywood quickly became relics in the 1960s, forcing them to do whatever they had to do to continue to earn a living, even if it meant signing up for series television. His best friend, Ronald Reagan, might have given the best performance of his career as the villain (a role Reagan hated) in Don Siegel's *The Killers* in 1964. After that, he was reduced to TV's *Death Valley Days* before getting elected governor of California, having migrated politically from Roosevelt Democrat to right-wing conservative. Fred MacMurray, who had been so effective as mild-mannered yet twisted villains in *Double Indemnity* and *The Caine Mutiny,* now earned his living by drawing paychecks from the milquetoast *My Three Sons* TV series and Disney's inane *Flubber* comedies. Glenn Ford, who'd been motion pictures' number one box office draw in 1958, would soon be heading to TV himself.

Holden had avoided the TV trap, but he was increasingly becoming less relevant; mediocrities such as *The 7th Dawn* and *Alvarez Kelly* did nothing to win him young moviegoers. To make matters worse, he took a step that alienated his core older fan base. To avoid American taxes, Holden became a citizen of Switzerland. Nothing could be more unpatriotic among conservatives of the time than to forsake American citizenship. Meanwhile his drinking continued to escalate.

Holden's alcoholism had reached the point that he'd have to check himself in at different "spas" from time to time to dry out. In July 1966, he was in such a spa in Montecatini in Italy. One night, Holden gave up his attempt at sobriety at the spa and had dinner and drinks with friends, two of whom, sisters both in their early twenties, persuaded him to drive them to Viareggio, a Tuscan resort city on the Tyrrhenian Sea. Holden had just purchased a Ferrari, and while the days of racing on dry lake beds in the Mojave were far behind him, he could not resist the chance to try out his new sports car on the autostrada. Soon he was tearing along the highway, the young women tucked in the Ferrari with him.

One witness to events that occurred that night said he was driving his own Porsche at one hundred miles per hour when Holden passed him with ease. Holden was driving so fast that he was unable to stop when he came upon a slow-moving Fiat ahead of him. He smashed into the smaller car, killing the driver, Valerio Novelli, a forty-two-year-old textile salesman struggling to support three generations of his family. Italian authorities prosecuted Holden for manslaughter, and in October 1967 he was found guilty, although in the end, the judge gave him only an eight-month suspended prison sentence.

Holden may have avoided time behind steel bars, but the publicity surrounding the wreck and the conviction only made matters worse for the public image of the actor, who was about to turn fifty and who was already in many quarters considered washed-up. His eight months' probation was still in effect when he agreed to play Pike Bishop in *The Wild Bunch*. The part would give him the opportunity to use all the skills he'd learned over thirty years as an actor as he portrayed a character who was by turns remorseful, exuberant, hollow, insightful, courageous, cowardly, haunted, determined, clever, angry, and in charge, always in charge. All these qualities would come into play as Pike Bishop leads his wild bunch from blundered railroad-office robbery to encountering a corrupt warlord, Mapache, in revolutionary Mexico to successfully stealing rifles from a train to returning to Mapache's lair, where he and his men decide they must lay down their lives for a comrade.

10.

One night, my wife and I sat down to watch *The Wild Bunch*, which she had never seen. She sat transfixed through the whole tale of robbers who had fled to Mexico, from the botched holdup at the beginning to the final shoot-out. Her first question, after the credits ran to that haunting *canción de despedida* "Las Golondrinas," was "Were Pike and Dutch in love?" My answer: Yes, though not in a romantic way. Walon Green's story, as remolded and refined by Peckinpah, fit squarely into a common mold for classic works of American literature, a story about the relationship of men without women.

At its heart was a love affair between two men—a *bromance*, to use the pop term that began to turn up during the 1990s. In this, *The Wild Bunch* was like such timeless American novels as *The Last of the Mohicans* (Natty Bumppo and Chingachgook), *Moby-Dick* (Ishmael and Queequeg), and *The Adventures of Huckleberry Finn* (Huck and Jim on the raft). This motif had been widely discussed on American college campuses in the 1950s and '60s, thanks in part to the rediscovery of D. H. Lawrence's 1923 book, *Studies in Classic American Literature*. Also, the works of the popular if controversial American critic of the time Leslie Fiedler prompted literary seminar discussions about the theme, particularly his essay "Come Back to the Raft Ag'in, Huck Honey!" and his books, *Love and Death in the American Novel* and *The Return of the Vanishing American*.

Fiedler was bold enough to use the term *homoerotic* in describing these relationships between men who flee the complexities of proper society and the demands of marriage to a woman for adventures in the wilderness. He took things a step further: He noted that the homoerotic love in these books most often concerned a white man and a man of color— Natty Bumppo and an American Indian, Ishmael and a South Seas islander, Huck and an African American. This dynamic also turned up often in the genre novels that Fiedler devoured by the dozen, especially Westerns. None of this could have been lost on the well-read Peckinpah.

In *The Wild Bunch*, Green and Peckinpah complicated the motif by including a "bromantic triangle" involving Pike, Dutch, and Pike's former partner Deke Thornton, whom Pike had abandoned to capture. Deke was out to save himself from a lifetime behind prison walls while exacting revenge on the man who had forsaken him. Yet Deke also retained strong feelings for Pike: He described Pike and his cohorts as "the best. They never got caught." And Pike knew that Deke was in every way justified in seeking retribution against him, yet he still maintained his own strong feelings for his pursuer. It would take three gifted actors to pull off this dynamic on-screen. Holden had shown he had the stuff for it. Peckinpah needed equally gifted actors for the other two roles.

From the moment the wild bunch robs the railroad office early in the movie, Dutch is at Pike's right hand. After Pike shoots the injured gang member who can no longer ride, Dutch supports him and his decision to move along while the Gorch brothers want to take time to bury their former comrade. Dutch pulls a pistol to support Pike during the show-down with the Gorch brothers over shares of the loot that follows. That night, Pike and Dutch bunk next to each other and talk about the future. "How about us, Pike? You reckon we learned—being wrong, today?" Dutch asks. "I sure hope to God we did," says Pike. Dutch serves as translator to Pike and the others when they deal with Mexican troops under Mapache. At times, Dutch seems to be the conscience of the bunch as well. When, in Mapache's compound, Pike jokes about the gang being similar to the thieving general, Dutch sternly rebukes him: "Not so's you'd know it, Mr. Bishop. We ain't nothin' like him! We don't hang nobody! I hope, someday, these people here kick him, and the rest of that scum like him, right into their graves." Dutch seems to be the second-in-command throughout the gang's adventures, but especially during the train robbery and the retreat with the stolen rifles back into Mexico. He's also flawed. After the wild bunch has transferred the stolen rifles to Mapache, Dutch betrays Angel, the young Mexican member of the gang, to the general. Dutch is filled with self-loathing, until Pike makes the fateful decision to attempt to rescue Angel.

Robert Culp had urged Sam to hire Sammy Davis Jr. for the part of Dutch. Culp and Davis were the closest of friends, and Culp knew something about his friend that few other people were aware of. Davis might have been a sophisticated song-and-dance man with roots in Harlem, a master of tap, and a regular at Rat Pack gatherings in Vegas, but he also had a deep and abiding interest in the West and its mythology, especially cowboy movies. He became obsessed with mastering the fast draw, practicing constantly, and he eventually liked to show off his technique at parties as the clouds of cigarette smoke grew thicker and the martinis flowed steadily. Certainly, casting Davis opposite Holden would have mirrored one of Fiedler's homoerotic relationships involving a white man and a person of color.

But Davis was nixed, as were several other actors Peckinpah considered: Steve McQueen, George Peppard, Charles Bronson, Richard Jaeckel, and Culp himself. Then Ken Hyman told Peckinpah that he wanted to cast Ernest Borgnine. Sam didn't see Borgnine as right for the role. Moreover, he'd never worked with the *McHale's Navy* star, and for this picture Peckinpah didn't want to take chances with an unknown quantity in such a pivotal part. Hyman insisted—and Hyman was right.

Borgnine was born Ermes Effron Borgnino to Italian immigrants in Hamden, Connecticut, shortly before America's entry into World War I. After his parents split up temporarily, Borgnine moved with his mother

Ernest Borgnine gave one of his best acting performances as Dutch in *The Wild Bunch*, but it was not an easy shoot for him. He played the role with a broken foot, and the dust in Parras stirred up his allergies and made him miserable. Here he takes a break from filming. Stuntman/actor Billy Hart and actor L. Q. Jones (back to camera) play cards behind him. Photo by Bernie Abramson, courtesy of Tonio K.

to Italy. He grew up there and then back in Connecticut after his parents reconciled. He was a rough-and-tumble kid, showing no inclination toward drama or any arts while he was attending public schools in New Haven as a teenager. After he finished school, Borgnine signed up for the peacetime navy, serving for six years, mostly on a minesweeper. Then he reenlisted once World War II broke out.

Borgnine came home after the war and looked around for work in factories, but he couldn't see spending his whole life on an assembly line. He kicked around the idea of returning to the navy. Then one day his mother said to him, "Have you ever thought of becoming an actor? You always like to make a fool out of yourself in front of people. Why don't you give it a try?"

"I was seated at the kitchen table," Borgnine said, "and I saw this light. So help me. It sounds crazy, doesn't it? But I saw this light. And I said, 'Mom, that's what I'm going to be.'"[53]

The gruff Italian guy toughened up by all those years in the navy applied for an internship at a small theater in Virginia. Within a couple years, he was a local favorite on the stage. Two years after that, he was in New York, playing character roles on Broadway. Then he moved to Hollywood and signed on at Columbia Pictures, where a role in a military drama changed his career. James Jones's novel of the peacetime army in Hawaii just prior to Pearl Harbor, *From Here to Eternity*, was both a massive bestseller and a favorite of the critics'. Director Fred Zinnemann cast Borgnine in the role of Fatso Judson, a switchblade-toting staff sergeant who is in charge of enlisted prisoners at the post stockade. The script called for Fatso to be a loud, explosive, sadistic bully, and Borgnine fit the part to a T, even if he did thereafter have to carry the onus of having beaten star Frank Sinatra to death.

In 1955, Borgnine played the title character in the big-screen version of Paddy Chayefsky's teleplay *Marty*. Borgnine was particularly effective playing the lovelorn title character, an Italian American butcher in the Bronx. The film was an international success, and Borgnine, just ten years after being goaded into acting by his mother, won the Oscar for Best Actor. The golden door he'd envisioned in his mother's kitchen had opened for him indeed. One of the hallways it opened to was surprising, given his background. He proved to be successful in Westerns as slowly, very slowly, Hollywood was beginning to present a more realistic view of the West.

An Italian in chaps and boots actually made perfect sense. In frontier days, the West was very much a multicultural place, though you'd never guess it from watching most Hollywood Westerns of the 1950s and earlier. Those movies presented it as territory inhabited by white people who spoke with generic accents. American Indians were present, but mostly as threats in blanketed stereotypes on horseback. Occasionally Mexicans turned up as well, but usually as sombrero-wearing, knife-clutching clichés.

In fact, the cattle drives from South Texas to Kansas were carried out by armies of cowboys who were far from pure white. African Americans comprised maybe a third of the hands. Mexicans maybe another a third. American Indians worked as cowboys on these drives as well. The cavalries that battled Indians were multiethnic, too, with many European immigrants and Natives among them. A Seventh Cavalry roster from 1876, compiled just prior to the Battle of the Little Bighorn, lists the names Stab, Bull in the Water, Bush, Climbs the Bluff, Curley Head, Foolish Bear, Forked Horn, Good Face, Goose, Horns in Front, One Feather, Owl, Red Bear, Red Foolish Bear, Rushing Bull, Soldier, Strikes the Bear, Strikes the Lodge, White Man Runs Him, White Swan, Curley, Goes Ahead, Hairy Moccasin, and Half Yellow Face.

The white men who rode with Custer were a varied lot who spoke with many accents, including privates born in England, Ireland, Bavaria, Denmark, France, Silesia (part of Poland), Prussia, Switzerland, and Italy. The army's melting pot failed to extend to African Americans, as no companies were racially integrated. Still, segregated regiments of black cavalry and infantry played important roles in the history of the American West, affecting everything from battles with Native peoples to the saga of Billy the Kid.

Borgnine found acting in a Western to be a good fit for his skills, starting with his appearance in a 3-D picture directed by André DeToth and starring Randolph Scott called *The Stranger Wore a Gun*. After that, Borgnine acted in *Johnny Guitar*, *Vera Cruz*, the contemporary Western *Bad Day at Black Rock*, *Jubal*, and a number of TV cowboy series, including *Zane Grey Theatre*, *Wagon Train*, and *Laramie*. The appearance of Borgnine on a horse made a Western seem different and more realistic; he presented the image of someone who had arisen from the dirt itself.

But Peckinpah had good reason to question Borgnine's suitability for the role of Dutch. Borgnine had delivered nuanced, praiseworthy performances in pictures such as *Marty* and *Jubal*. Too often, though, he mistook opening a fire hose of emotion, particularly anger, as good acting. A case in point was Borgnine's scenery-chewing performance in

Robert Aldrich's *The Dirty Dozen*, though it was a popular film. An encounter with a schoolkid who knew more about TV stars than movie stars prompted Borgnine to accept the starring role as a World War II PT boat commander in the television sitcom *McHale's Navy*. The series increased his fame, but his performance as McHale ranged from sloppy to predictable. The series diminished Borgnine's standing as a serious actor, but Peckinpah was stuck with him by orders of the studio and moved toward production with Borgnine as his Dutch. Little could Peckinpah have known that Ken Hyman had given him a gift of gold with Borgnine. It's hard to imagine any other actor owning the part in the way he did. The moral outrage over Mapache's practice of hanging Mexican villagers, the Nosferatu-like grin during the train robbery, the mask of self-damnation he wears while whittling outside the whorehouse, the demonic giggle just before the final shoot-out—all were pure Borgnine.

11.

Dutch is not Pike's original right-hand man. Before him, Deke Thornton held the position. If anything, Thornton was closer to Pike than Dutch ever was. Things changed once Pike selfishly abandoned a wounded Deke to capture by Pinkerton agents. Deke is tried, convicted, and sentenced to prison in Arizona for his crimes against the railroad, while Pike is free to continue to rob and live freely. Harrigan, the corrupt, soulless railroad official, offers Deke freedom in exchange for leading a pack of bounty hunters to kill Pike and his gang. Deke accepts, although he has a kind of love for Pike despite having every reason to hate him. Deke respects Pike for who he is and what he represents. In the early moments of the Starbuck shoot-out, Deke has the chance to shoot Pike but hesitates for just a moment, enough time for a tuba player to take Pike's place in his gun sights. Harrigan has provided Deke with "gutter trash" to be his bounty hunters. Deke realizes that Pike's men are in every way superior to what he's been given. Yet he moves ahead. He cannot allow himself to be sent back to prison.

For the third point of the bromantic triangle, Peckinpah selected Robert Ryan. It was an easy choice. Ryan was thin, tough, and just a tad grizzled, with a deeply lined face that seemed to be cut from boot leather. While never a major movie star, he had time and again shown himself capable of being one of the best actors in Hollywood. His performances in films such as *The Set-Up*, *Horizons West*, *The Naked Spur*, *Bad Day at Black Rock*, *Day of the Outlaw*, and *The Professionals* were as good as any to turn up on-screen. He worked with many of the most interesting directors around during his time, Nicholas Ray, André DeToth, Fritz Lang, Budd Boetticher, Robert Wise, and Richard Brooks among them.

Ryan worked regularly in film, but his sensibilities were more attuned to live theater. Movies? They were a way to get a paycheck. This is not to say he wasn't a professional. He showed up prepared, was always on time, and performed his work. He refused to bring any personal issues to the set, and he expected his directors to do the same. Ryan wanted to get his scenes shot, do his looping, and then move on to the next project. Typically, he didn't bother seeing the movies he acted in.

As 1967 began to bleed into 1968, moviemaking was not high on Ryan's list of priorities. His focus was fixed on political developments in the U.S. Democratic Party. Politics had been in his blood since his childhood in Chicago. His father was active in the party, so Ryan witnessed the city's take-no-names politics firsthand, not to mention the blood-drenched tactics of the Chicago Outfit, which were intertwined with elections. His father had gone bankrupt during the Great Depression, but somehow the family found money to send Ryan to Dartmouth, where he found success as a collegiate boxer. He knew how to take a punch, he knew how to throw a punch, and he never lost a fight during his college career. He returned to Chicago hoping to become a writer. Instead, he was forced to take on one hard-labor job after another to get by. Bored out of his skull, he one day showed up for an audition at a play and received a part.

In an age when men still dressed up to travel, Robert Ryan (right) and William Holden arrive in Parras to begin working on *The Wild Bunch*. Photo by Paul Harper, courtesy of Nick Redman and Jeff Slater.

He was a success and soon enough turned up on the West Coast looking for work in films.

He, too, became a marine when World War II called. Moreover, he became a drill instructor. As such, he had to become the hardest of hardasses as he attempted to turn men into fighters for the war machine. The experience gave him insight into the absolute worst as well as the best America had to offer, insight he used when he returned to acting after the war.

In *Bad Day at Black Rock*, he played Reno Smith, an out-and-out racist, and he was convincing, but he couldn't have been more different. His political journey had taken him to the farthest reaches of Hollywood's left, short of the Communist Party. Just before the start of World War II, he married a Quaker. Over time, Ryan more and more adopted his wife's pacifist beliefs and supported a range of leftist causes, from progressive schools to the civil rights movement. He especially wanted to see the end of American's involvement in Vietnam and soon became one of the war's most eloquent critics: "The thought of sending [American draftees] off to a war we shouldn't be in is something that's awfully hard to live with."[54]

The Ryan family had moved from California to New York City, where they lived at the Dakota in the same apartment that John Lennon and Yoko Ono would eventually buy. Ryan became a familiar figure at high-profile antiwar functions in the city. When liberal Democratic U.S. senator Eugene McCarthy of Minnesota announced he would challenge the incumbent pro-war Democratic president, Lyndon Johnson, for the party's nomination in 1968, Ryan signed up to support "Clean Gene." With the New Hampshire primary looming in early 1968, Ryan focused more on helping his candidate than on his own career. Shooting for *The Wild Bunch* wouldn't begin until after the primary, so Ryan had plenty of time for campaigning. He never spoke publicly about the irony that a dedicated servant to the cause of peace was getting ready to appear in a picture that elevated violence to new levels. He seemed to approach it as just another day at the office.

12.

The Gorch brothers were the least likable members of Pike Bishop's gang. Shortly after *The Wild Bunch*'s opening railroad-office robbery debacle, they show themselves to be self-obsessed and bigoted. They want to cut Angel out of part of his share of the loot. They say it's because he's the newest member of the bunch, but it's clear that they don't like him because he is a Mexican. Angel understands this. So do Pike, Bishop, and Old Man Sykes. The brothers also want to cut out Sykes, who has been a part of the gang longer than anyone else, from receiving any shares because he's an "old goat" who just watches the horses. They later challenge Pike's leadership, for a second time in the movie, after the gang's horses tumble down an embankment of desert sand. In response, Pike says, "We're going to stick together just like it used to be. When you side with a man, you stay with him, and if you can't do that, you're like some animal. You're finished! We're finished! All of us!" But the Gorches still question him, especially after Pike falls while attempting to mount his horse. Three things seem to motivate the Gorches: money, women, and booze. Honor and loyalty seem to be beyond their comprehension. Yet time and again, they fall in line and support their team and, in the end, sacrifice their lives for the Mexican they loathed earlier in the movie. They are a measure above the soulless bounty hunters under Deke Thornton's command because they possess some elemental humanness.

Peckinpah turned to actors he knew well to portray Tector and Lyle Gorch. For Tector, Sam selected Ben Johnson, the real cowboy from Oklahoma. For Lyle, he went with Warren Oates. Like other members of Peckinpah's stock company, Oates came from an unfashionable part of flyover country—in his case, the hamlet of Depoy, Kentucky, birthplace of the state's coal-mining industry.

Oates's father ran Depoy's general store, so the family had a bit more money than most people in the area, but Oates still grew up during tough times in a tough place. He showed dramatic flair even as a teenager. He courted the daughter of the owner of the Depoy picture show, the Palace, which meant he could get in for free, and after he'd seen a movie, he'd place a tin can on the end of a broomstick as a pretend microphone and act out what he'd just seen. He became so good at it that kids who lacked the wherewithal to buy a ticket at the Palace would show up to take in his reenactments. Oates later claimed these performances instilled the acting bug in him.

But Muhlenberg County was not exactly the land of opportunity, and Oates's mother wanted her children to escape "this mud hole" as soon as they could rather than spend their lives in the dark, dreary mines that country singer Merle Travis, also from Muhlenberg County, warned about. After Oates's dad shut down the general store, the family moved to Louisville. Oates took a stab at high school in the big city before dropping out to become a marine. After he mustered out, he enrolled at the University of Louisville, where he participated in theatrical productions. Then he set his sights on making it as an actor in New York City.

The Oateses were a conservative, Southern Baptist family, and the prospect of Warren's trying to be a professional actor concerned them. His brother, Gordon, had read that the odds of making it as an actor were a slim seven hundred to one. Warren promised that he'd give it five years. After that, if he had not become a successful professional actor, he'd retreat to Kentucky and live a normal life. After three years, he departed New York for California. In L.A., he joined the herds of would-be TV cowboys who strolled Sunset Boulevard practicing their best drawls and slouches in hopes of finding work on a Western series.

Oates was steps ahead of the others. He already had the voice, walk, and face for it. He looked something like a demon chipmunk with an unsettling gap-toothed grin and a beard that was more like fur than facial hair. His eyes could burn with rage or be as innocent as an infant's, all within seconds. As a result, Oates quickly found work on TV Westerns, including *The Rifleman*, which gave him his first contact with Peckinpah. Oates became a regular in Sam's circle of colleagues and drinking buddies, and eventually he appeared unbilled in Peckinpah's series *The Westerner*. In 1962, Oates landed the part of Ves Painter on ABC's rodeo series, *Stoney Burke*. Within weeks of *Stoney Burke*'s premiere, Oates was receiving more fan mail than star Jack Lord, who fumed about that.

Warren Oates in costume as the character Lyle Gorch outside Parras. Oates's personal life was in turmoil when he left for Mexico to film *The Wild Bunch*, but his rendering of Lyle showed he was one of the best actors working in American movies. Photo by Paul Harper, courtesy of Nick Redman and Jeff Slater.

It may have taken a bit more than five years to achieve, but Oates was now an unqualified success—and a return to "normal" life back in Kentucky was out of the question.

Oates worked almost exclusively in television until Peckinpah gave him a part as one of the subhuman Hammond brothers in *Ride the High Country*. Oates played the most cretinous of a family of cretins, a man who all but slavers as he ponders the Hammonds' fraternal tradition of gang-raping the bride whenever one of the brothers marries. He's also so wedged into his own filth that he'd rather engage in a knife fight than take a bath. The psychopathic edge Oates brought to the part was quite unlike any other performance that had ever turned up in a Western. It was chilling.

After appearing in Peckinpah's *Major Dundee*, Oates signed on to star in *The Shooting*, a low-budget Monte Hellman film that pushed the revisionist Western into theretofore unexplored territory; it is by most measures the first existential Western. Made under the auspices of Roger Corman, with Jack Nicholson producing and costarring, it was an early New Hollywood film. The screenplay was by Carole Eastman, who'd go on to acclaim for writing *Five Easy Pieces*.[55] Her playwright brother, Charles, actress Millie Perkins, and actor Will Hutchins filled out the cast. All were young, still in their thirties, part of the new generation out to make a new kind of movie. Oates did some of the finest acting of his career in *The Shooting*. He also demonstrated that he was more than just a character actor; he could carry a picture as its star. The problem for him was that virtually no one in the United States had a chance to see the film when it was released in 1966. *The Shooting* first played theaters in France, where it was lauded by critics. One theater in Paris showed it and its companion picture, *Ride in the Whirlwind*, for years. It was finally released in the United States after Nicholson had become a star with his role in *Easy Rider*.

Around the same time he made *The Shooting*, Oates starred in Dale Wasserman's play adapted from Ken Kesey's novel *One Flew Over the Cuckoo's Nest*. As R. P. McMurphy, Oates gave impressive performances night after night. Some of the seats at the Players Ring Gallery were filled by directors, producers, and studio execs, and Oates's acting in Wasserman's play did much to increase his reputation in the film industry. His role as the voyeuristic Deputy Sam Wood in Norman Jewison's hit movie *In the Heat of the Night* likewise showcased Oates's dramatic prowess. His star was ascending when his friend Sam Peckinpah contacted him to play one of the Gorch brothers in *The Wild Bunch*.

13.

From the opening of *The Wild Bunch*, the gang is pursued by a ruthless set of bounty hunters who will follow them into Mexico, ride after them after the theft of rifles from the train, give chase through the canyon country, and finally collect the bodies of Pike, Dutch, and the Gorches for reward money. Paul Harper, a Texan, played Ross, an animal of a man. (Harper was also an amateur photographer and took many pictures on location.) Another Texan, stuntman and actor Billy Hart, played Jess. Buck Holland was also a member of the motley crew. Two members of the bounty-hunter gang are beyond redemption. T. C. and Coffer demonstrate the lowest elements of human behavior. Matted with filth, they are anxious to get the bloodshed under way as they wait on a rooftop to ambush the wild bunch after it robs the railroad office. They are like demented schoolchildren. They argue between themselves over who deserves credit for shooting whom. They strip bodies of boots, pry gold out of corpses' teeth. From the Texas border into Mexico and then finally to their witnessing the carnage following the massacre that ends *The Wild Bunch*, they never once demonstrate any good qualities. They are pure bad—and half-witted. Once they retrieve the bodies of Pike, Dutch, and the Gorch brothers, they set off for Texas singing "Polly Wolly Doodle." Their ostensible boss, Deke Thornton, stays behind, glad to be shed of them. When he hears distant gunfire a few minutes later, which he knows means his former charges have been ambushed and killed, Deke smiles. There was nothing to love about T. C. and Coffer.

Peckinpah recruited L. Q. Jones to play T. C. For Coffer, Peckinpah chose a man who'd become one of America's favorite character actors in the fall of 1967.

Strother Martin's performance in *Cool Hand Luke* caught the fancy of American filmgoers struggling through the discord of the fractious 1960s.

His line "What we've got here is failure to communicate" would be repeated ad nauseam as the decade closed down. Martin showed particular skill in playing the mild-mannered sadist who runs the prison camp, and while he'd worked steadily in the years before *Cool Hand Luke*, he became much more in demand afterward.[56]

Martin was of average height at best ("5'8" and that's stretching the hell out of it")[57] with a high twang of a voice. He was given to fretting nervously. His fellow character actor Denver Pyle worked with him on John Ford's *The Man Who Shot Liberty Valance* and noticed that whenever Ford bellowed Martin's name, Strother would leap a foot straight up in the air from his chair. Ford noticed this, too, and afterward he would call out Martin's name just to see him jump. Martin also seemed afraid of horses and was never a particularly good rider.[58]

But Martin was a near-world-class athlete who'd done his share of stunt work when he first arrived in Hollywood. Martin was born in Kokomo, Indiana, and grew up there, except for a short time when his family lived in San Antonio. From early childhood on, he was a good swimmer and an excellent diver. When he was seventeen, he won the National Junior Springboard Diving Championship. Later, he became a member of the diving team at the University of Michigan.

"I was Michigan's number one diver," he said, "and Michigan was national and intercollegiate champion all the time I was there in school, and I made number two national springboard diving champion. My nickname was T-Bone Martin, and I was sort of half-assed famous that way." He came close to making the U.S. Olympic team, but in the end, it didn't matter: In 1940 there were no Olympics for the U.S. team to compete in because of World War II. Instead of diving for Olympic gold, Martin entered the U.S. Navy and became an officer, serving in the safety of Hawaii as the war blazed away in the South Pacific. There, he was charged with teaching sailors to swim. Because he was far removed from combat, he would tell an interviewer that he fell into the category of what were called "ball-bearing WAVES."[59]

After Japan surrendered, he returned to Michigan and fell in with a group of "Bohemians from New York" involved with campus theater. That led to his performing in a couple of plays, which was enough to interest Martin in acting. Then he saw Frank Capra's *It's a Wonderful Life* and was taken by James Stewart's performance. It prompted him to try to make a living from acting. Martin headed to Hollywood.

Strother Martin was on a career high in 1968, following his breakout role in *Cool Hand Luke*. He acted in the classic Westerns *Butch Cassidy and the Sundance Kid* and *True Grit*, but *The Wild Bunch* gave him one of his best roles ever, Coffer. Here he poses in costume with Ralph Jr., Hope Marie, and Zina Anne Prieto, members of a stranded Mexican American family for whom Peckinpah found work on *The Wild Bunch*. Photo courtesy of Ralph Prieto Jr.

Martin's swimming and diving prowess helped him get a foot in the door. He gave swimming lessons to actors, appeared in front of the camera as an extra in swimming scenes, and sometimes performed swimming-related stunts. He began to get nonswimming bit parts here and there as well. Casting directors detected, as he described it, a smell of horseshit on him. His father, Strother D. Martin, had grown up across the river from Indiana in Kentucky, where'd he been a sharecropper with only a third-grade education. Strother was not a particularly uncommon name among people from the Kentucky backwoods. Strother found himself emulating his father's rural persona in parts in movies and on TV.

Martin turned out to be a fit for the ever-expanding TV Westerns market of the 1950s, and he worked steadily. A part in 1955's big-screen production *Target Zero* paired him for the first time with L. Q. Jones. Martin played a Korean War soldier injured early in the film. Jones, also cast as a soldier, was required to carry Martin over his shoulder for the film's duration. The two men became friends on the shoot and afterward found themselves working together often. By the time they were cast for *The Wild Bunch*, the two actors were like jazz musicians who'd jammed with each other for years and knew how to anticipate each other's licks to come together as a unit.

14.

Casting the pivotal role of Angel, the Mexican member of the gang, proved tricky. Peckinpah's first impulse was to use Robert Blake. From a twenty-first-century perspective, the thought of casting Blake for anything elicits groans. In late 1967, he was one of hottest young actors in Hollywood. He'd been around the business for years, landing roles at MGM when he was only six years old and working steadily thereafter. As an adult actor, Blake could tap into a vast reservoir of tortured emotions, which culminated in a stunning 1967 performance in Richard Brooks's *In Cold Blood*. He received enough accolades for it that Blake decided to focus on lead roles only.

That left Peckinpah still needing to find his Angel. He wound up selecting a New York actor with a background in musical theater, of all things. His choice was a Latino with Spanish as his first language, though he was not an ethnic Mexican. Jaime Sánchez was born in Rincón, Puerto Rico, in 1938, making him significantly younger than other leads in *The Wild Bunch* (William Holden was twenty years older). In ways, Sánchez was far more versed in the territory *The Wild Bunch* encompassed than any of the other top-billed actors.

Sánchez had grown up around horses in Puerto Rico, and his father was a competent rider, although Jaime himself preferred going to the library to mounting a saddle.[60] As a kid, he found his way to movies regularly, and the Spanish-language cinemas in his hometown exhibited many films from Mexico's golden age, the same movies that had been playing in Mexico City when Peckinpah made his first visit there in the late 1940s. Several years after the picture became a sensation at Cannes, Sánchez saw Emilio Fernández's masterwork *María Candelaria (Xochimilco)* with Gabriel Figueroa's rich black-and-white images of nationalistic Mexican iconography. *María Candelaria*, set just prior to the outbreak of the Mexican Revolution, became a favorite movie of Sánchez's. Its male lead, Pedro Armendáriz, became one of his acting heroes.

Much of the recorded music Sánchez heard in Puerto Rico likewise came from Mexico. In particular, he liked the recordings of Jorge Negrete, whose best-known platter, "Mexico lindo y querido," became an anthem for Mexican nationalism, though it was popular in Spanish-speaking regions outside Mexico as well. Sánchez developed a tenor singing voice himself as time went by, and he never forgot those Mexican songs he heard when he was young. One afternoon nearly fifty years after Peckinpah signed him for *The Wild Bunch*, I talked to Sánchez on the phone, and he interrupted our conversation to sing the first verse of "La Adelita," his voice as high and affecting as it had been in the late 1960s.

Sánchez left Puerto Rico after he finished high school and traveled to New York with the goal of making it as an actor. In a relatively short time, he was admitted to the Actors Studio, where he studied under Lee Strasberg, and began appearing in off-Broadway plays. Sánchez's big break occurred when he was cast as Chino in both the original off-Broadway and the Broadway productions of Leonard Bernstein and Stephen Sondheim's *West Side Story*. Sánchez was just eighteen years old, but *West Side Story* gave him the chance to work with the towering genius of American musical theater Jerome Robbins, who had first conceived of retelling the story of Romeo and Juliet as a musical set in 1950s New York; Robbins also choreographed *West Side Story*. The play proved that Sánchez could sing and dance, but his dramatic skills were his ace in the hole. He felt a debt to Robbins, to whom Sánchez would eventually liken Peckinpah.

Sánchez demonstrated just how well he could act when he took part in the New York Shakespeare Festival, where he played Puck in *A Midsummer's Night Dream* and the clown in *Othello*. In 1962, Robbins staged Arthur Kopit's *Oh Dad, Poor Dad, Mamma's Hung You in the Closet and I'm Feelin' So Sad* with a cast including Sánchez at the Phoenix Theater, a significant off-Broadway venue where actors of the likes of Montgomery Clift and Robert Ryan had earlier taken to the stage. When Robbins took *Oh Dad, Poor Dad* to Broadway's Morosco Theatre in 1963, Sánchez remained in the cast for its forty-seven-performance run.

In between *Oh Dad, Poor Dad*'s performances at the Phoenix and the Morosco, Sánchez played Carlos in Frank Perry's 1962 film, *David and Lisa*. Perry, though only in his early thirties, was turning out to be one of New York's most important filmmakers in the 1960s. Hollywood films greatly outnumbered what New York produced, but at the time New York played the lead in creating art films. Perry's *David and Lisa*, largely set in a residential psychiatric treatment center, concerns young people attempting to work their way through severe psychological impairment. *David and Lisa* was warmly received and won Academy Award nominations for Perry and for his feminist wife, Eleanor, who wrote the screenplay.

Sánchez's work in theater also continued, including appearances with Michael Douglas and Raúl Juliá in Frank Gagliano's *The City Scene*, which comprised two one-act plays, *Paradise Gardens East* and *Conerico Was Here to Stay*. And Sánchez acted in the one-act play *The Toilet* by Amiri Baraka (still writing under the name LeRoi Jones). It was a heady time for experimental theater in New York, with leading lights such as Sam Shepard exploring uncharted dramatic ground. Sánchez was plugged into the whole scene.

In 1964, Sánchez played a significant role in Sidney Lumet's *The Pawnbroker*, one of the first American films to deal with the Holocaust from a survivor's point of view. In it, Rod Steiger portrayed a German Jew who'd witnessed the rape of his wife and the death of his family at the hands of the Nazis during World War II. His only way of coping later in life was to refuse to get in touch with his emotions and to concentrate solely on his work at his pawnshop in the Puerto Rican neighborhood of Spanish Harlem, as East Harlem was frequently referred to at the time. Sánchez was the pawnbroker's helper, who both idolized and attempted to strike up a friendship with the older man. The dynamic between Steiger's and Sánchez's characters became one of the strongest features of *The Pawnbroker*, which won Steiger an Academy Award nomination.

The film, which was highly influenced by the work of French New Wave director Alain Resnais's *Hiroshima mon amour*, certainly caught Peckinpah's eye. Among other things, *The Pawnbroker* brought a visceral power heretofore unseen in American films with its depiction of graphic violence and nudity, and Lumet made inventive use of flashbacks to reveal backstory. This landmark movie certainly was one to impress Peckinpah. Sam liked Sánchez's performance enough that he dispatched envoys to New York to try to find the young Puerto Rican actor. Sánchez stopped into a bar one evening and heard that people from Warner Bros. were looking for him to offer him a role in *The Wild Bunch*. Later the phone rang at his apartment. Peckinpah was calling from Mexico, and Sam confirmed to Sánchez that he wanted him for the picture.

Sánchez was under contract to appear in a play, but in a testament to Peckinpah's desire to have Sánchez for *The Wild Bunch*, Warners reached

Jaime Sánchez and Sam Peckinpah during the filming of the Angel's-village scene.
Photo by Bernie Abramson, courtesy of Tonio K.

a financial settlement with the play's producers to release the actor from
the contract. Sánchez immediately signed up for riding classes in New
York so he could get comfortable on the back of a horse. He also set about
practicing Spanish spoken with a Mexican accent. From the movies he'd
seen and the music he'd listened to growing up, he'd heard plenty of
Mexican Spanish, which was different from the Spanish of his native
Puerto Rico, much as American English is different from British English.
He dedicated himself to getting a Mexican accent down pat. He also had

to work on how he pronounced English. "The Mexican inflection in English is different from Puerto Rican," he told me, "and I did work very, very much on that, the melody of a Mexican speaking English. And I think I made it sound authentic because I had Mexicans ask me what part of Mexico I was from. I had a good ear for that."[61]

Though it was not unheard of, the casting of a Latino actor to play a Latino part, especially in a major role, was still not common practice. Sam broke some ground of his own here. He would break a whole lot more as *The Wild Bunch* went into production.

PART IV

"This Time We Do It Right!"

1.

As *The Wild Bunch* moved into production in early 1968, a number of other pictures with cowboy, or at least cowboyish, themes were in production as well, all aiming toward release during 1969. The financial triumph worldwide of the Sergio Leone/Clint Eastwood movies certainly played a role in encouraging studios and investors to put their money into Westerns, as did the success of such films as *The Magnificent Seven* and *The Professionals*.

Moreover, the image of the cowboy as a man alone, unrestrained by society's mores, was gaining favor with the baby boomers. Thousands of young men in the West and Southwest began kicking it in boots and hats in response to Paul Newman's portrayal of Hud—a phenomenon that horrified Newman, who considered Hud to be morally bankrupt and didn't understand why anyone wanted to emulate him. George Harrison appeared on the back cover of the Beatles' seminal *Rubber Soul* album wearing cowboy boots and a Western hat; the front-cover photo shows John Lennon in a roughout leather jacket with snap pockets. The Buffalo Springfield held the creative edge among West Coast rock bands, and when they performed live, Stephen Stills often donned a Western hat, while Neil Young, looking something like a Canadian Indian (he wasn't), took the stage in a suede coat with fringe on the sleeves. It wasn't unusual to see the Grateful Dead's Jerry Garcia sporting a poncho that looked much like Eastwood's.

Within a couple of years, the Byrds, the Grateful Dead, and Bob Dylan himself would be recording country music. If this was the apogee of the cowboy and the hippie, the nadir occurred in 1968, when a movable commune of mostly middle- to upper-middle-class runaways and dropouts first set foot on the five-hundred-acre Spahn Movie Ranch northwest of L.A. near the Santa Susana Mountains. The ranch's venerable Old West town set and surrounding mountains were where King Vidor had shot *Duel in the Sun*; Spahn Ranch was used for several TV shows, including *The Lone Ranger* and *Bonanza*. Now the dusty street once roamed by Hoss and Tonto became home to the followers of Charles Manson.

The American movie industry had committed itself to a cluster of films dealing with the mythology of the cowboy; all would be shot in 1968 and released in 1969. Some would fall flat artistically but would have some elements of interest. In the latter category was Tom Gries's *100 Rifles*. Gries had filmed a minor masterpiece the previous year with *Will Penny*. Thought but a shadow of that film, *100 Rifles* introduced fiery interracial sex scenes between Jim Brown and Raquel Welch, the likes of which had never before been seen in an American Western. As with the Leone/Eastwood pictures, it was shot with Spain doubling for Mexico. Like *The Wild Bunch*, it took place during the Mexican Revolution. Though it was not much of a movie (costar Burt Reynolds said, "It just didn't work"), it did set the tone for what those Westerns of 1969 had in common: pushing boundaries, taking revisionary views of the mythical West.

Charles Portis was an Arkansas boy who made it to the big leagues of American newspapers during the 1960s, rubbing shoulders with the likes of Tom Wolfe, Dick Schaap, and Jimmy Breslin before throwing it all away and returning to Arkansas to write novels. In 1968, the weekly *Saturday Evening Post* serialized Portis's second novel, *True Grit*, with a book publication date set for the summer. This extraordinary book was a work of black comedy, which was popular at the time as exemplified by the works of Terry Southern and Bruce Jay Friedman, among others. *True Grit* set the mythological West theories of Leslie Fiedler on their ear: This was the story of the adventures of a young woman full of spunk and of a bloated sot of an older cowboy hero in the wilderness—in this case, that part of current-day Oklahoma known at the time as Indian Territory. *True Grit* was that most remarkable of novels, one that was groundbreaking and literary yet immensely popular. Preproduction on the movie version of it was under way before the serialization began. Filming, under the direction of legendary hard-ass Henry Hathaway, began scarcely two months after the hardback's publication. John Wayne, who'd lost a lung and several ribs to cancer just a few years earlier, played the over-the-hill alcoholic Rooster Cogburn. Wayne would look fat and haggard in the film, a far cry from the sort of cowboy Übermensch image for which he was well-known.

Nineteen sixty-eight was the year that Leone's *Il buono, il brutto, il cattivo* hit American theaters as *The Good, the Bad, and the Ugly* and became a massive hit for United Artists. Leone had intended to retire from spaghetti Westerns after *The Good, the Bad, and the Ugly* was completed and ready for release in Italy in 1966. However, Paramount had offered him a large budget if he'd return to the well one more time. Leone enlisted the aid of new writers, Bernado Bertolucci among them, and a whole new cast of American lead actors to create *C'era una volta il West*. It would appear in Italy in December 1968 and then in the United States in 1969 as *Once Upon a Time in the West*, with Jason Robards, Charles Bronson, and Henry Fonda, who would be particularly effective as a blue-eyed killer.

Plenty of other cowboy pictures made their way through 1968 with release dates set for 1969: the John Wayne programmer *The Undefeated*, the James Garner comedy *Support Your Local Sheriff*, *More Dead Than Alive*, *Guns of the Magnificent Seven*, Audie Murphy's final film, *A Time for Dying*, Elvis Presley's *Charro!*, *The Great Bank Robbery*, and a host of spaghetti Westerns, including the cult classic *Sabata*. The stilted, didactic *Tell Them Willie Boy Is Here*, with Robert Blake, Robert Redford, and Katharine Ross, also made its way toward a 1969 release, as did that gasbag of a musical *Paint Your Wagon*, replete with wooden performances from newly made millionaires Eastwood and Lee Marvin.

The big fish in the 1969 Western sea was, of course, *Butch Cassidy and the Sundance Kid*. It starred Ross, who had skyrocketed to major-star status with her performance as Elaine in the counterculture favorite *The Graduate*, along with cinematic golden boys Redford and Paul Newman. The director was a pal of Newman's, George Roy Hill, whose slick work Andrew Sarris once dismissed as "idiosyncratically odious oiliness."[1] Everything and everyone was first-class and top paid on the *Butch Cassidy* project.

Other films going into production in 1968 were not exactly Westerns, though they certainly played off the mythology of the West and the image of the cowboy. From the get-go, Peter Fonda and Dennis Hopper considered *Easy Rider* to be a kind of Western, as well as a biker flick/road movie. They envisioned it as a kind of ironic cowboy picture with the action moving east toward the Atlantic Coast, the old America, instead of toward the frontier. The outlaws (Fonda and Hopper) score in Mexico a powdery drug we might assume is cocaine, which they sell to a dealer in a Rolls-Royce (Phil Spector) for big money—the equivalent of a bank robbery in a cowboy picture. The posse that pursues them is nothing less than America itself. Though seldom used in the movie, the names of the outlaws were derived from Western icons Billy the Kid and Wyatt Earp. The film would be shot with Harley-Davidsons supplanting horses.

Nineteen sixty-eight saw the release of Don Siegel's *Coogan's Bluff*, which starred Clint Eastwood and was produced by Eastwood's company, Malpaso. *Coogan's Bluff*, the first of five collaborations between Eastwood and Siegel, was not particularly good. However, its contemporary depiction of a sheriff's deputy from the West (in this case Arizona) alone in New York City in some ways foreshadowed another picture going into production for release in 1969: *Midnight Cowboy*.

Midnight Cowboy was based on a tough novel by the same name written James Leo Herlihy. Herlihy was a protégé of Peckinpah's playwriting hero, Tennessee Williams, and, like Williams, was not afraid to tackle previously taboo subjects in his own plays and in his novels. Formerly blacklisted screenwriter Waldo Salt was hired to adapt *Midnight Cowboy* into a script, and he softened some of the more violent elements in the novel while also expanding the character of Ratso Rizzo. Salt also made New York City itself more of a character in his screenplay. Salt tightened the focus of the story, making it a love story of sorts between Jon Voight's simple-minded Joe Buck and Dustin Hoffman's streetwise Ratso. *Coogan's Bluff* opens with scenes in rural Arizona, then the remainder of the story plays out with Eastwood's Coogan as a singular cowboy in the wilderness of New York. *Midnight Cowboy* opens in Joe Buck's hometown, Big Spring, Texas, then, like the earlier movie, plays out with stark images of the cowboy in the city.

Nineteen sixty-eight was a particularly disruptive year in American history, with political assassinations, continued racial unrest, violence in the streets, a rising crime rate, and American's involvement in Vietnam hitting its nadir with the Tet Offensive and the Mỹ Lai Massacre. It was also a profoundly creative time in both foreign and American filmmaking. Peckinpah was especially influenced by European and Asian movies, which were getting easier to find in the United States. Nineteen sixty-nine would be one of the great years for American film releases. It would also be the last great year of the cowboy in American cinema. *The Wild Bunch* would set the bar for filmmaking excellence in 1969 as well as being representative of the turbulent times during which it was made. It was also different. It was a real Western. *Midnight Cowboy* and *Easy Rider* succeeded in large part because they were departures, playing off the Western form. *The Wild Bunch* was unabashedly a full-on Western, with real cowboys and horses. But it doubled down on everything that came before it, upping the ante in violence. It also went far beyond anything John Ford, Anthony Mann, or George Stevens ever attempted in complexity of character and situation.

2.

Peckinpah had been accorded the welcome of a returning prince when he connected with Ken Hyman at Warners. Compared to the cubbyhole Paramount had provided him to work on the *Villa Rides* script, his digs at the studio off Olive Avenue were palatial and befitted an important Hollywood director. Peckinpah put in long hours as he refined the *Wild Bunch* script. The electric Panasonic sharpener ground away as he went through pencil after pencil scrawling rewrites to hand off to his typist, Gay Hayden, who could decipher Sam's all-but-illegible handwriting. When Peckinpah wasn't writing, he was planning the production of the epic film to be shot entirely in Mexico. When the working day wound down, he escaped to the bar of the El Chiquito Inn.

The El Chiquito, an unimposing restaurant, sat across Olive Avenue near the Warner Bros.-Seven Arts studio entrance. A sign out front featured the clichéd image of a *bandido*, replete with thick mustache and sombrero. Inside, everything was tufted red Naugahyde, red carpeting, and red petticoated dresses for the waitresses. The bar area had large booths that provided a comfortable setting for conversation, with an unwritten understanding that any talk that grew too angry would be taken out back. The place was popular with stuntmen, and with Hollywood's biggest stars. Peckinpah could unwind here and sometimes held conversations about his project.[2]

The Wild Bunch would be a huge undertaking involving many actors, stuntmen, and extras as well as dozens of head of livestock. A town had to be found as the location of the opening sequences, including a long, complicated shoot-out; Peckinpah and Warners executives knew much work would likely have to be done in the town to make it resemble a place in Texas. A functioning early twentieth-century locomotive and train cars had to be secured for the centerpiece train robbery and for Mapache's

157

battle with Pancho Villa's forces. Another town in the desert with adobe and stone buildings was necessary for Mapache's sanctuary, which was called Agua Verde in the script. And there was more, much more. When the topic of *Major Dundee* arose, Peckinpah blamed problems on producer Jerry Bresler and Columbia suits. His actions going into *The Wild Bunch* indicated that Sam was also aware of how his own shortcomings had damaged the earlier film. For one thing, he was taking no chances on an unfinished script as he had on *Dundee*. He continued to polish and polish the screenplay right up to February 1968, when he completed what became the shooting script.

The Wild Bunch was also beginning to take on a visual reality. Jim Silke, his exile for fibbing to Peckinpah over, came back into the fold when Sam asked him to create illustrations for the costuming, which Silke did after poring over books of photographs from the time period. Warner Bros.-Seven Arts assigned Tyrus Wong, one of Hollywood's best illustrators, to make watercolors depicting scenes from *The Wild Bunch*. Peckinpah also recruited other key personnel for his picture, two of whom were William Faralla and Edward Carrere.

The Brooklyn-born Faralla was a cohort of Peckinpah's from the TV world. Faralla was in his late fifties and had begun his Hollywood career in the late 1930s as an assistant director, working mostly on Hopalong Cassidy serials. He followed William Boyd and company as they transitioned to television. Faralla was a good fit for the new medium, where he continued to work as an AD and as a second-unit director. Peckinpah gave Faralla his first gig as a production manager when he enlisted him to work on the premiere episode of *The Rifleman*, "The Sharpshooter." Faralla later worked as AD on the pilot episode for *The Westerner*, "Trouble at Tres Cruces." Sam needed a confederate he knew well and trusted as production manager for *The Wild Bunch*. Among other things, Faralla would oversee the money on location. He wound up being something of a fish out of water in dealing with the realities of making a movie in a remote desert town in Mexico.

If Faralla had scrapped his way through the business as one of TV's junkyard dogs, art director Edward Carrere had a gilded work history by comparison. He was a Warner Bros. man through and through, first arriving at the studio as a draftsman in 1932. He had worked there, except for one break of five years, ever since. He became a full-fledged art director in 1947, collaborating with directors of the likes of Raoul Walsh and Michael Curtiz on big-budget productions. He'd just handled the bloated musical *Camelot* when he was named art director for *The*

Wild Bunch. It was a good match. Carrere had been born in Mexico and possessed a strong visual concept of just how the borderland would have looked at the time of the Mexican Revolution.

Peckinpah also hired Gonzalo "Chalo" González, who, outside of Peckinpah himself, worked harder than anyone else on *The Wild Bunch*. Never mind that González had never been employed in the film industry before Sam put him on the payroll, Chalo was, in the description of his friend the actress Isela Vega, the film's *el mil usos*, a jack-of-all-trades who performed essential chore after essential chore to ensure that *The Wild Bunch* made it onto film. González was a controversial figure during the shoot, through no fault of his own, but people working on the ground as the cameras rolled knew González was indispensable. Without him, there would have been no *Wild Bunch*.

Like Peckinpah, González was a native of Fresno. He and Sam were just a month apart in age, and their fathers knew each other from before the boys were born and occasionally hunted together at Peckinpah Mountain. The boys might have gotten to know each other had it not been for an equestrian accident in Mexico. The González family left on vacation from Fresno and traveled to Tepatitlán de Morelos in the state of Jalisco when Chalo was still an infant. There, González's father was killed when a horse he was riding plunged off a precipice. Chalo's grief-stricken mother remained in Tepatitlán close to family, so Chalo grew up there. He didn't make it back to the United States until he was around twenty, after he'd spent some time playing professional soccer and studying law and engineering at college in Mexico. In America, he worked at a number of jobs, among them truck driver, chauffeur, railroad man in Alaska, and metalworker. Finally, he set up his own business exporting lumber products from the United States to Tijuana. He never particularly liked the work, but he was earning a handsome living with his company.

One Saturday, González stepped inside a Tijuana bar, and "there was a guy that everybody wanted to kill" in a corner, fending away attackers with a chair. "Do you speak English?" the distressed man shouted to González.

"Yep," González said.

"Well, please help me!"[3]

The man with the chair was Peckinpah. Peckinpah told Chalo that he'd offered to buy the house a drink and made a toast in Spanish. But, to his surprise, everyone became angry at him at once. Peckinpah spoke more Spanish than most Anglos of his generation, but he never acquired

Sam Peckinpah, Chalo González, and González's wife at a birthday celebration at composer Jerry Fielding's house. Photo courtesy of Katy Haber.

a native fluency. As his friend Elsa Cárdenas told me, "Sam could understand some things, and he could say some things, but his Spanish was not good."[4] Sensing Sam's gullibility when it came to speaking Spanish, a man Sam knew had coached Peckinpah on how to make what Sam thought would be a toast to the house—but, in fact, the man had taught Sam how to *insult* everyone by claiming he had had sex with the mothers of every man in the bar, and that they were all the sons of bitches, God damn it. Once Peckinpah recited the words the man had instructed him to say, the fracas was on. "So I calmed them down," González said. He explained to the angered bar patrons that Sam had been the victim of a practical joke. Everything was okay again. "And he and I became friends."[5]

Peckinpah grew close to González. Peckinpah had attempted to hire him for different projects in the business, including *Major Dundee*, but González always declined. He continued to make good money with his lumber business, and much as the two men's friendship had grown over the years since the bar fight, González wasn't about to walk away from a steady flow of cash. He did convince Peckinpah to audition his niece Begoña Palacios for *Major Dundee*, and that was how Peckinpah met his second wife. As for himself, no, Chalo wasn't interested in moviemaking.

By the time of preproduction for *The Wild Bunch*, things had changed for González. His lumber business in Tijuana was no longer doing so well, and he was ready for a change. This time when Sam offered him work, Chalo said yes. González asked what he would be doing. Sam told him, "You're going to do a lot for me."[6]

González was paid to act as a technical adviser. Peckinpah had jobs in mind for him that extended far beyond the typical for that role, including finding the filming locations in Mexico. Phil Feldman disagreed that such an important undertaking be left in the hands of González, an industry outsider. The producer insisted that Sam employ well-experienced Warner Bros. location scouts, who would likely recommend sites in Durango, Mexico, where many American Westerns had already been filmed, a landscape familiar to many American filmgoers. Peckinpah wanted fresh locations for *The Wild Bunch*. Sam won out over Feldman's objections.

González set off in a Warner Bros. Chevy with $3,000 in Warner Bros. cash (the equivalent of more than $20,000 in 2010s money) and headed to Mexico. Chalo had a network of acquaintances to call upon to help. He remembered a professor from college who worked with the Mexican government for economic development of desert areas in Mexico. "That's what I needed for the show, desert areas," González said. So he contacted his old professor and gave him a copy of the *Wild Bunch* script. The professor decided that Chalo's best bet was a small town in the state of Coahuila called Parras de la Fuente, "the source of grapevines," which was built on an oasis in the Chihuahuan Desert and was the hometown of the martyred hero of the Mexican Revolution, Francisco Madero. Parras made sense to González. He remembered the town from when he'd traveled there on vacation back in his younger days with the professor and his family. The professor wrote a letter of introduction for Chalo to the state's governor and also one to the mayor of Parras.[7]

González set off for Coahuila. It is the third-largest state in Mexico in area, bordered on the north by the Rio Grande and home to two Mexican metropolises, Satillo, which is the state capital, and Torreón, which sits on the state line with Durango. Beyond the big cities and the smaller border cities facing Texas, much of Coahuila is desert and mountain country that witnesses little human activity, the kind of place where rattlesnakes, centipedes, and scorpions thrive.

González honed in on Torreón as the base of operations for *The Wild Bunch*. It had an airport with direct flights to and from Los Angeles, plus banks, hotels, and other amenities. Torreón hugged the Río Nazas on the north, which served as the boundary with the state of Durango. Short drives away from Torreón, especially on the other side of the river in Durango, were areas of stunning landscapes that would provide ideal settings for a Western. Yet the region had been ignored for the most part by Hollywood as well as Mexico's domestic film industry. A couple of years earlier, John Sturges had traveled to Torreón to film some scenes for his bleak Wyatt Earp fantasy, *Hour of the Gun*. Ten years earlier, parts of Richard Fleischer's Mexican Revolution thriller *Bandido!*, with Robert Mitchum and Gilbert Roland, were likewise shot there. Beyond that, only a handful of Mexican silent films had made use of the Torreón area.

A federal highway connected Torreón with Satillo to the east, and at about the halfway point between the two cities, a spur road dropped south to Parras. There, stone-lined canals fed the Estanque La Luz ("pond of light") at the foot of Monte Sombreretillo, and large trees grew in the plaza, making the town an inviting retreat. The town's crippling poverty offset its oasis lushness. The town had been too poor to tear down old buildings and construct more modern ones. It struck González and other outsiders as a place frozen in time, never mind a newish country club on its outskirts. For the most part, little had changed during the fifty years since the Mexican Revolution, when Pancho Villa had encamped here while moving his troops toward Torreón for a great battle. The utility poles with their old-fashioned glass insulators looked as if they had been installed during the Porfiriato. "Here in Mexico, time doesn't exist, no?" Lupita Peckinpah, Sam's daughter with Begoña Palacios, said many years later when she visited Parras. "Of course, Mexico can give you that feeling of no time, of no frontier, that you can do whatever you want."[8]

González found most of what the movie would need in Parras and just outside its city limits: a plaza that could be converted to look like a Texas border town; a shady area along a stream in the country club that could be converted to Angel's oasislike village; a nearby corral that would be perfect as the rendezvous point for the gang after the railroad-office robbery; and on and on—all of it close to the center of town. González hit real pay dirt when, following leads he'd picked up in town, he drove on a rutted-out, all-but-impassible gravel road to the Hacienda Ciénega del Carmen, built by the Spanish in the 1700s, where he saw an astonishing set of ruins. Parras took its name because it had been the center of Mexico's wine industry. Vast acreages of vineyards had once flourished here, hence the town's name. Wine was still big business in Parras when Francisco Madero was born there in 1873, and it remained so through the early years of the revolution. In 1916, an earthquake shook much of the Mexican heartland, including southern Coahuila. It shifted the water table in and around Parras, with disastrous results. Natural lakes and springs abruptly dried up. With no water flowing through irrigation ditches, most vineyards disappeared quickly, though some wine production still continued in the area, particularly the vintage that carried the Madero family name.

The Hacienda Ciénega del Carmen's ruins stood as testament to what the wine industry at its peak had been like in the region. A large span of an aqueduct that once had transported water from a lake in the mountains to the grape fields still stood atop massive Romanesque arches built of stone. Abandoned hacienda buildings, some attached to the aqueduct structure, remained standing as well—roofs gone and walls crumbling but bar-covered windows still intact, as was a broad stairway to a large *porche*. Desert sand and scrub had invaded what must once have been a grand courtyard. To González, who busily snapped Polaroids of it all, it seemed to be the ideal setting for Mapache's stronghold in *The Wild Bunch*, the fictional town of Agua Verde. He returned to Parras convinced that most of the movie could be shot in the town and at the hacienda. No one had ever shot a movie in Parras. González had discovered cinematic virgin turf.

González scouted out other scene locations for which the Parras area was not suitable. For the centerpiece train-robbery scenes, he found suitable trackside locations outside Otinipa, Durango, about 150 miles southwest of Torreón. The Río Nazas could double for the Rio Grande and serve as the site of *The Wild Bunch*'s spectacular bridge-explosion scene. Caves and canyon country in Dinamita, across the river in the state of Durango, could serve as the setting for an encounter between the American outlaws and the Huertista troops commanded by General Mapache. Two weeks after he first left to scout locations, González returned to L.A. with a satchel of Polaroid shots. As Peckinpah thumbed through them, he grew excited, focusing especially on the shots from the hacienda, the porch, the arches, the barred windows. It was a dream come true.

Faralla, Carrere, Peckinpah, and producer Feldman traveled to Mexico to inspect for themselves the locations González had scouted. To Sam's eye, they were even better than the photos suggested. "My father was like a little kid," Lupita Peckinpah said, describing Sam's joy at what he found.[9] But not everyone shared his joy. One day, Faralla drove Feldman out to take a look at the Hacienda Ciénega del Carmen. Red flags immediately popped up for Feldman as soon as Faralla turned off the highway and the car sank to its hubcaps in desert sand. They managed to free themselves. Then came eighteen agonizingly slow miles of rocks, ruts, and dust before the ruins of the hacienda buildings came into view. The place was visually compelling, to be sure, but Feldman thought it was insane to attempt shooting there for weeks and weeks. There was no electricity, the nearest power lines being miles away. Likewise, there was no running water, no septic tanks to support a sewage system, nothing. Just these great ruins, and then a whole lot of alfalfa growing on the irrigated desert. To Feldman, this wasn't going to work at all. He was convinced it was a mistake as he and Faralla made the tortuous trip back into Parras.

As soon as they were back in town, Feldman tried to talk Peckinpah out of using the hacienda. Sam told him no. "I can't get along without that winery; it's the greatest. I've got it all in my head, I know just how I'm going to shoot all the scenes," Peckinpah said.[10] It was almost half-true, to borrow a favored expression of L. Q. Jones's. Sam had nothing *completely* mapped out; certainly nothing was on paper. But he had a clear vision of what he wanted to achieve. Hacienda Ciénega del Carmen fit the bill. Feldman caved, no doubt shuddering at the cost of bulldozing a new road for all those generators, portable toilets, trailers, horse trailers, and buses.

3.

B ack in Hollywood, the script for *The Wild Bunch* was submitted to the Motion Picture Association of America for review to ensure it met standards for decency. Those standards were in serious flux. For years, the Motion Picture Production Code, or Hays Code, had regulated morality in movies, largely in response to Protestant-church criticism of displays of seminudity and sexual material in American movies, not to mention gossip-sheet accounts of the decadent lives of Hollywood stars. It had remained solidly in effect through the 1950s. In the 1960s, enforcement began to slip, allowing the release of movies such as Warner Bros.' own *Who's Afraid of Virginia Woolf?* Also, European films' nudity and cursing had established a solid fan base at art theaters in American cities.

Seeking to attract audiences back into theaters, the MPAA determined that it should allow American movies to deal with adult themes in a more realistic way. The government-controlled TV broadcasts of the 1960s would never allow swearing, exposed nipples, and spurting blood to show up in American living rooms. The movies were all but free from government control when it came to content, outside of local decency ordinances. Still, the industry had to find a way to placate churches, especially the Protestant churches, whose clergy held enormous sway at the time.

In the mid-1960s, under the leadership of Jack Valenti, a former top aide to president Lyndon Johnson, the MPAA began to roll out a system for alerting moviegoers if a picture included nudity, swearing, or other content that some might find offensive. At first it was just the simple tag *For Mature Audiences*. By 1968, it expanded to an alphabet soup of movie ratings: *G* for "general" audiences; *M* for "mature" audiences; *R* for "restricted" audiences, meaning no one under seventeen could see the movie unless accompanied by an adult or guardian; and *X*, meaning no one under seventeen could be admitted under any circumstances. Porn, such as it was in 1968, was not even taken into consideration, though the *X* rating would eventually be associated with it. *X* at the time was to be applied to studio-produced movies with such mature themes that kids should not see them. From their inception, the ratings were controversial.[11]

At the time, Valenti's system seemed to be a well-intentioned attempt to expand Hollywood's grown-up content while offering some protection for exhibitors, especially those in the Bible Belt. Politics may have made a significant turn toward the left in the early part of the 1960s, but by and large America remained a morally conservative, religious nation. In small cities and towns in the heartland, many Southern Baptist preachers excoriated their flocks for attending *any* movies, even biblical epics, as well as for dancing, playing cards, and imbibing liquor. A movie that showed a woman's bare breast or included dialogue taking the Lord's name in vain was certain to stir up protests, unless theater patrons had some warning in advance. Valenti's system provided just such an alert. However, the rating a picture received would affect its revenue. A *G* rating suggested family fare, Disney pictures, kids' stuff that would turn away the maturing baby-boomer demographic. On the other hand, *X* went too far the other direction, ensuring a limited audience. Even an *R* rating would drive away many people from the box office. *M* became the coveted rating, promising a picture with some coarse language, maybe a flash of an exposed nipple, and maybe a little bloody violence—content that would be censored on TV but still not overly risqué.

The *Wild Bunch* screenplay came back from the MPAA with two pages of recommended cuts: reduce the cussing, graphic killing and maiming, nudity, and, in general, lewd behavior by the gang members. No one involved with the production took these recommended cuts seriously. If anything, Feldman was something of a provocateur about censorship. Later, as the picture was nearing release, he might suggest edits, but never did he recommend cutting *The Wild Bunch*'s violence. The production team gave no more heed to the MPAA and its two pages of suggestions than it would to a doddering great-grandmother offering up a list of Bible verses.

4.

M eanwhile, from his office in Warners' studio in Burbank, Peckinpah fleshed out his crew for *The Wild Bunch*. A key recruit was
Gordon Dawson as wardrobe supervisor. *The Wild Bunch* was going to
be a costumer par excellence, no glitz or glamour, many people dressed
in period wardrobe. Peckinpah never considered anyone except Dawson,
who had stepped in to resolve costuming issues on *Major Dundee*. Scenes
from *The Wild Bunch* as written in the shooting script and as they developed in Sam's head were going to require intense effort by the picture's
wardrobe department, in part because Peckinpah planned to make heavy
use of squibbing for the movie's shoot-outs. Each time a squib went off,
it ripped a hole in a costume and left a bloody stain. All the costumes
would have to be reused and then reused again and again. Peckinpah
believed Dawson could best manage the wardrobe crew. He also seemed
to be one of those few people in Hollywood who could understand what
Peckinpah wanted in spite of Sam's sometimes less-than-articulate instructions. The man who had walloped the hell out of Jim Hutton for screwing
around on *Major Dundee* seemed perfect for the job. However, Dawson's
fortunes in the industry were changing.

Despite having one of the essential and most difficult roles on a movie
set, a wardrobe supervisor fell low on the Hollywood pecking order.
Dawson sometimes felt as if he were in the eyes of stars and directors
nothing more than a glorified valet. Wardrobe was the family business;
Dawson's dad was director of wardrobe at Columbia. Dawson was ready
to step out on his own, so he'd taught himself how to write scripts and
found success placing them on TV series. So when Phil Feldman called
him to say Peckinpah wanted Dawson on *The Wild Bunch*, Dawson
responded, "Oh, absolutely not, not even in question." Feldman then

began a courtship over several weeks, upping the salary offer with each phone call.

Finally, Dawson's phone rang one day, and he picked up the receiver and heard a voice so soft that he could barely make out the words: "Well, Dawson, you chickenshit, it's time for guts poker. You up for this or not? Come on, you want to take a walk on the wild side?" Fucking Peckinpah. Dawson agreed to visit Sam and talk about it in person. Peckinpah was succinct when they huddled together: "I've got a motherfucker, I don't know how to do it, it's too fucking big, it's all fucked-up, if wardrobe goes in the bucket, they're going to have my balls. It's my big chance, it's my comeback." Dawson couldn't say no to that and agreed to come on board. That Sam offered him twice as much money as any wardrobe supervisor had ever made on any picture made saying yes easier.[12]

5.

The obvious choice for director of cinematography was Lucien Ballard, who had teamed with Sam so successfully on *Ride the High Country*. Ballard was an Oklahoman, born in the small county seat town of Miami (pronounced *my-am-a*), located in the zinc-mining country near the convergence of Oklahoma, Kansas, and Missouri. The area around Miami was home to the reservations of the Miami, Ottawa, Modoc, and other Native tribes that had been uprooted from their homelands and relocated in the 1800s to what was then Indian Territory. There were Indians and cowboys aplenty surrounding Ballard as he came of age; Will Rogers had grown up just sixty miles away.

Like many Oklahomans of his generation, Ballard wanted to experience more out of life than what he could find in a sleepy town that seemed to be a hundred miles from nowhere. He felt no calling to enter any trade or profession. With nothing better to do, he made a stop at the University of Oklahoma after graduating from high school. Then he headed to China for a while. He returned to the United States, where he traveled the West Coast, working in sawmills, lumberjacking a little, and surveying. He wound up in L.A., where he found a job at a lumber company.

When not working, Ballard began to keep company with an old friend at her job as a script girl at Paramount. Many of the studio's new sound-stages had been destroyed during a fire the night of January 16, 1929, and Paramount was shooting at night while rebuilding went on during the day. One night, a Paramount worker asked Ballard to stop flirting with his lady friend and help out setting up scenery. Ballard agreed and was soon employed by the studio at night while holding on to his lumber-company job during the day. He worked on a circus picture starring Clara Bow, at the time the movies' hottest leading lady, who took a liking to him and invited Ballard to a sure-enough Hollywood party at her house. Ballard was hooked and soon gave up his day job at the lumber company.

It was Ballard's good fortune to wind up as an assistant cameraman at Paramount, even though nothing in his background indicated he would have any aptitude for photography. Eventually the studio assigned him to work on *Morocco*, a feature starring Gary Cooper and Marlene Dietrich. This brought him into the demanding gaze of director Josef von Sternberg, one of Hollywood's best. Sternberg had a gilded cinematic career that included mentorship by Emile Chautard and other French filmmakers who had relocated to New Jersey during the earliest days of American cinema. After a few hits and misses in the United States, Sternberg traveled to Berlin, where he directed one of the most significant movies in film history, *Der blaue Engel* (*The Blue Angel*), which made an international star of Dietrich and came to be regarded as a masterpiece of German expressionism. Sternberg returned to America as a director of note. He brought Dietrich with him and proceeded to make *Morocco*, their first Hollywood collaboration.

Sternberg took note of his assistant cameraman on the picture, and a mentor-protégé relationship ensued as Sternberg requested Ballard be assigned to subsequent pictures of Sternberg's.[13] Ballard's plainspoken directness appealed to Sternberg. "Other people were frightened of him," Ballard said, "but I wasn't, and that's why we got along. I could never sit

Sam Peckinpah and Lucien Ballard on location at the Río Nazas outside Torreón. Photo by Bernie Abramson, courtesy of Jeff Slater.

on a fence, I was always honest and would speak my piece, and he appreciated that." But things often grew contentious. Sternberg fired Ballard almost as many times as Ballard quit. After simmering down, the two men always resumed working together. Ballard even resigned from Paramount to follow Sternberg to Columbia. There Ballard came into his own. He remained at Harry Cohn's fiefdom even after Sternberg left in a snit.

Columbia had none of the luxuries of Paramount. The work was fast, the work was furious. No time for fancy lighting. No time to set up unusual camera angles. Yet in the rush to churn out product, Ballard, now a full-fledged cameraman, continued to learn and increase his range of skills. His contract called for him to work for forty weeks a year, during which he shot mostly forgettable features. Then he had a twelve-week hiatus, during which he'd go across the street to Columbia's short subject unit to shoot Three Stooges comedies. Because it gave him a chance to experiment with camera trickery, his cinematography with the Stooges was the most satisfying thing he did at the studio. Also, Ballard was introduced to Westerns at Columbia, sometimes working with Sam Nelson, who had a prolific career as a first assistant director but who also directed a couple of dozen shorts and B Westerns himself. By the time Ballard left Columbia in 1940, he was one of the best black-and-white cinematographers in the business.

In the late 1940s, Ballard worked with Max Ophüls, a European director who revolutionized the way the camera is used in motion pictures. Ballard then spent the next years constantly in demand for the realism he could achieve in screen photography. His preference was to shoot in the muck and dirt, in the trees and rocks, wherever. He would take the camera where it needed to go to tell the story most effectively. By the mid 1950s, he seemed to have worked everywhere and shot just about everything for just about everybody. Nothing was new for him.

During that decade Budd Boetticher wanted to find a location for a feature he was working on at Lone Pine, California, from which no director had ever before shot. He explored the countryside on horseback and on foot until he found just the spot, one where he could film a cowboy riding with a tremendous expanse of rocks and land as a backdrop. He took "Loosh" to the precise point and said he wanted to shoot with a twenty-five-millimeter lens "right here." Ballard shrugged, walked over about twenty feet, and dug in the sand until he found a spike. Ballard said, "Come here a minute and tell me which one you like best. Raoul Walsh and I made one right here twenty years ago."[14]

By this time, Ballard was shooting color, something he'd earlier resisted: "I turned down color because I didn't want to work with the color men. You know, you always had to have one or two consultants with you, and all they wanted was plenty of exposure for their negative. You couldn't control the photography with them around."[15] But, finally, he realized that he had to take up color if he wanted to continue working in Hollywood. He may have loved black-and-white movie photography, with its mood-setting lights and shadows and shades of gray, but he would do his finest cinematography in color. As he grew older, he seemed comfortable with technical changes. Peckinpah had used him as his videographer on "Noon Wine," shot using the new medium of video-tape, and Ballard merits most of the credit for its stunning look (by mid-1960s TV standards). Ballard was old-school, closing in on sixty years old by the time Peckinpah hired him for *The Wild Bunch*, but Ballard was in more demand than ever as a director of photography. The year he worked on *The Wild Bunch*, he also shot both Henry Hathaway's *True Grit* and Boetticher's *A Time for Dying*.

In the late 1960s, Ballard was a tough character, no one to be trifled with. Director Carroll Ballard (no relation) remembered Ballard carried himself like a Confederate general. He was almost always seen with a swagger stick tucked under his arm and a scowl on his face. Sometimes, when he was in what passed for him as a playful moment, he used the stick to goose unsuspecting men or to lift the skirts of women who'd let their guard down. His health was iffy; he suffered from severe back pain, which eventually became so bad that to stand up and walk he'd have to lace himself into a corsetlike device.[16] Yet his work ethic was unsurpassed. Nor was anyone his better when it came to understanding complicated cinematographic challenges. Peckinpah had plenty to throw Ballard's way. Sam planned to have as many as six cameras rolling at different speeds to film action sequences. Other shots would require a row of operators—holding what in 1968 passed for handheld cameras—lying on their backs in the dirt while shooting at horses and riders galloping above them. Ballard could make it all happen. It was worth the occasional swagger-stick poke to get what Ballard could deliver.

Ballard had been director of photography on Boetticher's *The Rise and Fall of Legs Diamond*, for which the two men successfully reproduced the look of newsreel footage from the 1930s. Peckinpah and Ballard now set about attempting to accomplish something similar for *The Wild Bunch*. They studied *Memorias de un mexicano* as well as any other newsreels they could find from the Mexican Revolution. They also plowed through books of photographs taken in Mexico during the years of the revolution. Ballard noted the "shallow" nature of the images. "We selected out lenses in an attempt to recapture this same kind of visual texture," Ballard said.[17]

6.

Chalo González's title might have been technical adviser, but in Mexico, he was assuming a role as de facto production coordinator, filling voids that William Faralla couldn't handle. "He didn't know how to do what a production coordinator has to do in Mexico," González told me. "He didn't know Mexico."[18] It fell to González to begin finding places for the cast and crew to stay once filming began. With his knowledge of the town and the connections provided by his old professor, Chalo knew just which doors to knock on. It was no easy task, given how small and remote Parras was. When he'd finished, he'd rented many of the town's houses and had booked every available hotel room in Parras.[19]

González also negotiated the deal with Parras civic leaders to allow filming in the town. Among other things, the town agreed to postpone a planned upgrade of its municipal utilities until after completion of the movie to allow vintage power, telephone, and telegraph lines and poles to remain in place. Warner Bros.-Seven Arts recorded a cash payment of twenty-five thousand pesos (roughly $1,300 in 1968 dollars, based on the exchange rate at the time) made by Chalo González to the alcalde of Parras as *la mordida* to ensure the mayor's cooperation. Peckinpah had the location he needed. Parras was the real deal, remote, harsh, demanding.

Permissions in place, Carrere and others from Hollywood descended on Parras to work with a mostly Mexican crew to transform the town into the early twentieth-century border town San Rafael/Starbuck. From that point on, most of the people involved with the production of *The Wild Bunch* would be from Mexico, ranging from virtually all the laborers to some of the people filling professional roles to the majority of the extras to the billed actors themselves.

Mexico's film *sindicatos* were heavily involved, and at times they were at odds with American union and guild members. The wages paid to the

Mexicans were minuscule compared to what American workers north of the river might have received, which could only please the bean counters back at Warners' corporate offices. Parras nevertheless benefited. *The Wild Bunch* provided a cash flow into a remote town with many financially desperate people. Carrere's transformation work required scores of carpenters, painters, truck drivers, and people with a back strong enough to handle a shovel. Tons of soil were hauled into the plaza to remake its main street from flagstone to dirt. Gritty false facades went up over the rather charming nineteenth-century adobe and stone buildings in the heart of Parras's small business district. As more and more Hollywood gringos poured into the small town, resentment among some of the locals grew over what they took to be the dismissive arrogance of the white men, starting with the pronunciation of the town's name. Almost all of the Anglos insisted on calling it Paris, some out of a sense of irony, but most out of ignorance of Spanish. They never seemed to want to learn how to say it correctly.

Warner Bros.-Seven Arts reached an agreement with the owners of the Hacienda Ciénega del Carmen, the Bedegas family, to lease the ancient winery and aqueduct. The contract called for the conversion of the site into a more or less permanent movie set for *The Wild Bunch* and for subsequent pictures to be shot there. Warner's paid the Bedegases sixty thousand pesos (just under $3,400) for its use. If any production companies rented the location in the future, proceeds would be split fifty-fifty between Warner Bros.-Seven Arts and the family. If no one was interested in using the site by mid-1970, the Bedegases were free to tear down all the work done there and use it however they pleased. The family also agreed to mow down the alfalfa growing, with the aid of irrigation, in the fields surrounding the winery. The land had returned to desert sand by the time filming began. Finally, the Bedegases agreed to allow up to two hundred soldiers of the Mexican Army serving as *Wild Bunch* extras to camp in the former alfalfa fields.

7.

For *The Wild Bunch*, Peckinpah's first assistant director would be his primary implementer, his scene-choreographer collaborator, and, often, his communication conduit to the rest of the crew on a complicated production. Phil Rawlins was tapped for the job. Rawlins and Peckinpah had been friends for a number of years, occasionally lifting a cup together. A native of Glendale, California, Rawlins grew up rodeoing, as did his brother, David, a film editor who'd eventually cut Peckinpah's final feature, *The Osterman Weekend*—Phil was a roper, while David was a rough-stock rider. Phil entered the business as stuntman, a contemporary of Roy Sickner's.

Rawlins had been working mostly in TV before Peckinpah hired him for *The Wild Bunch*. As a stuntman, he doubled for Clint Eastwood on *Rawhide* and had worked on *Gunsmoke*. By the early 1960s, he'd begun to shift to functioning as an AD. He was good at it, at least as far as TV went. His credits included *Maverick, Cheyenne, Hawaiian Eye, 77 Sunset Strip, The Outer Limits, F Troop*, and *Star Trek*. Most recently he'd been working on the *Dragnet* spin-off, *Adam-12*.

Rawlins, never mind his friendship with Peckinpah, was a problem from the start. His vision of *The Wild Bunch* was at odds with Sam's, beginning with the locations. One night the two men argued at the El Chiquito Inn, with neither man willing to give up his position. Sam invited Rawlins to step out back, where he sucker punched Rawlins between the eyes. Peckinpah watched in astonishment—and dread—as Rawlins sank no more than an inch and a half before he righted himself. What followed was for Sam a blur of fists and cowboy boots smashing into him, which finally left him unconscious on the ground in the alley. Rawlins might have just delivered Peckinpah the soundest thrashing he'd ever received, but he remained on the picture, at least for the time being.[20]

Rawlins was hardly the only staffing problem Peckinpah encountered. If Warner Bros.-Seven Arts production chief Ken Hyman was showing himself to be one of the most creative studio heads of production in town, he had also inherited hundreds of Warner employees, protected by unions, who had been with the studio for decades. Some, such as Carrere and the makeup artist Al Greenway, proved valuable to Sam. Others were entrenched paycheck drawers content with a cookie-cutter approach to filmmaking, inventiveness be damned. Peckinpah found himself saddled by the studio with just creative dullards when it came to props. Props were "in the bucket," as Gordon Dawson put it, from the beginning.[21] Dawson, who understood what he'd be in for on a Peckinpah picture, loaded up Warner's entire collection of Old West costumes, plus he rented even more from the legendary Western Costume, which had been supplying wardrobes for motion pictures going all the way back to D. W. Griffith's *The Birth of a Nation*. As the *Wild Bunch* company began to move to Mexico, Dawson showed up at a port of entry with 150 hampers of costumes and 500 feet of piping to hang all of those clothes.

Dawson passed by the property master and his crew as they checked in through Mexican customs with just a few cases of ammo. Dawson, being a seasoned Peckinpah hand, offered some friendly advice: "You better take more ammo, I'm telling you." The old-time Warners' men told him not to tell them what the fuck to do. "I've been in this business longer than you've been alive," one said. Dawson went about his business.[22] Sure enough, the ammo was completely gone by the second day of shooting, as was *The Wild Bunch*'s original property master.

Sensing this would happen, Peckinpah tucked away an ace up his sleeve. Stephen Ferry was one of the top property masters working in Hollywood. Roughly the same age as Peckinpah, the two men had known each other for many years socially, and they had worked together— Peckinpah had hired Ferry to be the property master on *The Cincinnati Kid*. Sam trusted Ferry. At the time, Ferry wanted to focus on acting. Over the years, he had landed roles here and there, mostly on TV series, going all the way back to *The George Burns and Gracie Allen Show*. Ferry was capable enough as an actor, but the parts were few, brief, and, usually, far between. For *The Wild Bunch*, Peckinpah offered Ferry the role of Sergeant McHale, a tousled noncom who leads a platoon of green American soldiers on a passenger car in the movie's train-robbery scene. It was a bigger and better part than any Ferry had previously played. While he signed on to act, it was understood between Ferry and Peckinpah that

Ferry would be available to step in if the props department went south. That was exactly what happened. Peckinpah fired everyone Warners had lined up to work props until, at last, Ferry took over as property master. Ferry became as integral to the team as Gordon Dawson, Lucien Ballard, and Cliff Coleman, though he never wound up in the movie's credits, except for his acting role.[23]

8.

Warner Bros.-Seven Arts budgeted $3,451,420 for the making of *The Wild Bunch*, a large amount to shoot a picture in 1968. It also allotted 225,000 feet of film, also significant for the time. Studio production head Ken Hyman had to know those figures were both just place-holders. The real numbers were likely to be greater—and they were. That was okay. Hyman seemed to take a let-the-big-horse-run attitude from the beginning, even if his producer Phil Feldman expressed doubts.

By mid-March 1968, the *Wild Bunch* film company had decamped to Mexico. With shooting set to begin on March 25, the cast began gathering in Parras. The image cast by William Holden when he arrived wound up burned into L. Q. Jones's memory. The Academy Award winner wore clothes Jones could only describe as the nicest he'd even seen—high-end safari casual replete with ascots. Holden brought with him huge suitcases with even more fabulous garments neatly folded inside. Holden's attire was the only thing fancy about him. His face showed every year of his half century of life on earth, and then some. He felt old and used up and was not motivated to try to look different from that. He had not dieted or used any of the other actor's rejuvenation tricks before heading to Mexico. This time he was going to be who and what he was in front of the cameras.

Jones had no worries about Holden's health, but it was a different story for Edmond O'Brien, who had come on board to play the cantankerous Freddie Sykes, the oldest member of the wild bunch. Sykes, even more so than Pike Bishop or Deke Thornton, was the living connection to the Old West of Billy the Kid and Wild Bill Hickok. Pike says that Sykes was once one of the best, who'd done his share of robbing and killing back in the old days. He adheres more thoroughly to the Code of the West than anyone else in *The Wild Bunch*. He has become decrepit by the early

1910s, but Pike keeps him around, even if he can hardly do more than watch the horses—and does his killing now with his bad coffee, not his pistol. In spite of his physical limitations, Sykes remains the kind of man Pike would "ride the river with." Pike is loyal to his longtime friend. In one of *The Wild Bunch*'s central ironies, it is Old Man Sykes who survives the carnage and, at the end, points the way to salvation for Deke Thornton: joining the Mexican Revolution on the side of Pancho Villa. Several people working on *The Wild Bunch* feared that O'Brien, unlike his character, might not make it to the end.

To Jones, O'Brien looked so frail that L. Q. fretted about O'Brien throughout the shoot. Jones made it a point to swing by the house rented for O'Brien daily to make sure the fifty-two-year-old actor was okay. Like Holden and Peckinpah, O'Brien had established a reputation as one of Hollywood's two-fisted drinkers. It was widely believed that boozing, and the resulting inability of O'Brien to control his weight, had hampered his career from developing into what it might otherwise have been. Nevertheless, he had become one of the best character actors in the business.

O'Brien was a Brooklyn native trained by Sanford Meisner, who, along with Stella Adler and Lee Strasberg, was applying the acting principles of Russian Konstantin Stanislavski to the American stage. O'Brien's proving ground was New York's Neighborhood Playhouse School of the Theatre, whose list of alumni would come to include Gregory Peck, Robert Duvall, Sydney Pollack, Steve McQueen, and Tony Randall. O'Brien also appeared alongside the likes of Laurence Olivier in productions of Shakespeare. Then O'Brien went to Hollywood to work for RKO.

O'Brien had a major role in the studio's production of *The Hunchback of Notre Dame* when he was just twenty-three years old. Then he moved on to post–World War II noir films such as *The Killers*, *White Heat*, and *D.O.A.*, as well as the Ida Lupino–directed *The Hitch-Hiker* and *The Bigamist*. In 1954, he won the Academy Award for best supporting actor in Joseph L. Mankiewicz's *The Barefoot Contessa*. After that, O'Brien's career went into something of a slide as he appeared more and more frequently on TV shows and in mediocre, at best, movies. Then John Ford cast him as the hard-drinking newspaper editor Dutton Peabody in *The Man Who Shot Liberty Valance*. It marked O'Brien's return to better-quality films, and he made the most of it. He followed *Liberty Valance* in short order with *Birdman of Alcatraz*, *The Longest Day*, and *Seven Days in May*. His

Edmond O'Brien (right) in full makeup for *The Wild Bunch*. He patiently sat for hours daily while makeup artists transformed him to the character of Freddie Sykes. Here he rides with Chano Urueta, who played the jefe of Angel's village. Urueta was a significant director during the Golden Age of Mexican cinema. Photo by Paul Harper, courtesy of Nick Redman and Jeff Slater.

drinking and weight gain continued, however, and by 1967 he was back to squeezing by on paychecks from TV shows such as *The Virginian* and *The Outsider* and roles in third-rate movies.

O'Brien was battling a bloated waistline when Peckinpah hired him for *The Wild Bunch*. The Academy Award winner was also burned out on the movie business, acting having become drudgery for him. However, he was excited by the quality of *The Wild Bunch* script and the opportunities a role such as that of Freddie Sykes provided him to ply his craft. Before he left for Mexico, he and his son, Brendan, rented horses at Griffith Park stables and hit the trails so O'Brien could start getting in shape. Soon he was feeling more invigorated than he had in a long time, never mind that Warner Bros.-Seven Arts' insurance company was expressing concerns about O'Brien's working in the high desert elevation at Parras (roughly the same as Denver's) or a vague leg injury from which O'Brien was recovering.[24]

No role in *The Wild Bunch* provided more challenges than that of Sykes, starting with the hours in makeup required every day as O'Brien was aged into a grizzled, battered character at least twenty years beyond his own age. It was all done the old-fashioned way—spirit gum and fake whiskers—with Al Greenway and crew performing precise work on O'Brien day after day.

But O'Brien's becoming the character of Sykes required much more than just prosthetics and a false beard. What O'Brien did with his body, his facial expressions, and his voice was more essential than Greenway's makeup magic. *The Wild Bunch* was a bit of an homage to *The Treasure of the Sierra Madre*, with Sykes clearly drawn from that movie's character Howard—played by Walter Huston—the veteran of gold prospecting in the mountains of Mexico. The trick for O'Brien was to make Sykes a similar character to Howard without falling into imitation. O'Brien had undertaken a similar task earlier in the 1960s, with results that left him less than happy.

O'Brien told Peckinpah that John Ford had asked him to reprise Thomas Mitchell's performance as the besotted doctor in *Stagecoach* when O'Brien played the newspaper editor in *The Man Who Shot Liberty Valance*. As a consequence, O'Brien had not done much digging into the character of the editor. He just gave Ford what he wanted—"which really amounts to bad impersonation and that is not creative acting."

In a note to Peckinpah, O'Brien wrote, "Right now, for instance, the town is full of pictures that imitate each other—and the other day I heard someone say—and at first I picked up the easy label—that *The Wild Bunch* is *Dirty Dozen* as a Western. Well, it isn't—and I don't think you want it to be. Any more than if you really examine your thinking—you don't want me to do an impersonation of Walter Huston's part in *Treasure*—because that's all it would be and there's no point in doing a part in a big picture that would not be my performance."

O'Brien saw Sykes as a character devoid of self-pity, who would refuse to comment at all when he was injured—just endure it and carry on. His general demeanor was "humor when necessary—inscrutable when necessary—mumbles when he doesn't care to be heard or shuts up. But he can talk damn clear if he has to and if it's important—but quite clear. I think he should laugh a lot, like hell, man, this is the only way to go. No hero, just screw it, endure and get it done and toss off the enduring. He can be old as hell, the face and the makeup will do that, but I don't want him to play old. He was *born* old and YOUNG/and one day he will die old and young." It was a hell of a goddamned part, O'Brien wrote to Peckinpah. "I think I'm starting to like acting again."[25]

O'Brien joined with the movie's other main actors at the Hotel Rincón del Montero, the small resort on the outskirts of Parras. There, at a long table, they went through several days of rehearsals, with Peckinpah gigging O'Brien to give him a more impassioned reading. "Oh, you mean how am I going to do the character? Do you want to see that now?" O'Brien instantly remade himself into Old Man Sykes, jumping up, dancing around the room, and cackling. Sam loved what he saw in O'Brien's "old and YOUNG/and one day he will die old and young" reading of the character.[26] It wasn't like doing a film. It was like making characters actually come alive. Something magic was going on in Parras. Actors such as Warren Oates could feel it. It wasn't just the acting. It was *everything*. All the parts seemed to be coming together in a magical way. Something extraordinary was occurring.

Typically, O'Brien marked up his copies of shooting scripts with soft-lead pencil. For *The Wild Bunch*, he used a pen for the only time anyone could remember. His green-ink notations showed he worked hard on the script. His lines for two pivotal speeches—the "Who the hell is they?" sequence and the movie's closing passage, "It ain't like it used to be. But it'll do"—were not a part of the mimeographed copies of the shooting script. They appear in green ink scrawled in O'Brien's hand on his copy of the script. It is unclear whether he came up with the lines himself or if they grew collaboratively out of the rehearsals or both. Whatever the case, the green ink turned to gold when O'Brien delivered the words in front of the cameras.[27]

In fact, something remarkable was occurring at those rehearsal sessions at the Hotel Rincón del Montero. Under Peckinpah's direction, the actors went beyond acting and were *becoming* the wild bunch and the other characters in the movie. It was intense, hard work, but the actors thrived on it. "We rehearsed the scenes for the emotions of it, for the movement of it," said Warren Oates. "And then we played it, but it was like life, it wasn't like doing a film. That's the most outstanding thing to me, is that it wasn't like a play when you think of playing on a stage, or doing a TV show when you're trying to do ten pages a day. We had time to work on what we were doing. There was no loss of movement or motion, and we were all pretty well balanced human beings in the first place." Oates added, "It was our life. We were doing our fucking lives right there and lived it every day. And if we ever forgot it, Sam created something around [us] to make us cognizant [that] we were there not just as characters in a piece. We were there in truth."[28]

Peckinpah also wanted truthful depiction of violence, determined to outdo Arthur Penn's use of squibs in *Bonnie and Clyde*. As the actors rehearsed, outside the hotel the special effects crew experimented with squibbing wardrobe. The crew had set up a cutout of a person against a corral fence. Peckinpah watched them as they practiced blowing holes in clothing but stopped them by shouting, "That's not what I want! That's not what I want!" He produced a pistol loaded with live ammunition and began shooting the cutout. The bullets pierced the cutout and emerged from the other side. "That's the effect I want." The crew now used bigger squibs on both the front and the back of the cutout, simulating the passage of a bullet through a body. They also added hamburger meat to give the illusion of tissue flying with the impact in addition to spreading stage blood.[29]

9.

Jaime Sánchez saw something inspiring about Peckinpah from the read-ings onward. It was hard to put his finger on just what it was, because Sam hardly spoke. Yet it was "very special," in Sánchez's words. "I didn't know the man, I didn't know anybody in Hollywood. I realized this guy is going to do something incredible, because you can sense when someone is great." Sánchez saw that the other actors felt the same sort of thing he did. "Sam made everybody feel that you go for broke. Not to go for broke was an act of dishonor." Peckinpah did one thing that was completely different from the ways of the film directors Sánchez had worked with in New York. He was used to an environment in which a director conducted meetings over coffee to discuss character development, with the director offering up plenty of advice to the actor on how to play a role. Peckinpah, on the other hand, challenged the actor to create the character him- or herself. It forced the actor to do plenty of thinking. Sánchez felt exhilaration as an actor working with Peckinpah and the talented *Wild Bunch* cast and crew.[30]

Sánchez's presence did cause some consternation among the actors and crew members he'd be working with in the upcoming months. It wasn't a personal thing so much as the result of a long-standing Hollywood resent-ment of New York actors. O'Brien may have been a native New Yorker, and Ernest Borgnine, Robert Ryan, and Warren Oates certainly had New York experience, but they'd all been making films on the West Coast for long enough to be considered part of the Hollywood community. Not Sánchez, who, in addition to freshly arriving from New York, was also a generation younger than the other leads. Any dislike the Hollywood people felt toward him went unnoticed by Sánchez. Years later, he told me that he considered working on *The Wild Bunch* to be gratifying, a completely positive experience. It was one of the great accomplishments of his career.[31]

PART V

"I Wouldn't Have It
Any Other Way Either"

1.

The *Wild Bunch* cast and crew settled into Mexico just days before the assassination of Martin Luther King Jr. in Memphis on April 4, 1968, which unleashed social unrest the likes of which had not occurred in the United States for more than one hundred years. Rioting broke out from coast to coast, with more than a hundred cities suffering violence, looting, and burning. Particularly great destruction hit Kansas City, Baltimore, Washington, D.C., and Chicago, where arson fires blazed out of control across the West Side. Responding to calls for help from Mayor Richard Daley, more than three thousand Illinois National Guard troops supported by U.S. Army troops began to patrol the city. The soldiers took sniper fire from burned out buildings. Similar scenes played out in other cities. Forty-five people died nationwide during the rioting. Police, especially in Chicago, were not nearly as restrained in their responses to such situations as they would be in years to come. They could swing nightsticks and blackjacks freely and fire off tear gas, and Daley authorized them to "to shoot to kill any arsonist or anyone with a Molotov cocktail in his hand . . . and . . . to shoot to maim or cripple anyone looting any stores in our city."[1]

In Vietnam, the deadliest year for American forces began with the first phase of the Tet Offensive, which blindsided U.S. military commanders when it rolled out in late January. Over the next three months, Americans viewed TV reports depicting U.S. forces struggling against North Vietnamese and Viet Cong fighters in such places as Khe Sanh, Hue, and Saigon itself. Casualties were staggering. A month and a half before King's assassination, nearly 550 American troops died in Vietnam in just one week, with 2,500 wounded.

Just three weeks before King's death, Lyndon Johnson came close to losing the New Hampshire Democrat Party primary. Robert Ryan—who played Deke Thornton, leader of the bounty hunters, in *The Wild Bunch*—had celebrated the news that his candidate, Eugene McCarthy, scored 42 percent of the vote to Johnson's 49 percent. Four days later, Senator Robert F. Kennedy renounced his support of Johnson, clearly indicating that he was planning to make a run for the nomination himself. Then, on March 31, 1968, Johnson shocked the nation when he announced that he was withdrawing from the election. Kennedy began firing up his political machine, much to the chagrin of McCarthy supporters such as Ryan. Contrary to later reports, Ryan was feeling little love for Kennedy when the *Wild Bunch* company arrived in Parras. The previous summer, the folk-rock band the Youngbloods had released "Get Together," the song that urged people to smile on their brother and try to love one another. By the spring of 1968, no one in the United States seemed to be smiling at all, let alone doing much in the way of loving. It was not a bad time to be out of the country. For the months that they were in Mexico, the *Wild Bunch* cast and crew by and large felt disassociated with the turmoil going on back home.

They settled into the digs that Chalo González had secured in Parras, with Peckinpah, Holden, Borgnine, and a few others occupying near-palatial houses. From that high standard, the quality of the dwellings dropped off precipitously. Lower-billed actors had lesser houses, in some cases doubling up with each other. Four Mexican actresses shared a house that was cramped by American standards but the envy of impoverished people in Parras, who lived in tiny adobe structures with no running water or electricity. For the most part, the crew took over the town's hotels and motels, such as they were. The crew quickly learned the wisdom of employing the seasoned desert rat's trick of placing the legs of beds and cots into pails of water before retiring at night. The next morning, they'd find drowned centipedes, tarantulas, and scorpions in the buckets that would otherwise have crawled between the sheets.[2]

2.

Of the forty actors who received credits at the end of *The Wild Bunch*, twenty-four were Latinos, with all but one, Jaime Sánchez, being Mexicans or Mexican Americans. Though only a few people in American audiences, by and large ignorant of Mexican entertainment, could have known it, *The Wild Bunch* included some of Mexico's top acting talent, all widely recognized in their own nation. The best-known of the Mexican actors working on *The Wild Bunch* was Don Emilio Fernández, who had been given the vital role of the Huertista general Mapache. In the movie, Mapache is commanding troops fight pro–Pancho Villa insurgents, as well as raiding pueblos for whatever he can steal for himself. He later hires the wild bunch to hijack a load of U.S. Army rifles across the Rio Grande in Texas.

Fernández was Mexico's greatest director as well as one of its best film actors. An icon in Mexico, he was known as much for his dark excesses and violent temper as he was for his creative genius. He was typically drunk during his waking hours yet had the stamina to have sex with different women every chance he had. Plenty made themselves available to him—never mind that he was now in his midsixties, overweight, and long married. He never went anywhere unarmed, and he was quick to pull his pistol if anyone crossed him. Stories spread across Mexico concerning the number of people he had shot and killed, most of them fantasy but in at least one case true.

Fernández had been born in 1904 in a small mining community that was, at the time, part of the municipality of Juárez, not far from the American border. His father was an army captain; his mother, a Kickapoo Indian. Unlike most mestizos at the time of Fernández's youth, he began to embrace his Indian heritage, not his Spanish heritage, and continued to do so throughout his life. He became known far and wide

Mexico's greatest film director, Emilio "El Indio" Fernández, as General Mapache in *The Wild Bunch*. A controversial man, he gave a brilliant performance but scandalized cast and crew members by fondling actresses on the set and by the "harem" of young women he brought with him to Parras. Photo by Paul Harper, courtesy of Nick Redman and Jeff Slater.

as El Indio. After he was a well-known film director, Pope Pius XII offered him a contract to make devotional films for the Catholic Church. Fernández wrote back to the Holy Father to decline: "Forgive me, Your Holiness, but I am a Mexican Indian, those who failed to conquer the Spaniards. I still believe in Huitzilopochtli, and saints and miracles do not mean anything to me."[3]

The Mexican Revolution, on the other hand, meant a great deal to him. While still a boy, Fernández disappeared into his country's bloody warfare as it played out in his native Coahuila, and it left an impression on him that lasted the rest of his life. By the time he was in his late teens, he had sided with a faction in an unsuccessful attempt to overthrow Mexican president Álvaro Obregón. As a result, El Indio was captured and imprisoned, then forced to leave Mexico. He went to the United States, winding up in Los Angeles, where he worked as a laborer to survive.

While on a construction job at a film studio, he was hired as an extra for a movie, which was life changing. From that point on, his future was in cinema. He began learning the business from the bottom up, hiring out for whatever employment was available at the studios. Legend has it that in the late 1920s he even posed nude as the model for the Academy Awards statuette. By 1930, he had become a billed actor, but he yearned to direct and didn't see a way he could accomplish that in Hollywood. A shifting political landscape made it possible for him to return to Mexico in 1933, where within a year he became one of Mexico's most famous actors. Shortly after that, a screenplay he'd written was filmed, and then, a few years later, the opportunity to direct came his way.

His timing couldn't have been better. Spanish-language films found a steady market throughout Central and South America, as well as in the Caribbean. Mexico became the primary supplier, with the government providing incentives to film studios. This created the Golden Age of Mexican cinema. El Indio directed the first masterpiece of the period in 1943 with *Flor silvestre*. The film starred his friend Dolores del Río, whom he'd met when she was a major star in Hollywood. Fernández paired her with Pedro Armendáriz, an up-and-coming actor with roots in both Mexico City and Laredo, Texas. The screenplay was written by El Indio and Mauricio Magdaleno. Gabriel Figueroa was the cinematographer. Fernández, del Río, Armendáriz, Magdaleno, and Figueroa collaborated on several important pictures.

Flor silvestre was a Mexican cinema blockbuster, both a box office and critical success. Next came the release of Fernández's *María Candelaria*. It was even better than *Flor silvestre* and became a benchmark for quality in Mexican cinema. It was the first Mexican movie to be exhibited at the Cannes International Film Festival and won the Grand Prix (now the Palme d'Or), Cannes's biggest prize. El Indio hit other creative peaks directing *Enamorada*, *Las abandonadas*, and *La perla*.

El Indio became wealthy, adopted an opulent lifestyle at his fortress-style house in Mexico City, and moved among the most powerful men in the country. As the luster began to fade from the Mexican film industry in the second half of the 1950s, Fernández turned to acting to maintain his lavish way of living. He often went to Hollywood to appear in front of the camera, usually in a sinister role. In the years just prior to his work on *The Wild Bunch*, he had roles in three American Westerns, *The Appaloosa*, *Return of the Magnificent Seven*, and *The War Wagon*.

Now he settled into one of Parras's grandest houses with an entourage of women. In this, he was not unlike his *Wild Bunch* character, Mapache, who maintained a stable of courtesans at his Agua Verde stronghold. Some of the other members of the cast referred to the women as "El Indio's harem," noting that a portion of the "harem" were scarcely of what would be legal age in the United States. If there were disapproving glances, Fernández gave them no heed. He did whatever he wanted. As filming progressed, he allowed his hands to run freely over some of the female cast members, ignoring any complaints they might have registered.[4]

To some of the *Wild Bunch* company, it was clear that El Indio's acting technique was to *become* the character he was playing. Without question, El Indio and Mapache had similarities: Both were hard men, violent drunks who kept strings of women at hand. El Indio also was an artist and had moments of sensitivity. In Parras, he surrendered to his sinister inner Mapache and became one of the most memorable of villains to ever appear in an American Western.

3.

E l Indio was hardly the only actor on *The Wild Bunch* who was on a loose moral tether. Albert Dekker played the railroad man Harrigan, charged with eliminating Pike Bishop and his band of outlaws once and for all. Harrigan appears relatively briefly in *The Wild Bunch*, as a remorseless, bloodthirsty tool of the railroad interests. A sociopath, he has not a concern about innocent townspeople slaughtered in the cross fire when his miscreant band of bounty hunters attempts to kill Pike Bishop's gang. "We're holding you and your whole damned railroad responsible for this carnage!" one outraged townsman says to him. Harrigan replies, "We represent the *law!*" Later, Deke remonstrates with him: "Tell me, Mr. Harrigan, how does it feel, getting paid for it, getting paid to sit back and hire your killings, with the law's arms around you? How does it feel to be so goddamned right?" Harrigan says smugly, "Good." Harrigan is as violent and vile as Mapache, maybe more so; during one sequence, Mapache at least demonstrates that he possesses a modicum of human decency. Harrigan, the white businessman, has none. He is every bit as cruel and ruthless as Faulkner's character Popeye in *Sanctuary*—and then some.

Peckinpah had wanted his regular collaborator R. G. Armstrong to play Harrigan. Armstrong was a character actor who had appeared on many TV series (including working with Peckinpah on *The Rifleman* and *The Westerner*) and in a number of movies (including both *Ride the High Country* and *Major Dundee*). He'd had a tough upbringing in Alabama that included immersion in blood-and-thunder Christian fundamentalism. In his best roles, he tapped into some inner part of himself still tortured by the hard-core religion and violence he experienced as a youth. It seemed logical to cast him as Harrigan, but Armstrong refused the part, pissing off Sam to no end. "You better not turn me down again, you son of a bitch!"[5] Peckinpah said to Armstrong. And Dekker got the part.

Dekker came across as a cold outsider among the Americans in the film, many of whom had worked together on a number of occasions. Dekker had appeared in a few Westerns, both movies (Anthony Mann's *The Furies*, Robert Parrish's *The Wonderful Country*) and TV shows, but he was hardly known as a cowboy actor. Instead, he was a Broadway star of significance before he boarded a train for Los Angeles to work in the movie business. Most of his picture work was in run-of-the-mill melodramas and light comedies. From time to time he was good in noir movies, especially *The Killers*, where he appeared alongside Edmond O'Brien. Dekker was a committed liberal, serving a term as a Democrat in the California State Assembly in the 1940s, where he represented a left-leaning district that included Hollywood. Around that time, he lived in Canoga Park in a Rudolph Schindler–designed house, an architectural masterpiece that Dekker subsequently sold to cult writer A. I. Bezzerides. By the time the late 1960s rolled around, Dekker was in his sixties and still working regularly on TV. He was also completely nuts.

Dekker arrived in Parras with a thirteen-year-old girl who would share his house. He introduced her to L. Q. Jones as his wife. In the days that followed, Dekker told Jones and others that while he had been acting for more than forty years onstage and in front of the cameras, he was actually a medical doctor, and the time had come for him to leave the thespian's art behind and to start practicing medicine. *The Wild Bunch* would be his last movie. After that, he and his "wife" were going to relocate to Africa, where Dekker planned to use his medical degree to help impoverished people. In fact, as a young man, Dekker had briefly studied premed at Bowdoin College in Maine, but he was no physician. He was certainly not married to the thirteen-year-old. He was divorced at the time and dating a former fashion model back in L.A., who apparently had no notion about his activities with a teenage girl in Mexico. The cast and crew of *The Wild Bunch* included a number of people with strong personalities, some as eccentric as hell, but Dekker took the prize as the weirdest of them all. And he was a criminal, a pedophile, who showed no remorse.

4.

The scenes making up the first half of the released version of *The Wild Bunch* were shot in Parras and at the nearby Hacienda Ciénega del Carmen. This would include the railroad-office robbery, the wild bunch's fleeing to Mexico, a visit to Angel's village, an encounter with Mapache and his troops, and striking the deal for the theft of rifles from the train back in the United States. The last twenty-five minutes of the film were shot there as well, including the delivery of the stolen rifles and the final shoot-out. A middle section of the movie, running about thirty minutes, was filmed later in and around Torreón and just across the state line in Durango; it included the centerpiece train robbery, the bridge explosion, and scenes in the canyon country.

Roy Sickner, who'd first dreamed up the movie all those years ago, was in place as associate producer and de facto stunt coordinator as work began in Parras. Sickner had pulled together a virtual who's who of stuntmen to work on the picture. Among them were Joe and Tap Canutt, sons of Yakima Canutt, who had raised stunt work to an art form on John Ford's *Stagecoach* thirty years earlier. Sickner's popularity among his colleagues aided him in rounding up the best of the best, but he also spread word that he could arrange for the stuntmen to get paid more per "gag" than the going Hollywood rate. That proved incentive enough.[6]

Stuntmen mostly considered themselves outsiders on a picture. They often had little respect for the actors they doubled for, even less for authority figures such as producers. On *The Wild Bunch*, they boarded together separate from the cast and rest of the crew in a large building that Chalo González had rented. Poker games, fistfights, drinking, and various kinds of debauchery occurred there. Several of the stuntmen also acted in the film, most notably Texan Billy Hart, who played one of the bounty hunters, Jess. Sickner's early *Wild Bunch* collaborator and buddy from high school, Buck Holland, was in Parras with a contract for stunts and acting. Holland was a Sickner loyalist and cool toward Sam from the beginning.

Three days before filming commenced, Sickner gathered Holland and stuntmen Louie Elias, Mickey Gilbert, the Canutt brothers, Bob Herron, Buzz Henry, Archie Butler, Erwin Neal, Jack Williams, Joe Yrigoyen, Bill Shannon, and Jim Sheppard to work out some of the gags needed for the opening shoot-out scene. Sickner was present for the first few weeks of shooting, receiving $250 for each stunt he cast and gaffed, which would include those performed in the Starbuck shoot-out. Then his name abruptly disappeared from Warner's call sheets, and Whitey Hughes took over stunt coordination.

Holland remembered that Sickner had to leave Mexico for vague legal reasons. L. Q. Jones said rumors held that Sickner and a friend were drunk and on a roof in Parras, dropping condoms filled with water on people strolling along the sidewalk. According to the buzz around the set, a high-ranking Mexican government official was in town to observe filming and stepped out of a doorway just when Sickner let one of the condoms fly. The soaked official was outraged.[7]

Mexican authorities ordered Sickner out of the country and even distributed photos of him to ports of entry with instructions that he was not to be allowed to cross the border. Just before Sickner left, he took Holland aside and asked him to send him updates on the production of what Sickner continued to consider *his* movie. Holland agreed to do so. After Sickner's departure, Holland became convinced that Peckinpah wanted to fire him but kept him on the picture only because of his connection with Sickner, although that surely was not true. Sam would fire anyone who wasn't working up to par, including a friend of the associate producer's. Holland stayed only because Peckinpah wanted him there.[8]

5.

First assistant director Phil Rawlins traveled to Parras with the rest of the crew and set about performing his work, though nothing had improved much between him and his director. He also drew ire early on. The Sunday before shooting began, he'd sent a call for Lucien Ballard to appear on the set, believing Ballard was receiving a flat rate for his work on the picture. Not so. Production manager Bill Faralla had to shell out $300 in extra pay to Ballard at a time when the highest paid among most American workers earned $300 for an entire week. Producer Phil Feldman got wind of Rawlins's error and was miffed.[9] Two days into the shoot, Peckinpah determined enough was enough and gave Rawlins his walking papers, although Rawlins didn't believe he was truly fired. Sam was sometimes known to fire some of his closest associates two or three times in a day, but then expected them to show up for work the next morning. In this case, Sam was serious.

Cliff Coleman was strolling across the Warners' lot in Burbank when he was approached about becoming the new first assistant director on *The Wild Bunch*. This was the same Cliff Coleman who raced Triumph motorcycles with Steve McQueen and Dave and Bud Ekins, the same Cliff Coleman who had won the gold medal at the International Six Days Trial (ISDT) as a pioneering American rider in the event. Coleman took the job, though it meant he had just hours to board a jetliner bound for Torreón.

Coleman was—and remains—the proverbial piece of work. I drove up from L.A. one December morning to visit him at his place in Frazier Park in the mountains south of Bakersfield. Ever the gearhead, he greeted me wearing a jacket displaying the name of a local tow-truck company. As soon as we were inside his house, he asked if I had Gordon Dawson's phone number handy. I did. Shortly he had Dawson on the phone. "This

Stratton guy is here," he said to Dawson. "Well, I don't know. I can tell by the way he's dressed that he's not gay. He's too tall to be a Jew. He's got some kind of beard that suggests he has serious psychological issues . . . No, he hasn't offered me any money. Has he given you any?" That was my introduction to Clifford C. Coleman, the man who went on from *The Wild Bunch* to have a solid career working as an AD on movies (*The Longest Yard, Shampoo, Animal House, Tom Horn*) and TV series (*The Rockford Files, Kojak, Airwolf, Magnum P.I.*).[10]

Coleman explained that he had always suffered from ADHD and thus wasn't much of a reader. But he had an incredible memory that allowed him to recall images with precision. "Two years from now," he said to me, "I might not remember exactly what we talked about, but I'll remember that you were here wearing brown cowboy boots with Levi's and a Pancho Villa T-shirt, along with a tan corduroy jacket." His gifts for that level of recall would serve him well on *The Wild Bunch*.[11]

Coleman hustled to LAX that March day in 1968 and was soon on a plane to Torreón. Sitting next to him was a tall man with a blanket covering

Sam Peckinpah and first assistant director Cliff Coleman set up a shot during the Battle of Bloody Porch. Throughout the production, Coleman wore a campaign hat with cavalry braid he liberated from wardrobe. Photo by Paul Harper, courtesy of Nick Redman and Jeff Slater.

a large item on his lap. Regulations about such things on airliners were laxer in the late 1960s than fifty years later. Once the plane reached cruising altitude, the man introduced himself as James Dannaldson. The Nebraska native was well-known in the movie industry for providing exotic creatures for use in action/adventure films. Twenty-five years before his encounter with Coleman on the airplane, Dannaldson led a film crew into the lower reaches of the Amazon to photograph his interactions with wild animals to use in the quasidocumentary *Jacaré*. Dannaldson had nearly been killed by a twenty-foot anaconda. The attack was all captured on film, and Dannaldson won praise for his derring-do. Dannaldson asked Coleman if he was on his way to Mexico to work on the Warners' picture being filmed there. Coleman said yes, and Dannaldson said he was, too. He pulled the blanket away to reveal a large glass container teeming with twelve thousand western harvester ants captured in the Mojave Desert. Peckinpah had put in an urgent call for ants. God only knew what he needed them for.[12]

Soon enough, Coleman learned the answer. The film opens with shots of children torturing ants as a prelude to a massive shoot-out involving the wild bunch and bounty hunters, with innocent residents of the town caught in the cross fire. Coleman's first task in Parras was to create minia-ture stick corrals around ersatz ant piles that included the stinging red insects transported by air all the way from the desert outside Los Angeles to Coahuila. The concept had come from Emilio Fernández. He'd told Peckinpah that the opening scenes of the shoot-out in San Rafael/Starbuck reminded him of when, as a child, he and his chums would build a corral around an ant den, then toss live scorpions onto it and watch the ensuing battle. Once the ants had killed the scorpions, El Indio and his friends would set fire to the ant den. Now Sam was re-creating those experiences from El Indio's childhood for the opening of *The Wild Bunch*. The close-ups of the giggling children torturing the creatures showed them with the most innocent of faces. The point was clear: Something sinister lurks within us all, even children. Moreover, Peckinpah believed that the men who made up the wild bunch were like those scorpions dropped "into an anthill that sooner or later was going to eat them up."[13] He used the footage of the scorpions and the ants to bookend the opening railroad-office robbery and shoot-out. Those shots inside the tiny corrals worked to both set up the ambush, hint at betrayal, and show the suffering of living things.

Much more complicated than the scorpions-and-ants sequence was staging the shoot-out in San Rafael/Starbuck, which involved dozens of actors and stuntmen. Making it all work called for precise choreography, a major challenge for Coleman as the newly recruited first assistant director. At night, Coleman retired to his room in the same hotel where Rawlins was waiting to be called back into action. There, Coleman read the script for the next day's sequences and mentally replayed the conversations he'd had with Peckinpah. Then he lay back on the bed and stared at the blank wall ahead of him. Each shot would then begin to pop up as images on the plaster. Soon he would have each shot for the scene mapped out in his mind the way Peckinpah had described it to him. The next morning, he'd organize the scene as he'd envisioned it the night before.

Coleman spent hours barking at extras and actors in the streets of Parras, running through the action over and over until everything clicked into place. Then Peckinpah would arrive and observe what Coleman had worked out. There would be adjustments—and sometimes disagreements, sometimes out-and-out arguments, with Sam inevitably winning if push came to shove. Sometimes it seemed to Coleman that Sam had no idea what in the hell he wanted, which Coleman found maddening. The opposite was actually true. L. Q. Jones knew that Sam played out scenes in his brain dozens of times before he headed off to location. But Peckinpah became the most intuitive of directors once filming was under way, readily changing his mind from one day to the next as the movie took shape. Once, the special effects crew loaded down a wall of an abandoned building outside Parras with dozens and dozens of squibs, then covered them with stucco and paint. After hours and hours of the crew's work, Peckinpah decided that he wanted to shoot the sequence someplace else. When Coleman told me about it nearly five decades later, he said he assumed those unused squibs were still implanted in that wall way down in Mexico, ready to be exploded.

The shoot-out sequences in San Rafael/Starbuck removed any doubts about Coleman's effectiveness on the picture. That section of the movie began as a relatively peaceful meeting of the local temperance union in a revival tent, with actor Dub Taylor as a reverend named Wainscoat preaching to the teetotalers. They are the good, wholesome people of the town, the smug new citizens of Starbuck, out to stifle whatever wild times remain from the days of the Old West. They epitomized much of what Peckinpah loathed about twentieth-century social niceties.

The teetotalers sing "Shall We Gather at the River?"[14] The hymn was familiar to fans of Westerns. John Ford had used it in *Stagecoach*, *My Darling Clementine*, *3 Godfathers*, *Wagon Master*, and, notably, *The Searchers*, among other films, including his last feature, *7 Women*. By the time Ford was making his Westerns, "Shall We Gather at the River?" had for years been a popular hymn sung by American Protestants, especially at funerals. Ford employed it to reinforce both the power of faith and the importance of community.[15] In *Major Dundee*, Peckinpah made use of it in a Fordian manner during a burial scene, with both Yankee and Confederate soldiers coming together to respect the dead. In *The Wild Bunch*, he turned "Shall We Gather at the River?" on its ear; community is blown to smithereens in a hail of rifle bullets and shotgun blasts. It's every person for himself or herself as guns rumble and blood explodes from those shot.

Wainscoat is a windbag spewing Bible verses and artificial values. Taylor played him expertly. A Virginia native, the son of a cotton broker, Taylor got his start in vaudeville. He broke into pictures with Frank Capra's Oscar-winning *You Can't Take It with You* and became one of Hollywood's busiest character actors, most often appearing in cowboy movies and TV shows. He became a member of Peckinpah's stock company after playing a horse thief in *Major Dundee*. Taylor had a twang and an ability to stretch out words that suited him ideally for Westerns, and he could be equally at home as a bartender or a Bible-thumper. He demonstrated his mastery of the latter as Wainscoat.

Taylor as the Reverend Wainscoat admonished his flock not to indulge in wine or strong drink, warning that it "biteth like a serpent," as the wild bunch rode into town. Coleman, acting on Peckinpah's directives, had had much going on in the gaps in Wainscoat's tent to set up the opening of the movie's action—soldiers on horses, townspeople going about their daily duties, children at play. There was no disputing Coleman's success at manifesting Peckinpah's vision. Phil Rawlins hung on at the hotel for a while. As the San Rafael/Starbuck street sequences played out over the next few days, it became clear that he was never going to be called back to work on *The Wild Bunch*. Rawlins quietly packed up and returned to California. He never spoke to Peckinpah again.[16]

Other issues came along. Early on in the shoot-out, Ernest Borgnine, the war veteran, panicked when he heard the distinctive whizzing sound that meant live ammo was being fired, not blanks. "What the hell is going on here?" Borgnine said to himself. He called out to stop the action. "Those guys are using real bullets!" he shouted, pointing toward Mexican soldiers who were working as extras in the scene. Mexican law required soldiers to have live ammunition on them at all times. The troops had mistaken their "live" loads for blanks.[17]

6.

Whatever criticisms could be leveled at Peckinpah, no one could question his dedication to a film project once it was under way. He labored away at it like a fiend. It became *the thing*; nothing else much mattered. He was too deep into his alcoholism to give up drinking altogether, but he cut way back. Compared to his consumption during the previous hunting trip in Ely, Nevada—when he took his nephew to the local whorehouses to get laid and Sam wound up dead drunk on wire spools in the back of a truck—he was almost a model of sobriety. He limited himself to drinking beer at night after work was complete. Contrary to the reputation he developed in the 1970s, he was never drunk on the set while he was working on *The Wild Bunch*. Too much was on the line for him, both professionally and artistically. His intensity was unmatched by anyone else's. He was at his creative best as he created *The Wild Bunch*, the story that had obsessed him for more than a year now.

Likewise, William Holden swore off hard liquor. He was a beer sipper in Parras, carefully eschewing entry into the blackout zone. He generally avoided the after-hours liquor-soaked high jinks that other members of the company engaged in after shooting wrapped for the day. He likewise stayed away from the *prostitutas*—some imported from Mexico City—and spent his evenings quietly. Several years earlier, he'd been on safari with the goal of killing an elephant in Africa. Once the guides had led him into place and an elephant was an easy rifle shot away, Holden was unable to pull the trigger. In an epiphany it came to him that he should be working to protect African wildlife, not destroy it. Conservation of African wildlife was now his passion—and would remain so for the remainder of his life. Evenings in Parras, beer in hand, he loved nothing more than to while away the hours talking about Africa to anyone who would listen.

One person who showed up at Holden's table night after night was Billy Hart, the Texas-born stuntman and actor, who hung on to every word Holden uttered about elephants and lions, totally fascinated.[18]

Holden's career and personal life may have been in a slide, yet he was part of Hollywood's royalty, at least in the eyes of many in the cast and crew. He had a regal air, but he also strived to be very much a regular guy, just Bill Beedle from South Pasadena. One day he went for a walk and encountered a large rattlesnake, which he shot, then brought back to show his *Wild Bunch* colleagues—the kind of thing that any guy might do, although Eddie O'Brien's son, Brendan, staying with his dad in Parras, saw Holden with the dead snake and was scared of the movie star thereafter.

Following Peckinpah's lead, the other members of the *Wild Bunch* company worked incredibly hard, Holden among them. He had his vanities to be sure. Holden may have shown up looking like a fifty-year-old who'd aged more than his years—face heavily lined, gut soft. But when Sam asked him to wear a mustache as Pike Bishop, that was too much. Holden replied, "The hell I will." But he didn't hold out long. He was soon sporting a mustache in front of the camera. Sharp-eyed observers noted that Holden's fake lip hair was similar to Peckinpah's real mustache.

Holden, the veteran of the old studio system way of making films, had never been a part of something like Peckinpah's free, improvisatory approach. It was nothing like the methods of, say, Alfred Hitchcock, with everything precisely storyboarded. Yet Sam stayed in control of everything, though it was a lot to manage. Day four of filming of *The Wild Bunch* was not atypical: 244 extras, 80 animals, 43 animal handlers. The caterer provided 372 lunches. Guns were everywhere, 239 of them as props. Hundreds more arrived in the hands of the Mexican Army troops, hired as extras for the film; they brought their service rifles with them. After the original supply of ammo ran out on the second day of filming, Phil Feldman ordered in more than ninety thousand rounds from Warners, a jaw-dropping amount by 1968 standards.

Film was disappearing faster than blank rifle cartridges. Peckinpah shot more than twenty-five thousand feet during just the first week from 131 camera setups. Each can of exposed film had to be transported from Parras to Torreón either by car or small aircraft. From there, it was moved through questioning Mexican and American governmental officials at a port of entry into the United States. Thence it went to L.A., where it was developed and printed. The dailies were then transported back to Mexico, where Peckinpah and others viewed them. The process was labor-intensive, to say the least. Though fraught with possibilities for mishaps, it worked. Records indicate just one batch of film was accidentally ruined during a border crossing.

Lucien Ballard was at his creative best, overseeing a crew of camera operators who filmed with a variety of cameras outfitted with different-size lenses. Typically, Ballard used six cameras for action sequences, each running at a different speed. To capture images at real time, a Mitchell or Panavision camera operated at twenty-four frames per second. To achieve slow motion, a cinematographer would run the film through the camera at a faster rate. Ballard had his cameras set at variety of frames-per-second rates: 30, 60, 90, even 120. Cameras were sometimes modified to allow them to achieve fast run rates, but even then, they would have to crank through yards and yards of film before they hit the increased speed needed. (Peckinpah's film editors would later monkey around further with speed of shots using an optical printer.) The dailies that came back from L.A. were stunning. Ballard the cinematic alchemist and Peckinpah had conducted tests with film-stock exposures with the goal of achieving a slight sepia cast to the images without diminishing the color palette. Ballard had succeeded. The effect gave *The Wild Bunch* a hint of being something of a relic.

Miles and miles of film were shot each week. The best frames, the ones that ended up in the movie, were like miniature works of art, in ways akin to Frederic Remington's paintings of rough and reckless cowboys. In Burbank, Warners vice president Edward S. Feldman was blown way: "Suddenly, the dailies came back with a yellow tinge on them. And the yellowness was fantastic. It was as if you could feel the heat coming off the film. But we're sitting in dailies and the head of postproduction at Warners then was a Teutonic editor named Rudi Fehr, and he said, 'Don't worry, Ed, we'll get it out in the lab.' But I said, 'You don't understand. This is genius, whoever did this.' He said, 'But it's not clear. It looks like the heat is coming off the ground.' I said, 'That's what they're trying to do.'" Feldman realized that Warner Bros.-Seven Arts was achieving a new kind of realism. "What Peckinpah wanted to show, basically, was that dying was not glorious and people getting shot was not heroic. And he brought that quality to the picture."[19] With the action shot at all those different speeds, Ballard's work created endless possibilities for Peckinpah's film editors.

Peckinpah and his crew were providing Ballard plenty of gold to capture on film. Gordon Dawson was in full pit-bull attack mode as he and his crew churned out the costuming needed for each sequence. Who knew what Peckinpah would ask of him? James Dannaldson, who transported the ants on the plane while seated next to Coleman, stood around six feet eight inches. With Anglo faces in short supply in Parras, Sam decided he wanted Dannaldson to appear in front of the camera as—well, how about a banker? How was Dawson supposed to achieve that on the director's whim when the guy was that tall? But Dawson sorted through all the clothes hanging on the hundreds of yards of piping and came up with something that would work.

Early on, Sam decided that he wanted Strother Martin, playing the bounty hunter Coffer, to look like a 1913 version of a Hells Angel. In typical Peckinpah fashion, he didn't elucidate just what he meant by that. It was up to Dawson to figure it out. He rushed into a trailer and furiously began to dig around until he found a rosary, never paying any attention to the crowd of curious locals, most if not all of whom were devout Catholics, who had gathered to observe what the yanqui movie man was up to. Dawson grabbed some needle-nosed pliers and tore the tiny crucified Jesus from the rosary cross and tossed it onto the sidewalk outside the trailer door. He then wired a rifle cartridge onto the cross in place of Jesus. He turned to leave the trailer and saw the crowd of Mexicans, mouths agape, staring at him as if he were Lucifer himself. The bullet cross hanging from rosary beads became a signature prop for *The Wild Bunch*. I felt more than a twinge of emotion when I visited Dawson at his house in Woodland Hills decades later and he allowed me to slip that very bullet cross, which he'd carefully preserved as a souvenir from the shoot, around my neck.

Dawson's challenges in dressing a cast representing people caught up in violent, changing times were not small. The costumes ran the gamut from then-contemporary knickers and newsboy hats for small boys to traditional cowboy attire. He had to outfit American soldiers in campaign hats with cavalry cords and Mexican federal troops as well. He had to come up with wardrobe for Anglo townspeople as well as Mexican villagers and revolutionaries. He was charged with telling a story through wardrobe. Martin's and L. Q. Jones's characters were the vilest to turn up in the movie, and they hardly looked like cowboys at all. Along with a newsboy cap, Jones wore an automobile driving coat that hung down to his knees, making it almost seem as if he were wearing a dress of some sort. Martin wore a filthy, battered narrow-brim hat with a wide hatband, a style with twentieth century stamped all over it, as if to say that he represents the depravity of new times.

Peckinpah certainly wanted to push the theme of the evil that awaited mankind in the age of technology. There was no small irony here. He believed that technology suffocated the elemental humanity of people, that it was purely malevolent, trumpeted by conservatives of the ilk of Richard Nixon, whom Peckinpah loathed. I remember my college mentor, an English professor who embraced many left-wing tenets, telling us in class one day that we all had an ethical obligation to go home that day and use a shotgun to blast the screens of our TVs. Peckinpah would have applauded that kind of sentiment even as he worked in cinema, the most technologically driven of all creative media of his day. He explained the contradiction: The movie camera was not the product of technology but rather a gift from the gods.[20] In this he was not unlike the aging members of the *Wild Bunch* gang, cowboys ill at ease with the modern era who nonetheless seemed to value such technological advancements as the Colt M1911 semiautomatic pistol, pump shotguns, machine guns, and hand grenades. They no doubt likewise considered such things to be gifts from the gods.

In depicting the technological evils sprouting up in the early twentieth century, Peckinpah introduced a few anachronisms. Internet gun nerds have pointed out that Martin's bolt-action rifle dates from the 1940s, not from the 1910s. The machine gun the gang acquires dates from late in World War I; it wasn't in service in 1913. Other anachronisms beyond the guns appeared here and there. At the time, Peckinpah was making a picture he assumed would be seen only on the big screen, with few people taking it in more than once or twice. That someone would watch *The Wild Bunch* twenty or thirty times at home, pausing to examine details of firearms in high definition, was inconceivable in 1968 and '69, and that led to small errors. It was of no great consequence if Sam filmed Old Man Sykes being shot in the right leg and then he showed up at the end of the film with what might be a bandage on his left leg. The sore-thumb mistake that stood out the most was a shot of Pike Bishop's gang fording what was supposed to be the Rio Grande, leaving Texas behind for Mexico. The water in the swollen river flows left to right. Anytime you leave Texas and enter Mexico, the Rio Grande below you will run from right to left as the river makes its way from New Mexico to the Gulf of Mexico.[21]

One day early on in the production, Holden had a day off from shooting, but Sam invited him to show up anyway to observe that day's filming. The sequences showed the aftermath of the San Rafael/Starbuck shoot-out, with Martin and Jones as the primary actors. Holden watched

Sam Peckinpah meets with extras for the Temperance Union shots early in *The Wild Bunch*. Photo by Paul Harper, courtesy of Nick Redman and Jeff Slater.

as Peckinpah directed the two actors, nudging them to put more and more into their performances. It clicked then with Holden that this was not going to be just another cowboy picture. He arose from his chair and began to walk away. Sam stopped him: "Wait a minute, where are you going, Bill?"

"I'm going back to my room."

"Well, why are you going back to your room?"

"Is that the way you're going to shoot the rest of the picture?"

"Yeah—"

"I'm going home and studying."

No one on the cast saw Holden until it was time for him to appear in front of the camera again. Jones, who witnessed the event, said, "He went back and started working on his script because he saw this was what Sam was going to do, and this is what the actors that he was working with were prepared to do. So Bill was going to carry his end of the load. He'd obviously seen the picture slightly different, and then realized, 'Wait a minute, this is what Peckinpah's going to do with the supporting actors, he's going to want the same intensity from me, so I better get my ass in gear.' And that's what he did."[22]

Holden was doing more than just studying his script. He also was studying his director. As filming continued, cast and crew noticed that Holden was developing Pike Bishop into a character very much like

Peckinpah himself, right down to the vocal inflections and hand gestures. One of the crew members told Peckinpah that Holden was "doing" him. Peckinpah said, "Ah, you're full of shit."[23] But the character of Pike Bishop began to have much in common with Peckinpah, a man who had lost his grip and was struggling to regain it. Holden captured the intensity of Peckinpah in Parras.

7.

Holden became something of a hero to the *Wild Bunch* cast for more than just the performance he was turning in. He took steps to quell their grumbling stomachs. By all accounts the quality of the food and beverages provided by the caterer was bad. When the actors showed up before dawn for makeup, they found instant, not brewed, coffee waiting for them. Matters only grew worse. Warner Bros.-Seven Arts had contracted Alimentacion Filmica to provide lunches at bargain-basement rates. Cast and crew hated the food. When the long days of filming were complete, people returned to their leased houses and hotel rooms, where local cooks prepared regional dishes such as goat stewed in its own juices or *machacas* made from beef jerky and fried eggs. On Sundays, Peckinpah, ever the self-styled grill master, held backyard cookouts at his leased house, but even he was limited by what meats he could find to roast over the open coals. The yanquis hungered for cheeseburgers or, better yet, thick, juicy steaks.

Holden took matters into his own hands and through some magic of communication arranged for a large shipment of steaks to arrive in Parras. The steaks were turned over to local cooks to prepare. The *americanos* slavered over their plates as they awaited sizzling steaks. Those steaks never arrived. From the meat the cooks prepared a dish that the Americans described as "chili," though it most certainly was not that, given that in general Mexicans abhor the American dish known as chili. Perhaps what the cooks concocted was closer to *carne guisada*. Whatever the case, the Americans were left wanting.

Holden had to leave Parras for a couple of days to attend a funeral in L.A. He loaded up all those big suitcases he'd brought with him, though they were mostly empty. When he returned, they were packed with steaks and dry ice. A fiesta took place in Sam's backyard, with Peckinpah himself overseeing the grilling of Holden's gift to cast and crew.

8.

In Agua Verde, *The Wild Bunch*'s fictional stronghold of the Huer-tistas, Mapache's inner circle is made up officers from the Mexican army and German advisers, in addition to the general's courtesans. Two officers are particularly close to Mapache: Zamorra, played by Jorge Russek, is Mapache's sycophant; Herrera, played by Alfonso Arau, is the accountant in charge of Mapache's money. Both actors were in their thir-ties and were familiar to Mexican audiences. In spite of his relatively young age, Russek had already appeared in almost fifty Mexican movies and was beginning to work in Hollywood, where he'd appeared in episodes of the TV series *I Spy* and *The High Chaparral*. With his sharp facial features and narrow eyes, he made Zamorra a base and sinister char-acter, suspicious of anyone motivated by anything other than women and booze.

Arau had a more challenging task in creating Lieutenant Herrera. The character is at once as sinister as Zamorra yet at the same time somewhat naïve. He can kill without compunction. He is also nervous when he seems to realize he is in over his head. Arau faced the challenge of breathing new life into what had become a Mexican caricature over the previous twenty years. Just as *The Wild Bunch*'s Old Man Sykes was much like Howard from *The Treasure of the Sierra Madre*, its Lieutenant Herrera was drawn from that movie's bandit chief, the wide-eyed, sombrero-wearing Gold Hat, played by Alfonso Bedoya. Gold Hat and his oft-misquoted line "We don't need no badges. I don't have to show you any stinkin' badges!" devolved into a cultural stereotype—the Mexican *bandido*—that turned up in other movies and in cartoons. Arau had to echo Gold Hat yet avoid creating an oversimplified character.

Arau and Bedoya shared more than a first name. They looked as if they might have been related—both men had big, toothy grins. There

Alfonso Arau as Lieutenant Herrera.
Though a TV star in Mexico at the time,
The Wild Bunch was his first American
picture. Photo by Bernie Abramson,
courtesy of Tonio K.

the similarities ended. Arau was a much more versatile actor than
Bedoya. Arau arrived in Parras to take part in his first American film
already an experienced actor and TV star in Mexico. He learned method
acting under Seki Sano, a Japanese expat living in Mexico who had
studied under the Soviet Union's Konstantin Stanislavski. Sano developed the reputation as one of the great drama teachers in the western
hemisphere.

Arau formed a comedy song-and-dance duo with Sergio Corona, and
billed as Corona y Arau, they became popular performers on Mexican
TV. Arau also acted in a dozen Mexican movies and one German film
before Peckinpah gave him the role of Herrera in *The Wild Bunch*. By
the time he met Sam, Arau was interested in directing movies himself.
His first conversations with Peckinpah centered on directing, not on the
character Herrera. Arau believed that he received his part in *The Wild
Bunch* mostly because he was a neophyte director whom Sam found
interesting.

But Arau discovered that his star standing in Mexico and Peckinpah's
interest in him as a director meant little when it came to getting lunch.
At noon during his first day on the set, he went to find something to
eat. He encountered a flunky from Warner Bros. who was directing
Mexican actors toward one dining area, white actors to another. Arau had
heard that the same sort of segregated dining took place on John Wayne
pictures shot in Durango, never mind that Wayne himself was married
to a Mexican. (I spoke to a woman from Durango who worked on

Wayne's *Big Jake*. She said there was no segregation on Batjac Productions movies by that time. If it had occurred earlier, it was an ugly memory by 1971.)[24]

Arau was outraged—"I got furious, I mean, I got *furious*! That was my *first* day on location!" Soon enough Arau was on the phone with the president of the Screen Actors Guild in L.A., Peckinpah's *Major Dundee* star Charlton Heston. "Listen," Arau said to Heston, "this is the situation here. You're not doing your job! How do you let your people come to this country and discriminate against us in our own country?"[25] Arau could hardly have found a more receptive ear in Hollywood. Heston would later gain a reputation as a conservative gun rights advocate, but in the 1960s he was one of the most liberal of American movie stars. He was passionate about civil rights, and he knew and had protested with Martin Luther King Jr. Heston joined Marlon Brando, Sammy Davis Jr., and Sidney Poitier as prominent guests at the King-led March on Washington, during which the civil rights leader delivered the "I Have a Dream" speech at the Lincoln Memorial. Heston was alarmed by the news from Arau about segregated dining in Parras and made calls to executives in Burbank.

By the end of the day, segregated dining was dismantled on the picture. That evening, Peckinpah found Arau on the set. It was the first time the two men had seen each other since filming began. Peckinpah, employing his rudimentary Spanish, said, "*¿Eres el rebelde?*" Arau briefly let the question sink in: Are you the rebel? How Peckinpah reacted could make or break Arau's future in Hollywood. Arau stood up straight and said yes. Sam paused, then clapped his hands and said, "Bravo!" He and Arau were bonded from that point onward.[26]

Peckinpah had taken to wearing off-white Levi's with either desert boots (chukka boots, of the sort Jimi Hendrix would wear at Woodstock the summer that *The Wild Bunch* was released) or lace-up combat boots, a bandanna tied around his forehead. It was an unfortunate choice of outfit, given that Peckinpah suffered from a major case of "the piles," an old-fashioned term for external hemorrhoids that are particularly swelled and bloody. Any sane person would have taken time away from the picture to have them surgically removed. Peckinpah refused to allow anything to slow down progress on *The Wild Bunch*, which without question he viewed as his make-it-or-break-it chance to prove himself as a director. Cliff Coleman could smell Peckinpah before he saw him, the stench of Preparation H, shit, and blood assailing all noses in his vicinity. The mess also soaked through the seat of his white jeans. Still, he didn't allow his condition to slow him down. Peckinpah pushed himself and pushed himself—never mind his pain—with days beginning at four A.M. and lasting until midnight. Peckinpah was also afflicted with insomnia and often couldn't sleep during the precious four hours between the end of one workday and the start of another. He found a way to fill that time.

"He started talking to me," said Arau. "He kind of adopted me. He started explaining to me what he was doing—and why. He gave me a lot of tips. He gave me incredibly valuable pieces of his wisdom." These conversations often occurred during the darkest hours of night. It might have been one o'clock in the morning. It might have been three o'clock, but Arau gladly roused himself. "He became my tutor, my mentor."

One predawn morning Sam said, "Alfonso, what do you think of clichés?"

"Well, we have to stay away from them."

"No. I love clichés."

"What do you mean?" Arau said, shocked.

"I love clichés because clichés establish an immediate communication with the audience. Clichés reside in the collective subconsciousness. And what is a film? A film is just a collection of clichés."

"Wow. Okay—"

"The work of the director is to love the cliché, adopt the cliché, and then work against it. You have to remake the cliché in a way that nobody has ever made it before. That is the creative work of the director." Both the director and the actor confronted that task with the character of Herrera.[27]

Arau, who wound up on the Warner Bros.-Seven Arts payroll for fourteen weeks instead of the four called for in his contract, could see that everything in *The Wild Bunch* was a cliché. Its sequences were programmed to push buttons in the minds of audiences who had already seen a hundred Westerns or more: the railroad-office robbery and street shoot-out in San Rafael/Starbuck, discussions of the future around a campfire, Mexican *bandido* jefes, conflicts between wizened old men and brash upstarts, American outlaws in a hostile Mexican village, a train robbery for a climax—cinemagoers had seen all these things dozens of times in cowboy pictures. Peckinpah either worked against everything already burned into the brains of moviegoers or pushed it to extremes.

Train robbery was the subject of the first-ever Western. A *Wild Bunch* scene in which the gang is crossing the desert and rides down a steep hill of sand mimicked many similar movie scenes, going all the way back to John Ford's *Straight Shooting*, a Harry Carey/Hoot Gibson picture

L. Q. Jones, Robert Ryan, Albert Dekker, and other cast members inspect the rooftop vantage their characters will have in *The Wild Bunch*'s opening shoot-out (top photo). Actors and crew prepare for the railroad office robbery, with Sam Peckinpah in the lower left-hand corner, shading his eyes (bottom photo). Photos by Paul Harper, courtesy of Nick Redman and Jeff Slater.

released in 1917; one of the most spectacular occurred in Buster Keaton's masterpiece, *The General*, from 1926. The scene had turned up as recently as 1968's *Bandolero!* Likewise, a bridge explosion was nothing new. Bridge explosions had become so common that Walon Green had avoided including one in his drafts of *The Wild Bunch*: He envisioned the gang crossing the river using a cable. Sam wrote an exploding bridge into the script, causing groans from many of the crew members: *Jesus Christ, hasn't it already been done?* The destruction of the bridge over the river Kwai in David Lean's film seemed to be the end all for such special effects, never mind that directors kept returning to the well. Sergio Leone's *The Good, the Bad, and the Ugly*, which hit American theaters just prior to the *Wild Bunch* company's departure to Mexico, included a massive bridge explosion. One had turned up just a couple of years before that in Henry Hathaway's *The Sons of Katie Elder*. There was no need to repeat it *The Wild Bunch*. Peckinpah insisted it be included.

The decision by *The Wild Bunch* gang members to make a valiant attempt to save their comrade at the end of the picture was just about the oldest chestnut in the book, to Peckinpah's thinking. That was precisely what appealed to him about it. "The whole idea," said Jim Silke, "was, Who would really do that—rob and kill, steal guns, and yet in the end give the guns away to the peasants and go back for Angel and die for him? That was the problem because everybody wrote that story: the outlaw with the heart of gold. It was really an old-fashioned Western. Sam said, 'What if we made a film where they really did that? What kind of guys would really do that? Walk in and sacrifice themselves like that?' Every guy that wrote a Western wrote that story, but it never works. It's pure romance. So that was the intent from the outset, to make that story work."[28]

9.

One evening in San Antonio a few years ago, I was talking to the Mexican American novelist Manuel Luis Martinez at a museum with a special display of Mexican Revolution artifacts. Manny told me he was a fan of *The Wild Bunch*, in part because he'd never before seen an American movie that portrayed so many Mexican faces. I understood what he meant. That had resonated with me when I first saw the movie at age thirteen. I felt as if I'd been transported into Mexico—not some Hollywood soundstage rendition of Mexico but the real thing, populated by real people. Peckinpah edited in dozens of close-ups of anonymous people he found in and around Parras.

From one Mexican perspective, each person "was either a saint or a monster," with no middle ground, Paco Calderón wrote. That served the story "splendidly, for it's meant to be an epic ballad and not a travelogue, but it does jolt the Mexican viewer because the 'good Mexico' is portrayed so idyllic it's unreal, while the 'bad Mexico' is very, very accurate; in fact, no American movie has captured the look, sound, feel, texture and carnage of the Mexican Revolution as this one has."[29]

Mexican actors took on all sorts of roles, in some cases playing Anglos. One of the most notable examples of this is in the shoot-out in San Rafael/Starbuck. The rare viewer would notice that one of the old men in the Temperance Union tent was Raúl Madero, younger brother of the martyred father of the Mexican Revolution, Francisco Madero. Raúl Madero was around eighty years old at the time *The Wild Bunch* was filmed, and his face was familiar to nearly all Mexicans. He was a hero of the revolution himself, having helped plot it with his brother in exile in San Antonio. Raúl Madero served as a major in Pancho Villa's legendary División del Norte before becoming governor of both Coahuila and Nuevo León. Peckinpah, no doubt smacking his lips at the irony, cast him as a teetotaling Protestant white man.

As the bunch made its escape from the railroad office it had robbed, the character named Crazy Lee, played by big-screen newcomer Bo Hopkins, was left behind to hold hostages. All the hostages are supposed to be Anglos. They are played by Mexicans from Parras, one of whom is a woman mostly lost to Hollywood history except for her screen credit: Señora Madero. She was a niece of Francisco Madero's. "You trash!" she says to Crazy Lee. With a brownish-blond wig and her pale complexion, Señora Madero certainly looks the part of a South Texas Anglo. She was an untrained actress, and Peckinpah was unhappy take after take with her performance. She failed to register the level of disdain her prim, proper white self would have held toward such "trash" as the bunch. Peckinpah took Hopkins aside and instructed him to walk up to her, kiss her, and then stick his tongue in her ear during the next take. Hopkins did just that. It worked: Pure disgust registered on Señora Madero's face as Hopkins lapped away at her.

Hopkins was the product of Carolina mill towns and had done time both in reform schools and the army before becoming an actor. A Roy

Bo Hopkins, in his first significant motion picture role, won undying loyalty from Sam Peckinpah as well as praise from cast and crew members for completing his scene even though he'd been wounded by a squib discharge. Photo by Bernie Abramson, courtesy of Jeff Slater.

Sickner protégé, he'd appeared in TV shows and made brief appearances in a couple of forgettable movies prior to *The Wild Bunch*. More than ten actors auditioned for Crazy Lee, but Sickner recommended that Sam give Hopkins a look. Sam liked what he saw in Hopkins's audition and awarded him the role.

Hopkins was understandably nervous in Parras, given that it was his big chance in a major motion picture. The shoot-out occurring outside the railroad office happens as the temperance band parades down the main street playing "Shall We Gather at the River?" The script required Hopkins to force his hostages in the railroad office to sing the hymn. Hopkins didn't know the lyrics. Try as he might, he kept forgetting them. His roommate on *The Wild Bunch*, Dub Taylor, stayed up all night with Hopkins to help the young actor learn the words. Hopkins was able to pull off the "Sing it!" sequence. Memorizing a hymn was one among many challenges.

Hopkins had never worked with squibs prior to *The Wild Bunch*. He'd never even heard of them until he showed up in Parras. After learning more about how they worked, he decided he would give the most realistic reaction to the "gunshots" hitting him if he could actually feel the squibs exploding. He asked the special effects people to tape them directly to his skin, even though many actors and stuntmen wore T-shirts between their costumes and squibs for protection. When a squib went off, it was akin to a firecracker exploding. It hurt like hell when it was taped directly to your body. Yet Hopkins did it time after time, without complaint. "I squibbed up twenty-six times," he said. "They had me in a truck with wires going up my leg, up my butt, up my other leg, and all over my chest." Once wired up, he thought, "Jesus Christ, I'm going to go to the moon."[30] During one take, a squib planted in a wall blew up, firing a piece of wood into one of Hopkins's eyelids. Blood began to run down his face.

"He's hit!" Peckinpah shouted. "That's a wrap. This will be the first thing we hit in the morning."

"No, sir," said Hopkins. "I'd just as soon finish it now."

"Are you all right?"

"Yes, sir."

"What do you want to drink?"

"Anything—"[31]

Tequila appeared, and Hopkins gulped it down. Then he did the shot again. This time, the crew had loaded his shotgun with half loads, which didn't work out. So he went through the shot again, and again, until it met Peckinpah's satisfaction. When it was over, the Mexicans working on the crew began to applaud Hopkins. Sickner, who was still working on the picture, stepped up and gave Hopkins a hug and told the actor that he'd made Sickner look like a million dollars. Peckinpah was smiling, then he and producer Phil Feldman invited Hopkins to dinner that night. When Hopkins climbed into a cab to go to his quarters to change clothes, something he never expected happened: He began weeping and couldn't stop. He had done something he thought he could never do—act—and he had earned acclaim for it.

Injuries popped up everywhere during filming. Hopkins was hardly the only person hurt. In modern moviemaking, computer-generated imagery (CGI) has so progressed that actors and stuntmen seldom have to do dangerous things. In 1968, everything that was filmed had to be created in real life, which often put workers and actors in hazardous situations. Medical reports and insurance claims began to pile up. In Parras, where desert dawns were frigid and the afternoons were brain-broilingly hot, wind was a constant. One day a gust blew a ladder over, and it struck crew member José Morales Villegas in the head, sending him to the hospital. Aurelio Barbosa Nuño was treated for a bruised thorax as the

Elsa Cárdenas was a major movie star in Mexico and had acted in the American block-buster *Giant* and the Elvis Presley vehicle *Fun in Acapulco* before appearing in a flashback with William Holden in *The Wild Bunch*. She had worked and been friends with Sam Peckinpah since she appeared in the pilot for Peckinpah's TV series, *The Westerner*. Shortly after *The Wild Bunch* wrapped, they became lovers. Photo by Bernie Abramson, courtesy of Tonio K.

result of an accident. One of the assistant directors provided by the Mexican *sindicatos cinematográficos*, Jesús Marin Bello, suffered a broken foot when a horse stepped on him. A sixteen-year-old boy, a laborer on the picture, was hit in the head by a flying plank. A makeup woman, after putting in long days in dehydrating heat and failing to eat sufficiently because of the bad food, collapsed with anemia. An electrician was hit by gunfire, requiring hospitalization and skin grafts. Phil Ankrom, destined to become one of the prop men to run afoul of Peckinpah, came down with typhoid fever.

Peckinpah, stricken by the piles and exhausted from lack of sleep and brutal work hours, was on his best behavior. He was heading toward a romantic relationship with the Mexican actress Elsa Cárdenas, whom he had known since the late 1950s. Cárdenas gained some notoriety around Hollywood for her affairs with Elvis Presley, with whom she had costarred in *Fun in Acapulco*, and with director Budd Boetticher. But she was a traditional Mexican woman of her generation when it came to romance. She wasn't the sort to bed a man before first establishing a relationship, with plenty of courtship. She told me that while Sam was directing *The Wild Bunch*, he had no time for romance with anyone, including her, even though he cast her in a cameo for the picture. She and Peckinpah both understood that romance would have to wait until after shooting wrapped.[32]

Still, Sam was not one to stave off all of his desires. He had sex regularly with a little-known Mexican actress who worked on the picture. Once her scenes had been shot, and she went off the Warners payroll, Peckinpah dropped her as a bedmate and found a willing replacement.[33] While he did curtail his drinking while directing *The Wild Bunch*, he also liked to visit a cantina in Parras and mix with the locals. As so often happened, he wound up one night in a violent confrontation, this time with some men from Parras and the surrounding countryside. Again Peckinpah was losing the fight. Actor/stuntman Billy Hart was in the cantina and decided Sam had had enough. "I hate to go into this," Hart told me at the Old Spanish Trail Restaurant in Bandera, Texas, just months before he died in 2015, "because Sam meant so much to me. I don't like to talk about bad things concerning him, but he was about to get seriously hurt. So, I waded into it to pull him out. Just as I was going in, this huge guy moved back as I was going forward. He stepped on my foot just right, and it snapped my ankle."[34] The picture moved ahead, with shots of Hart set up to disguise his cast.

Neither Hopkins nor Hart suffered nearly as much Yolanda Ponce, who was twenty-five years old and was yet another newcomer to film work, having appeared in just one movie. Ponce first appears in *The Wild Bunch* during the opening shoot-out, as a townswoman trampled to death by a horse ridden by one of the escaping outlaws. The shooting of the gag went just fine, but after filming cut, the stuntman riding the thousand-pound horse backed it up, not realizing Ponce was still stretched out on the ground. The horse stepped on her belly and upper leg. She was rushed to the hospital in Parras, where she was stitched up.

The cuts and abrasions were bad. The doctors decided she would eventually need plastic surgery. Moreover, the horse fractured her tail-bone. The claim filed with *The Wild Bunch*'s insurance carrier, Seguros Azteca, S.A., stated she would be incapacitated for a minimum of twenty days. The injuries would have a lasting effect; she would be partially incapacitated from the accident *indefinidamente*. Yet Ponce had more gumption and capacity for pain than anyone else who worked on *The Wild Bunch*.

Stuntwoman, actress, and singer Yolando Ponce suffered a major injury during the opening shootout of *The Wild Bunch*, yet somehow finished her work on the picture. Sam Peckinpah hired her as often as he could for future movies to show his gratitude. She sang "Santa Amalia," a corrido frequently associated with the Mexican Revolution, from the back of a caboose and portrayed a *soldadera* killed by a shotgun blast fired by Pike Bishop (above). Photo by Bernie Abramson, courtesy of Tonio K.

She picked herself up and returned to work after an absence of a few weeks, appearing as a *soldadera* in Mapache's army. With her big voice she sings "Santa Amalia" from the back of a railcar during a battle between Mapache's federal soldiers and Villistas. She also appears in a key sequence during *The Wild Bunch*'s bloody finale, during which, still as the *soldadera*, she shoots William Holden in the back with a pistol. "Bitch!" Holden cries, then turns and dispatches her with a shotgun blast. A crew member jerked Ponce to the floor with a hidden rope to simulate her being struck by the shotgun's pellets—no easy stunt for a woman who had undergone surgery a few weeks earlier. Peckinpah was so impressed by her dedication to the picture that he resolved to give her work in the future; and he followed up, as he tended to do on any promises he made to someone who went the extra mile on one of his pictures.

10.

The production progressed to sequences filmed at Angel's home village, the Eden of *The Wild Bunch*. The rest of the movie is set against harsh desert landscapes and sun-blasted towns. Angel's village is shady and cool by contrast. Innocent children splash naked in a swimming hole. The villagers prepare a feast for their guests, Pike Bishop and his gang. Everyone seems happy and relaxed, except for Angel, who realizes his *novia*, Teresa, has fled the village to become one of Mapache's women. Even the Gorch brothers turn loose of their hard-edged shells and reveal they are still boylike deep down. Pike and the village jefe observe this: "We all dream of being a child again, even the worst of us," says Don José, the community's elder. "Perhaps the worst most of all."

Peckinpah selected Chano Urueta to play Don José, bringing another noted director from Mexico's golden age of filmmaking into *The Wild Bunch*. Urueta began directing movies during the days of silent pictures. While his credits never included classics comparable to his friend Emilio Fernández's *Flor silvestre* and *María Candelaria*, he had directed more than sixty pictures before his work on *The Wild Bunch*. A diplomat's son, he, like Fernández, had gone through his childhood with the bloodshed of the revolution surrounding him.

Though his reputation was tame compared to that of El Indio, he was known to be a bit of wild man and more than a little eccentric. Alfonso Arau told me that Urueta occasionally used live ammunition in his movies to get realistic responses from his actors.[35] He'd begun acting in earnest a couple of years before *The Wild Bunch*. In his younger days, posing for a photographer with a cheroot planted in the corner of his mouth, he looked a bit like a dapper Jason Robards. To portray Don José in *The Wild Bunch*, he had allowed his white hair to grow long and sported a full goatee. This gave him the look of a mystic come down from the mountains, albeit one with a pistol stuck in his belt.

The *Wild Bunch* script revealed little about Don José, just that he was the village leader, possibly Angel's grandfather, and that he despised the Huertistas who victimized his people. Like the members of the wild bunch, he espoused a code. He was a *bandido* as well as jefe of his pueblo, and in this, he was not unlike Chico Cano, a famous real-life border figure from the time of the Mexican Revolution.

How you felt about Cano depended on your political bearing—and whether you were an ethnic Mexican or a Texas Anglo. Both Mexicans and white Texans engaged in banditry along the Rio Grande, and Cano was among them. Cano the *bandido* seemed only in part motivated by personal enrichment. As a child he'd been taught to value three things above all else: *su familia, su tierra, su hogar.*[36] They became a kind of holy trinity to him as an adult. More than anything else, providing for and protecting family, land, and home drove him to raid across the river. He eventually became a military commander in the Mexican Revolution for the same reasons: *su familia, su tierra, su hogar.*

Peckinpah's Don José was driven by the same principle. In his conversation with Pike Bishop, Don José is charming and welcoming yet tough as the desert country that produced him, with eyes burning hot as the Coahuila sun. Some allege Cano once used a twenty-pound stone to crush the head of a Texas Ranger who'd tried to kill him a year earlier. I have little doubt the character Don José would have smashed in the head of a lawman had he found himself in the same position. Yet he was hospitable as he could be in treating the wild bunch to a fiesta at his pueblo.[37] One of the themes Peckinpah developed in *The Wild Bunch* is the need for people to stand up for what they believe in, to be true to themselves and true to their land. The reward was the paradise of Angel's village.

The bunch's stay at Eden ends the morning following the fiesta, with Pike and company riding away to an uncertain future. As they depart, the whole village turns out, singing "Las Golondrinas." As the mournful tune progresses, a *muchacha* hurries to Borgnine's Dutch to give him a flower. Another young woman hands Oates's Lyle Gorch a sombrero. Angel's mother stops her son, places a bundle in his hands, kisses him, then blesses him with the sign of the cross. "That's what Mexican mothers do with their children when they are leaving, they bless them," Chicano filmmaker Edgar Pablos told me. "*The Wild Bunch* was the first

American movie I ever saw that had that in it."[38] Angel then sits up straight and rides onward, strong in the saddle as he understands the significance of the song. The villagers recognize that they will never see the members of the wild bunch again. The gang is doomed, riding away to the deaths of all its members, with the exception of one. "Las Golondrinas" is their song of farewell.

"Las Golondrinas" ("The Swallows"), or simply "La Golondrina," was written in 1862 as a *despedida* (good-bye) by Narciso Serradell Sevilla, a Mexican physician and composer who had been exiled to France during the French Intervention, although some claim Serradell's song is actually adapted from a much older *canción*. On the surface, the song concerns a swallow's struggle to return home. From the beginning, "Las Golondrinas" took on metaphoric significance to Mexican people. At first it was a requiem for lost lands, then a song sung to say good-bye. By the time of the Mexican Revolution, it was commonly heard at funerals, where it was often played and sung at the end of the mass as the casket was being carried away from the church en route to the graveyard.

One gentle spring day in San Antonio in the 1990s, I stood outside Mission San José as locals gathered for a wedding to take place inside its church. At this mariachi wedding, I spoke with a trumpeter, who wore black and silver and looked resplendent in the afternoon sunlight. He had played in different mariachis for more than twenty years—concerts, parties, weddings, funerals. Mariachi funerals particularly interested me. I asked the trumpeter why that song about swallows had become common at such events.

My trumpeter buddy told me *indios* in Mexico believed that when people die, their souls were transformed into swallows, which then winged their way to the next world. Spanish missionaries in the New World sometimes adapted *indio* beliefs to Catholic teachings to help with converting Native peoples to the Church. The swallow as the purveyor of a soul to heaven was just such a case, the trumpeter told me, and that contributed to its popularity as a funeral song. Years later, Juan Tejeda, an author, accordion master, and educator who cofounded and produced the Tejano Conjunto Festival en San Antonio, told me: "It gained popularity during the Mexican Revolution probably because of the intense civil war, in which over a million people died and the forced migrations because of this war that caused thousands of people to migrate to the U.S., which also explains the popularity on both sides of the river, even though you can see the relationship of this song with people who were already here on this side of the river for generations and the lament for the loss of land and culture, and the symbolic relationship with the common brown bird."[39]

Peckinpah certainly understood the loaded symbolism of "Las Golondrinas" when he determined that the villagers should sing it to the wild bunch as they leave the pueblo. It was important enough to him that he wanted to play the song over loudspeakers as the sequence was filmed. A version of it had been recorded in L.A. for this purpose, but the tapes were damaged and unusable after they were transported to Mexico. Peckinpah turned to Chalo González for help. González took off for Mexico City, where he located musicians and singers who would record a version of "Las Golondrinas" that would sound as if it were sung by villagers, not professional singers. He rushed the new tape back to Parras, arriving in time for Peckinpah to play it while shooting the bunch's departure from Angel's village. González's improvised version of "Las Golondrinas" was so good that it would wind up on the *Wild Bunch* soundtrack.[40]

11.

As the filming of the scene in Angel's village was wrapping up, Peckinpah encountered some destitute Americans who had become stranded in Mexico. Ralph Prieto had taken his family from their home in Indiana to Mexico to look up relatives. By March, the Prietos were broke, with no money for return train tickets to the United States. Stuck in Torreón, the family was in desperate straits, when Ralph saw a notice in a newspaper about a major American movie in production in Parras. He gathered up enough centavos to buy bus tickets for his family to travel to Parras. They arrived at the resort and golf course—which L. Q. Jones would describe as nine holes of mud[41]—where Peckinpah and company were filming the Angel's-village sequence of *The Wild Bunch*.[42] Ralph attempted to contact someone connected to the film, to no avail.

Then Cliff Coleman walked past Ralph Jr. and his brother one afternoon and overheard them speaking English—English with a Midwestern accent, no less. "Where in the hell are you guys from?" Coleman asked. Ralph Jr. told Coleman it was Indiana and explained that his dad was trying to get a job on the picture. Coleman asked the boys to introduce him to their father. "My dad gave him the story about how we had to get back home," Ralph Jr. said. "So they hired us as extras, all eight of us. We met Sam Peckinpah. Now Sam Peckinpah, like every other day he was on that set, was not having a good day. He never seemed to have a good day."[43]

Peckinpah also hired Ralph Sr. to be an interpreter for the film company—never mind that the elder Prieto's Spanish was not all that good, though he was able to get the job done. In one scene, Ben Johnson and Warren Oates frolic in wine vats in the company of some real prostitutes from Parras portraying prostitutes on film. (Johnson, pulling down the blouse of one, ad-libbed a line comparing the size of her nipple to the size of his thumb, a line censors in the United States choked on;

Sam Peckinpah with children from the Prieto family (left to right): Hope, Chris, Mitchell, Zina, Steven, and Ralph Jr. Some of them performed in front of the camera in *The Wild Bunch*. Photo courtesy of Ralph Prieto Jr.

it had to be expunged from the movie.) It fell to Ralph Sr. to exhort the women to "jump higher, jumper higher" in Spanish. Peckinpah put Ralph Sr.'s wife to work as an assistant animal wrangler. Though not in any great quantity, cash began to flow from production manager Bill Faralla's expenses stash to the Prietos.

Virtually all hotel space, good and bad, was already taken by members of the movie company who'd arrived well ahead of the Prietos. Not to mention that the payments from *The Wild Bunch* weren't great at all, leaving little to spend on room rental. The family moved into a hostelry that proved to be only a little better than sleeping out in the open in the desert night. The roof was thatched and infested by bats. Rats and mice scurried across the dirt floor at night.

By the time the Prietos first appeared in front of the camera, the Angel's-village scenes were in the can. The film company had now moved on to the Hacienda Ciénega del Carmen to shoot scenes of the outlaws' introduction to Mapache at Agua Verde, the death of Angel's former girl-friend, the planning of the train robbery, and the wine-vat romp. The sequences in which the outlaws first visit Agua Verde are significant. When Mapache makes his first appearance in *The Wild Bunch*, he does not ride up on a steed. Instead he is driven in a red Packard automobile.[44] Mapache is a force of evil, and in keeping with one of Peckinpah's themes, it is fitting that he embraces technology, which, in Peckinpah's eyes, is dehumanizingly evil. The outlaws seem uneasy as they inspect the automobile. They are more comfortable with animals and the land, not machines. Old Man Sykes says he's heard of a machine that can fly. Pike says, yes, it's true, and that such machines will be used in the inevitable European war, which would break out in August 1914. Riding in the car with Mapache is a German military adviser named Mohr (played by the German-born Mexican actor and TV director Fernando Wagner). Germany was the most technologically driven nation in the world in the twentieth century. Agents of the kaiser were busy in Mexico during the revolution to attempt to build some geopolitical advantage over England and France.

At four A.M. of their initial day of work, the Prietos went to wardrobe in Parras to get costumes before they boarded the bus that would make the long, bumpy drive to the ancient winery. Gordon Dawson's crew of mostly Mexican women gave the Prietos an icy reception. The tension of that morning would repeat itself for the Prietos as filming continued. "Mexicans from Mexico don't much like Mexicans from the United States," Ralph Jr. remembered.[45]

Peckinpah lined up Ralph Jr. and three of his siblings in a barred window at the winery for a sequence in which Pike Bishop and the gang stroll around Agua Verde on their first day in Mapache's stronghold. Sam told them to drop pebbles on Holden, Ben Johnson, Ernest Borgnine, and Warren Oates as they walked through a doorway below. Sam didn't tell his actors that the kids were going to do it. He wanted to capture their natural reaction. Sam got more than he bargained for. After the first take, Holden lost it, angered that a bunch of Mexican kids would mess up his shot. Sam could use only one brief "natural reaction" in the released version of the film: a perturbed Ben Johnson glancing up at the kids above him. "Ben Johnson looked like he wanted to beat our asses," Ralph Jr. said.[46]

The family had a loyal ally and protector in Peckinpah. He saw to it that the whole family was allowed to go through the line to get boxed lunches available for extras whether any Prietos worked that day or not. Ralph Jr.'s youngest brother, Mitchell, was just two years old and begged for milk, but the caterers never seemed to have it on hand. One day, Peckinpah walked past and heard Mitchell crying. He asked what the problem was, then ordered the caterers to ensure that Mitchell had milk every day. "Sam Peckinpah watched out for us," Ralph Jr. said. "He really watched out for us."[47]

12.

Peckinpah was working harder than ever, at times demonstrating the amazing efficiency he'd shown during his days as a TV director. He was improvising scenes and shooting extraordinary amounts of coverage. He freely adjusted schedules and seemed to have few worries about expenses. Producer Phil Feldman fired off memos of concern to Ken Hyman back in Burbank, who supported Sam. Magic was occurring in Mexico, and Hyman and other executives in L.A. knew it. The color images they were watching of Pike Bishop and his desperadoes in Mexico looked different from anything they'd seen in earlier Western films. The fighting during the opening shoot-out took portrayals of violence to new levels of realism. Sequences of the wild bunch fleeing Texas into Mexico, then confronting their mistakes and figuring out what to do next, followed by scenes of their uneasy and temporary alliance with Mapache, are all gritty and genuine. The acting was top-tier.

Sam gained the support of Hyman and others back in Burbank because he was careful about what he let them see. He'd learned some things from *Major Dundee*. He knew what a creative disaster it would be to have sweating execs in silk suits arriving in Parras to "fix" problems with the production as they had on his previous picture shot in Mexico. Early on, Peckinpah brought in a weapon to keep the suits at bay. Lou Lombardo was far from well-known in Hollywood outside TV circles, but he was destined to become one of the best film editors of his time.

Lombardo was a Missouri native who had the good fortune to end up in Kansas City at the perfect time. There he met Robert Altman, a former World War II bomber crewman turned industrial filmmaker. Altman had wiped out in the movie business in both L.A. and New York and was biding his time in Kansas City, hoping to get another shot at the big time. Lombardo went to work at the same industrial-film company that employed Altman. A group of Kansas City businessmen, hoping to strike riches in the film business, put together a few thousand dollars to fund a youth-exploitation movie entitled *The Delinquents*, which would star Tom Laughlin, later of *Billy Jack* fame. They enlisted Altman to write and direct it. Altman brought Lombardo on board to help. *The Delinquents* was a tremendous success financially and opened doors for Altman in Hollywood. Soon Lombardo was a production assistant on Altman's documentary *The James Dean Story*.

Lombardo developed a deep interest in film editing and became an apprentice film cutter at MCA's TV studio, Revue Productions. The apprenticeship stretched over eight long years, during which Lombardo worked on dozens of TV shows. "For six of those eight years," Lombardo said, "I was cutting this and that but never getting any credit for it. When my eight years were up, Altman was going to do a CBS pilot and asked me if I would do it. I was legally able to do it. Walter Grauman at Fox saw it, and he gave me a shot at a TV series he was going to produce. That was a big thing."[48]

Lombardo worked as a camera operator on "Noon Wine," which is how he met Peckinpah. Sam liked him. Lombardo was in his early thirties and a bit of a hippie. He possessed a dead-solid work ethic, which Sam always appreciated, and crackled with creative ideas. "About a year later," Lombardo said, "he called me and said, 'I've got this picture called *The Wild Bunch*, maybe you could do it. What do you have that you could send over that you're proud of?' On the *Felony Squad* TV series, I had a shoot-out where I had to manufacture slow motion, because they didn't shoot slow motion in television. You got one take and that was it. Joe Don Baker came out with a gun and was being shot by all these police. I printed every frame three times and created slow motion. I intercut him being shot, falling, this guy shooting, that guy running, Baker falling. Sam and Phil Feldman, the producer, saw it and said, 'You've got the job—and as a matter of fact, we'll use that kind of thing.'"[49] Never mind that Lombardo had never before cut a feature film.

In Parras, Peckinpah and Feldman set Lombardo up in a makeshift cutting room with a Moviola, film racks, film benches with racks and rewinds, trim bins, swivel chairs, sync machines, butt splicers, a Cinema-Scope bubble, and other equipment for editing at the golf course resort on the outskirts of Parras. He worked on the footage that Lucian Ballard and crew were shooting. Lombardo later recalled:

> *No, there weren't any storyboards and there were very few masters. Having done gunfights in police shows on television for a few years, you know how you're going to build a battle. I told Sam that my concept in [the opening shoot-out of* The Wild Bunch*] was to involve the audience. I wanted them to think they were in the middle of an explosion that went off around them. You sketch it out. The point is, everybody in the world is shooting at these guys and hitting everybody else except them—and they're shooting back. The street fight was twenty-one minutes long when I first cut it; that is three reels. It went on and on. I went the standard route, I had everything making sense. Then we started taking it down and meshing it. You let the film take you there.* [50]

Lombardo allowed the film to take him to extraordinary places, creating what cinema scholar Stephen Prince would call "complex montages of violence." [51] What Lombardo was doing echoed the work of Arthur Penn and editor Dede Allen on *Bonnie and Clyde*. Lombardo was pushing the cutting-room art to a whole new level. He had studied the work of the great masters of montage, beginning with Sergei Eisenstein. Like Peckinpah, Lombardo had been influenced by the movies of Akira Kurosawa, particularly the slow-motion montage, fashioned from footage shot with multiple cameras, that appears in *Seven Samurai*. Yet Lombardo possessed his own distinct artistic vision as a film cutter. He put together several reels that included the particularly violent opening shoot-out as well as other scenes from the early parts of the movie. The slow-motion sequences in particular were unlike anything that had ever appeared at an American cinema. Future director Kathryn Bigelow (*The Hurt Locker*) referred to Lombardo's bullet ballets as "almost *gestalt* editing" that was "radical and tremendously vibrant." [52]

Peckinpah was blown away by Lombardo's work. So, too, were Ken Hyman and the other suits back in Burbank. Warner Bros.-Seven Arts vice president Edward Feldman wrote to Sam, "We are absolutely thrilled with the wonderful footage we have seen . . . I think we have a tremendous film, and it's nice to see talent express itself." [53] Hyman knew Peckinpah was creating something special down in Mexico and, as he had since the earliest days of production, continued to hold Phil Feldman at bay when the producer complained about cost overruns and delayed schedules. Hyman's let-the-big-horse-run approach was working. It was the only time during his movie career that Sam had a studio head so committed to a Peckinpah project.

Still, issues continued between producer and director. Scores of memos were written by both of them. Peckinpah was never one to curtail his fire when angry. Phil Feldman sometimes responded with anger, sometimes with understanding, sometimes with sarcasm, sometimes with humor. "Dear Partner," Feldman wrote in one memo. "Your tearful, enraged, incoherent screams have been duly noted in part and frequently unduly attended to. Sometimes the problems are difficult, and then we attend to them immediately; when they are impossible it takes a little longer."[54]

Often Feldman composed memos out of complete frustration with Peckinpah, whose tantrums could extend beyond the infantile. The least little thing could set off Peckinpah's paranoia. "You're ruining my picture!" he growled time and again to even the staunchest of loyalists who had made the slightest misjudgment. More than once, Feldman attempted to rein him in:

"Now, partner, I'll let you in on a secret. The production problems are being handled very well by a man named Faralla with the help of a producer named Feldman. This Dago and this Jew have no help from the Mexicans; none from the assistant directors; and a limited amount from the department heads and staff. Your lack of interest in many things included Mr. Faralla's Pride caused Bill to tender his resignation to me a couple of weeks ago. However, he has remained. Without him, you'd have a disaster. The production has not been shabby; you are not asked to compromise on the film and most of all, Sam, you must realize you can't shake me up by making some of these uncalled-for statements so save those energies for the film."[55]

The last sentence was both current and prescient. In years to come, a procession of colleagues, friends, and lovers would all but pull their hair out trying to understand why Peckinpah, always simmering with paranoia, wasted so much energy and time engaging in piss fights, particularly with producers, studio bosses, and others he regarded as authority figures. On *The Wild Bunch*, Peckinpah used the tactic in a calculated strategy. Sam knew he was running over budget and schedule, and he knew his creative demands were the source of the problem. Sam sought to put Feldman on the defensive by blaming others on Feldman's team.

Producer Phil Feldman and Sam Peckinpah had a complicated relationship. Feldman was a hands-on producer who at times helped Peckinpah achieve his vision. But at other times, they had serious disagreements, one concerning Chalo González's contributions to *The Wild Bunch*. Photo by Bernie Abramson, courtesy of Tonio K.

It was a way to buy more time and get more freedom. Sam was hardly the only director to use this approach. No doubt Sam had observed it work going all the way back to his days as a dialogue director at Allied Artists.

Feldman was far from a saint himself, though as an attorney, agent, and now studio executive he had learned to keep much of his anger bottled up and allowed it to seep out mostly in nasty comments here and there, such as his lament that he received no help from the assistant directors. At times, he seemed blind to what was going on around him. Employing Mexican extras cost little; white extras imported from the nearby Mormon colonies received slightly better pay but were still cheap. Cliff Coleman and the other assistant directors, who included future producer Howard Kazanjian as well as hardworking ADs provided by the Mexican film *sindicatos*, were choreographing scenes that at times involved hundreds of people. Feldman responded with a memo critical of Coleman for employing too many extras: "From here on in, however, you must check with either Bill Faralla or in his absence, with myself."[56]

Feldman was continually irked by his encounters with Chalo González on the set. González had proved his value to the picture time and again, beginning with his discovery of the all-important shooting locations. He'd also coordinated deals with local government officials, convinced high-ranking officers of the Mexican Army to provide troopers to work as extras, served as a technical adviser to Mexican actors and musicians, driven many miles to procure dynamite for *The Wild Bunch*, and worked with Lou Lombardo to ensure lines of Spanish appearing in the film were correct, among many other accomplishments. Feldman seemed blind to those contributions. He raised stinks about González in Parras and in communications with executives in Burbank. Every day that González was on the payroll, he came under scrutiny. Faralla, who continued to resent Chalo's presence on the picture, wrote to Peckinpah urging that González be paid through Faralla's cash funds instead of by checks cut in Burbank. The memo dripped with irony, for if González was a "sore subject" with the studio, it was to a great extent because of Faralla's complaints to Feldman and others.[57]

Faralla penned a memo that seemed to be favorable to González but in retrospect reads as a passive-aggressive attempt to get Chalo under his control: "As you know, Chalo is a very sore subject with the studio and even though you promised, or told him, he would get paid for Saturday and Sunday, I think it advisable to let sleeping dogs lie. As a matter of fact, I would like to get him off the payroll and get him up here where we can accommodate him without all the static. If you talk to Lou Lombardo today or tomorrow, perhaps we can determine a stop day for Chalo and get him up here."[58]

Faralla had made a huge mistake when he failed to ensure that dynamite for *The Wild Bunch*'s most important stunt sequence—the bridge explosion following the train robbery—was shipped from L.A. to Mexico. That put Faralla in a bad light with Peckinpah and Feldman. Sam asked González for help. Chalo turned to his network of Mexican contacts and was soon on the road again, driving a great distance across Mexico to meet with an army officer who could provide dynamite. When González arrived, he negotiated with the officer, who insisted on treating Chalo to a full evening of hospitality. That included an invitation to shoot pool and down some drinks, which González graciously accepted, even though he'd never shot a game of pool in his life. Finally, as dawn neared, Chalo left with his car loaded with explosives.[59]

He was exhausted when he returned with the dynamite, and after he unloaded it from the car, he collapsed on a desk and fell asleep. Feldman happened upon the fully clothed and snoring Chalo. Feldman saw a drunk Mexican who was snoozing when he should have been working. Feldman never troubled himself to learn that González had just single-handedly saved one of the movie's crucial scenes. He added it to his list of reasons why Chalo should be fired. Later, González reported an incorrect line of Spanish in a reel of film that Feldman considered to be in the can. Feldman believed that González should have caught the error earlier and exploded in a memo to Peckinpah, releasing all the pent-up hostility he felt toward Chalo:

> *For eighteen months through illness, what I deem to be inefficiency, drunkenness that I have seen with my own eyes, charges by people of dishonesty necessitating investigation, pressure of management and practices and procedures which I don't agree with, I have defended and kept on salary Chalo González against more people's advice, exhortations, etc., than I would like to talk about. I have done this because you seem to have a special reason and I believe a partner is entitled to this consideration from another. But I do not need, to cap it all off, a eulogy after giving blood, sweat, and tears and getting the company to spend $8 million because "just now" (after a reel had practically been put to bed) an error in a line may have been discovered. Who did Chalo bring this up with? He never brought it up to me. He obviously never brought it up with us before "just now." I have felt for a long time and have expressed it to Mr. Lou Lombardo, who is Mr. González's direct supervisor, that Chalo has not performed his duties in a conscientious fashion to my satisfaction on the Spanish. I know you disagree and I have been mindful of that fact through what I advised you was a lot of questioning by management as to the need for Chalo's services . . . I really didn't need your memo on Chalo this morning.*[60]

Sensing that González's job might be in jeopardy, Lombardo wrote a memo of his own to Feldman, defending Chalo's work: "The first point being inefficiency and drunkenness. I have never witnessed this during working hours in my department. What happens after that is certainly none of my business."[61] Lombardo said that the need to fix the line in question was not González's fault at all. Lombardo and Peckinpah had inserted it *after* Chalo had approved the Spanish in the scene. Lombardo's memo did little to placate Feldman, who responded with a roar:

Since you have entered the contest to deify Mr. González, I think I ought to answer a few points . . . although I must advise you and Mr. Peckinpah both that I have never considered Mr. González worthy of my best efforts in this regard since I discovered him asleep on a desk in Parras one morning, passed out and reeking. However, since you and Sam are determined to carry on this crusade, let me advise you both by this memo that if indeed you have a desire to continue this, then I will be pleased to open a full-scale investigation into every facet of Mr. González from the beginning of his time with us up to the present day. I have no desire, but I suggest that if you and Sam wish to sanctify this fellow that Pope Paul VI has left room for him now, having demoted two hundred Saints. Since I don't run the Church, I hardly know the qualifications for Sainthood, although as a result of this picture I understand there is a movement at Warner Bros.-Seven Arts to make me the first Jewish Saint for tolerance, patience, forbearance, etc. Perhaps I will take my place beside Chalo González, who will be the Saint of Film Editors and Directors.

This González matter for me perpetuates and focuses a lot of the problems which I would like to forget about in connection with The Wild Bunch. *You have stirred up things that I had buried in my mind*

El mil usos Chalo González (right) got into costume for *The Wild Bunch*, playing one of Mapache's federal soldiers killed during the final shoot-out. In this shot, Ben Johnson as Tector Gorch also meets his demise. Photo by Bernie Abramson, courtesy of Tonio K.

and you have opened a raw wound, as Sam did with his memo yesterday morning. I had sought to fix May 31, which is the last possible date I could carry anyone on the payroll of The Wild Bunch *for post-production, as the date when Mr. González could disappear from my life and along with him I could forget a lot of things about* The Wild Bunch *that I would as soon not remember. I'm very sorry that you saw fit to write your memo.*[62]

Peckinpah clearly sensed racism at work in Hollywood, and while directing *The Wild Bunch*, he did what he could to boost the hiring of Mexican and Mexican American film workers. Elliot Silverstein, who had hit pay dirt as a director with *Cat Ballou*, was in Mexico in 1968 scouting locations for his upcoming movie, *A Man Called Horse*. He and Peckinpah corresponded about professionals in the Mexican movie industry whom Silverstein might want to employ. Sam provided him a list: José "Pepe" Cueto, *The Wild Bunch*'s chief wrangler; Aldolfo "Fito" Ramírez Jr., an important member of Gordy Dawson's wardrobe crew; Luis Ortega, Federico Farfan, and Raúl Falomir, all of whom were "special effects men" on Peckinpah's picture; physician Raúl Rosales, who'd been patching up so many people injured while working on *The Wild Bunch*; head grip Salvador "Apache" Serrano, "a miracle"; and assistant directors Jesús "Chucho" Marín and Mario Cisneros. Peckinpah recommended Chalo more than anyone else: "When we wanted something done, and done first, it was always Chalo who took care of it, and more important, followed through. I wouldn't work down here without him."[63]

Peckinpah advocated Hollywood careers for two of the Mexican actresses in *The Wild Bunch*, though their parts were ultimately small. In their effort to create a realistic story, both Walon Green and Peckinpah had avoided adding any artificial love interests to *The Wild Bunch*. A flashback that Peckinpah penned revealed that Pike Bishop had just one true love affair in his life—with a married Mexican woman portrayed by Aurora Clavel in *The Wild Bunch*. Angel had a girlfriend, Teresa, back at his village, but he leaves her behind to ride with Pike. Otherwise, the primary characters in *The Wild Bunch* seem to have few encounters with women except for prostitutes, whom the Gorch brothers enjoy "in tandem."

Interactions with women that made it into the movie are limited to a childlike encounter the Gorch brothers have with a young woman playing *juego de hilos* (cat's cradle) in Angel's village; two brief flashbacks to Pike's affair with the married woman; a night of Johnson and Oates cavorting with prostitutes in wine vats; an encounter three of the wild bunch have with two prostitutes during a fiesta at Agua Verde; and the chance meeting between Angel and Teresa at Mapache's headquarters in Agua Verde. Teresa, who appears on-screen for only a scant few minutes, during which she argues with Angel before he shoots her, is the most important female part in the whole movie. The abundantly talented Sonia Amelio played her.

Amelio was a performer famous throughout Mexico, although she was unknown in the United States. Born in Mexico City in 1941, she was a true piano prodigy, appearing in concert at El Palacio de Bellas Artes as well as performing on Mexican TV at age six. She studied music at Mexico's Conservatorio Nacional de Música as well as dance at Teatro de la Ciudad de Mexico, emerging from both institutions as a star student. Eventually she would earn high marks as a ballerina, conductor, and musical

Sonia Amelio was well established in Mexico as a musician, dancer, and actress when Sam Peckinpah cast her as Teresa, the most important female role in *The Wild Bunch*. She auditioned for the part by playing piano at the Mexico City home of Emilio "El Indio" Fernández. Photo by Bernie Abramson, courtesy of Tonio K.

educator. She became most famous as a *crotalista*, a master of castanets, which she used as she danced in a variety of forms.

Ever versatile, she also earned high marks in Mexico as a film actress, largely thanks to Emilio Fernández. El Indio had cast her in two of his late-1960s pictures, most notably as the female lead in *Un dorado de Pancho Villa* (*A Faithful Soldier of Pancho Villa*). As word spread that Warner Bros.-Seven Arts was preparing to film a major motion picture in Mexico, her agent sent her photos to Peckinpah. Sam liked how she looked and asked El Indio to arrange a meeting. Fernández invited Amelio and Peckinpah to dinner at his massive fortress of a house (known as La Casa Fortaleza) in the Mexico City borough of Coyoacán, which was and is recognized as one of Mexico's great centers of art and architecture. In the mansion's *salón de música*, Amelio played piano for Peckinpah. He was impressed by her performance and dinner conversation and offered her the part of Teresa.[64]

Teresa dreamed of bigger things than life in the pueblo and was frustrated by Angel's abandoning her. She became determined to do something to make her life better. When Huertistas headed by Mapache raided

"Go back to the fucking pueblo . . . No more will I be hungry . . . Now I am happy. Very happy. I live with my general Mapache . . ." Photo by Paul Harper, courtesy of Nick Redman and Jeff Slater.

her village, she saw her chance—she rode away with *el general*. She became one of a host of *mantenidas* in Mapache's Agua Verde court and clearly is the favorite. However demeaned she might feel by the situation, it is still better for her than starvation in the pueblo. Angel confronts her at a fiesta, during which she presented Mapache with the gift of a horse. Angel's and Teresa's eyes meet. For a moment, an expression of sadness, maybe even a bit of panic, is on her face. Then they speak, in Spanish, no subtitles needed. She quickly recovers her resolve. She tells Angel that she left the village willingly. She then tells him to leave, to go back to the fucking pueblo. *No more will I be hungry . . . Now I am happy. Very happy. I live with my general Mapache . . .*

In the brief sequence, Amelio pulled off an acting tour de force. Her laugh is maniacal as she leaves Angel behind, yet her face shows regret. Her eyes well with unshed tears. For the briefest moment, she seems afraid. *No more will I be hungry . . . Now I am happy. Very happy.* Maybe so. She's also clearly aware of the cost of the deal she's entered with the devil. She departs Angel and climbs the stairs to Mapache's table, where she begins to kiss the general. Enraged, Angel pulls a pistol—not a six-shooter of the Old West, but a Colt Model 1911, emblematic of the evil technology of the twentieth century—shouts "*¡Puta!*" and shoots her dead.

All told, Amelio's appearance in *The Wild Bunch* lasts about two and a half minutes. But that was enough. Peckinpah liked what he saw in her acting. He offered her a two-year contract with Warner Bros.-Seven Arts, just the kind of break that many young actors would kill to receive. Amelio knew little English, however, and a contract with Warner's also meant she'd have to move to L.A., far away from her musical activities in Mexico City. She demurred. She acted in Mexican movies and TV series for the next ten years, then focused on music and dance, performing with castanets to pieces composed by Liszt, Tchaikovsky, and Rimsky-Korsakov. She gained considerable acclaim for her musical performances, though she rarely appeared in the United States and never in another American movie.

For Mapache, the death of Teresa is hardly more than an inconvenience. He and his lieutenants hustle the mourning women of Agua Verde through their memorial rosary. The general is angry at Angel, mostly because Angel disrespected him by killing his main woman, but also because Teresa was on Mapache's lap when Angel shot her. The bullet could have hit Mapache instead. The general has no time to grieve. A kept woman called Lilia, played by Lilia Castillo, ascends to be the new favorite. She is usually at Mapache's side from the time the wild bunch departs to rob the train north of the Rio Grande through the slaughter that ends *The Wild Bunch*.

Castillo had already appeared in Mexican movies and on a Mexican TV series when her agent, an older German woman working in Mexico City, arranged for Castillo to interview with Peckinpah and Phil Feldman, who hired her immediately to join Amelio and the other actresses playing Mapache's kept women. Her appearance in *The Wild Bunch* was a huge step forward for her in an acting career that had already taken off rapidly.

Castillo was born in Mexico City, but when she was young, her parents divorced. She moved with her mother and sister to Los Angeles. Castillo always longed to return to Mexico. When she was twenty years old, she made a couple of trips south of the border and decided to stay. The Californian attire she and her sister brought with them to Mexico opened a door for Castillo. "We all had miniskirts," she told me. "On my sister's birthday, we went to a little nightclub in the highest building in Mexico City. We were there with my brother and my cousin. We were underage but still had one drink. On the way out, a man stopped us—because we were wearing miniskirts, everyone was just staring at us."[65] At the time, short hemlines were all but unknown in Mexico.

The man invited Castillo and her sister to watch a popular musical group as it recorded in a studio. While there, she was asked by a producer if she would be interested in appearing in a variety show on TV. She went back to the United States, then returned to Mexico City, where the producer hired her to dance on TV. That led to a gig modeling for Pierre Cardin. She auditioned for a small part in a Mexican movie, a spy thriller that starred bodybuilder Jorge Rivero, but wound up with a lead role. Then her agent sent her to meet with Peckinpah and Phil Feldman. "I didn't realize *The Wild Bunch* was going to be that big," she said. "For me, it was just another job."[66]

She left the comforts of Mexico City behind and moved into a house in Parras with two other actresses. It seemed to her that the movie company had taken over the whole town, leaving her to wonder what had happened to all those people who really lived there. She was befriended by Chano Urueta, the white-bearded actor playing the jefe of Angel's village. Urueta funneled money to poor children who were extras in the film, in particular a young boy who suffered from polio. Her encounters with William Holden were pleasant: "William Holden was very

Lilia Castillo was a Mexican American actress who had lived in both Mexico City and the suburbs of the Los Angeles when she was cast to play one of Mapache's courtesans. Within a few years of *The Wild Bunch*'s release, she decided to leave to movie business and focus on raising her family in Southern California. Photo by Paul Harper, courtesy of Nick Redman and Jeff Slater.

reserved but very nice." And Ben Johnson: "What a wonderful, wonderful man. His wife would send him homemade cookies, which he would share. He was really sweet."[67]

Of all the actors on the film, Castillo was closest to Warren Oates. She spent a great deal of time with him in Parras: "He was really, really cool."[68] He also needed someone to show him some kindness. Oates was turning in a breakout performance as he worked on *The Wild Bunch*. He was in as many scenes as anyone else in the movie, outside of William Holden in his role as Pike Bishop and Ernest Borgnine as Dutch Engstrom. Oates's character of Lyle Gorch is present at the opening railroad-office robbery and the massacre at the end—and most of the scenes in between. Oates rarely had as big a part as he did in *The Wild Bunch*, so he was able to show some range as an actor, from an innocent man-child at Angel's village to a killer at the end. Just before his death, he takes control of a machine gun and fires at Mapache's troops, emitting a primal scream as he does so. He had much to draw on from his personal experience. Oates's life frequently went off the tracks.

Oates was ahead of the Hollywood pack in using marijuana and psychedelics, which presented some difficulties for him with his fellow cast members. He held Ben Johnson in the highest esteem, but Johnson adhered to a stringent cowboy code against hippie favorites such as weed and psilocybin. He hated them. Oates took pains to keep Johnson from discovering his taste for pot and other illegal substances, but otherwise he was up-front about looking for fun in Parras. "Warren liked to party pretty good, and so did Peckinpah, and that was all you needed to start the parties, is have Peckinpah and Warren to get together," Johnson said.[69]

L. Q. Jones remembered that when Oates wasn't reveling in Parras, he was usually down in the dumps. "I couldn't help him," said Jones, who shared a house in Parras with him. "We all were trying to help him, but most of us were as screwed up as he was."[70] Ben Johnson said, "Warren opened up to me once or twice in his life, talked about his growing up and a lot of things that happened to him along the way, and he, like Peckinpah, had had a lot of things happen to him that shouldn't happen to a young guy, and he just never did forget it. Maybe he was trying to get even with somebody along the way, you know?"[71]

Among the issues Oates was dealing with was his impending divorce. When he had a chance, he boarded Warners' two-seater Cessna, which made back-and-forth trips from Parras to Torreón, where it was easier to make international telephone calls. He'd talk to his wife over a staticky landline connection in an attempt to salvage the marriage. The calls failed to improve things. Oates would be even more glum when he returned from Torreón. Jones tried to supply a sympathetic ear, but he was never sure that it helped much. "All you can do is listen, send him out to get drunk, and off you go again."[72]

The time Oates spent with Castillo did cheer him up. They never worked together in front of the camera—not really. In the movie, Castillo sticks her tongue out at Oates's character. That was accomplished through the magic of film editing. The shots of her and the shots of Oates weren't even filmed at the same time. Castillo was in fact sticking her tongue out at Peckinpah when the camera captured her.

For Castillo, working on *The Wild Bunch* was an adventure, even if it did mean a seemingly endless cycle of frigid predawn mornings, afternoon blast furnaces of heat, wind, and sand, and long hours of intense work in front of the camera, topped off by long bus rides back to Parras, cars ringing until deep in the night from all the gunshots and explosions on the set at the hacienda.

Once, a member of the Mexican Army working on the picture told her that peyote grew in the region, so they took a walk to a place where he showed her some buds. Castillo had hippie friends, plus she was young and open to trying something new, so she plucked one of the cactus buds and chewed it. "All it did," she said, "was give me so much energy. I started walking and walking." That was a problem, because she was in wardrobe: "I had these really nice outfits, but the shoes were very tight." Once she jumped off a section of aqueduct to the ground, a drop of about five feet. She felt okay right afterward, but the impact with the ground caused her a small hernia. She joined the numerous walking wounded at Parras and the Hacienda Ciénega del Carmen.

She had other difficulties, primary among them being unwanted contact with Emilio Fernández: "I'm probably not a good person to ask about him. I didn't have too much respect for him. He seemed like a dirty old man to me. There's this scene that I have. I'm the one who is with him after they murder his girlfriend [when Angel kills Teresa]. When they started dragging Angel, Indio started putting his hands on my breasts. He wasn't supposed to do that." Castillo didn't want to interrupt the shot, so she refrained from pushing El Indio's hands off her. "It really angered me. Of course, it shows up in the film, but it wasn't supposed to happen. So, I never did like him." But like many women victimized by sexual assault and harassment, especially fifty years ago, she kept her mouth shut about her disdain for him, and she did not allow his roaming hands to interrupt progress on the film. "I pretended I liked him because I didn't want someone to get mad at me and say, 'Oh, the reason we stopped [filming] was because of you.' But after that, I just couldn't stand him."[73]

Although she didn't see a great deal of Peckinpah, her relationship with him was good. She found him to be an amazing director. "He made you live the part. You didn't even have to think about it. He could get things out of anybody." As often happened in films, some of her best work never made it into the final cut of the movie.

One day Castillo saw Peckinpah sitting alone, looking sad. She'd just bought some chocolates at a little store in Parras and walked up to Sam to give him one, though she was careful not to disturb him beyond handing him the candy. "I think he liked that," she said. He certainly liked her work on the picture and demonstrated that by convincing Warner Bros.-Seven Arts to give her a two-year contract.

After her work on *The Wild Bunch* wrapped, the studio paid for her to relocate to Los Angeles and signed her up to study acting under Stella Adler, who had been Brando's mentor. What was not clear to Castillo or anyone else on the set of *The Wild Bunch*—with, perhaps, the possible exception of Phil Feldman—was that the marriage of Warner Bros. and Seven Arts Productions was unraveling. By the time *The Wild Bunch* was released a year later, the Hymans had sold their controlling interest in Warners to the Kinney National Company, a scandal-ridden conglomerate that specialized in parking garages and cleaning services. When Castillo's contract ended in two years, the new management at the studio had parted ways with Peckinpah and had no interest in renewing her.

"I was too young to be patient," Castillo said. "So, I went back to Mexico and went back to work in Mexican movies." Eventually she married, settled in Southern California, and gave up her career in film as she focused on family. She so divorced herself from her former movie life that she was unaware that critics came to consider her one American film a classic. She never forgot Peckinpah: "Sam was a great director, a *great* director. Except for his drinking, he was a great man."[74]

13.

Though the appearance of women in *The Wild Bunch* was scant by intent, Peckinpah, the cliché-makeover artist, still had plenty in the way of stereotypes to confront. American filmmakers had an especially egregious history in their portrayals of Mexican women, both in Westerns and in other movies, going all the way back to the early 1910s, when directors and producers applied tenets of lowbrow vaudeville melodrama to their story creations when they churned out films set on the border during the Mexican Revolution.

"Mexican women in these films are portrayed as attractive and exotic figures, who are willing to betray their own and submit themselves unconditionally to the 'superior' race," wrote Margarita de Orellana, a Mexican film scholar and editor of *Artes de México*. One such movie was *Saved by the Flag*, a Kalem Company production released in 1911. Kalem, founded in New York in 1907, was a precursor of sorts of Warner Bros. In many ways, the film set the mold for what would be depicted in American movies for the next five decades: An American in Mexico fell in love with the glamorous girlfriend of a Mexican general. She willingly tossed her boyfriend aside for the white *americano*. The two eventually fled to the United States, where they literally wrapped themselves in an American flag and defied the Mexicans on the other side of the border as the pictured ended. "This scheme is repeated in many films: Mexican women have to choose between an American and a Mexican, and the balance is weighted. In love, any low-rating American official outranks a Mexican general," de Orellana wrote.[75] This sort of thing still reared its head in the 1960s.

Eventually a highly sexualized image of the Mexican woman from the time of the revolution (and even before) developed in American movies, a beautiful *mexicana* with flowing brunette hair and fiery brown eyes in a low-cut peasant blouse and wearing double bandoliers crossed on her torso to emphasize her breasts. If she sported a long skirt, it was often split so that she could reveal plenty of leg. She inevitably had a temper that burned bright as her eyes. She was also helpless in falling head over heels in love with white men. The stereotype was expanded and modernized to become "the Mexican spitfire" portrayed by Lupe Vélez in 1939's *The Girl from Mexico*.

The stereotype was still very much alive and well at the time Peckinpah was filming *The Wild Bunch*. One example was *Bandolero!*, which starred Raquel Welch as the Mexican-born wife of an Anglo banker working in a small town in South Texas. Welch, who by the late 1960s was Hollywood's leading sex symbol, appears impossibly glamorous in *Bandolero!*, with an extravagant hairdo that never seems to get ruffled and clothes that never seem to get soiled. She's feisty and hot-blooded, a Latina who can only be tamed by a *real* man, as she demonstrates at the movie's conclusion. Nothing in the movie rings true, especially not the portrayal of the Mexican woman.

Peckinpah took pains to avoid falling into that kind of cliché snare as he filmed *The Wild Bunch*. To refute that most odious of stereotypes of Mexican women appearing in American movies, Peckinpah used an extra from among the people from "up in the hills"[76] and shot his answer to breasts and bandoliers. The plain-featured woman portrayed a Huertista *soldadera*, and—counter to the stereotype—she was far from glamorous. She wore battered clothes, her hair looked as if it had not been touched by a comb in weeks, and she was tired and dirty, far too exhausted to be a spitfire.

In the sequence, she wearily unbuttoned her practical, working-woman's blouse—nothing at all like the low-cut peasant blouse of a stereotypical spitfire—to bare a milk-engorged breast. The weary warrior then began to nurse her baby, holding her child against the ammunition-loaded bandoliers. The brief sequence was completely void of sexuality. Instead it summed up the life of *soldaderas*, those remarkable women from the time of the revolution who traveled with armies, sometimes fighting as full-fledged soldiers themselves, sometimes working at other tasks to support their soldier husbands, and all the while continuing to tend to their families.

Glamour akin to Raquel Welch's in *Bandolero!* or even that of Claudia Cardinale (a Tunisian actress portraying a Mexican woman) in *The Professionals* was nonexistent in *The Wild Bunch*. The closest to it occurred in a flashback scene in which Holden's and Ryan's characters cavorted with high-dollar prostitutes in a hotel suite following a successful robbery. In a cameo, Elsa Cárdenas played one of the prostitutes, sitting on William Holden's lap while stripped to her old-fashioned underwear, and she projected some element of glamour, at least in a 1910s provocative way— Cárdenas looked very much like a woman from one of those naughty picture postcards from the early twentieth century. She and the other women in the suite were sexualized, but then, they were *prostitutas*. The courtesans who tend to Mapache at his lair are attired fancier than any of the other women in *The Wild Bunch*, but they are the kept women of an army general who has plenty of money. It's to be expected that they would look the way they do.

Aurora Clavel appeared topless, briefly, in a flashback. Flashes of breasts occurred as Warren Oates and Ben Johnson splashed around in the wine vats with the real-life prostitutes, but the way Peckinpah filmed this was hardly amatory. Instead, it was realistic, within the context of the scenes, and nonprurient.

By and large, the Mexican female characters who appear in *The Wild Bunch* have no romantic attraction to the white men they encounter. In the scene shot at Angel's village, women treat gang members with kindness and courtesy. They dance with the white men in their midst during the *baile* held the night before the gang departs for Agua Verde. It is nothing beyond being hospitable to visitors, no ripping of bodices because white men are in the village. Bishop and a young prostitute have a touching encounter toward the end of *The Wild Bunch*. Earlier in the picture, we see their eyes meet, and they register attraction to each other. Now Bishop dresses while she washes her chest. Her baby is in the corner—a shot of the child crying, a shot of Bishop downing what's left of a bottle of alcohol, one life beginning, another at its end. The young woman seems to understand that the only coupling she will have with this man is over. She knows she will never see him again. Her eyes say she realizes his death is near. When Bishop pays her for their night of sex, her sadness grows—this wasn't about money, it was about honest feelings. Meanwhile the Gorch brothers haggle over money with another prostitute. That conversation, never mind the prostitute's anger, has a sadness of its own. Nothing is sexy here. Neither of these women is anything like the Mexican spitfire stereotype.

Peckinpah also avoided much of the ethnic stereotyping of Mexicans that had appeared in American movies for decades. The most loathsome characters in *The Wild Bunch* are the bounty hunters and their railroad-official leader, Harrigan, all of them white men. None possesses the slightest of redeeming qualities—Deke Thornton describes them as "gutter trash." The noblest people are the *indios* from Angel's village who retrieve their case of stolen rifles from Pike Bishop and company and nothing more. The other inhabitants from the village have a decency to them absent from most of the other people in *The Wild Bunch*. In the end, Don José, the village jefe, leads his people to join Pancho Villa's supporters in the fight against the Huertistas, a worthy cause. The most virtuous of the wild bunch themselves is Angel, the Mexican member of the gang who gives up his share of riches to give his people firearms to defend themselves. He faces his prolonged torture and death at the hands of Mapache's thugs for stealing the rifles with bravery. "He played his string right out to the end," Dutch, who betrayed Angel, says in remorse and admiration. Aristotle once said that a man doesn't become a hero until he can see the root of his own downfall. Angel gets it. His rash decision to kill Teresa leads to Mapache's discovery that Angel stole the rifles, which leads to Angel's death. He accepts it.

14.

Walon Green himself turned up in Parras, which allowed him to meet Peckinpah for the first time. Producer Phil Feldman had continued to doubt Peckinpah's ability to pull off the bridge-explosion sequence, which Sam described to Syd Field as the centerpiece of the film. Feldman hedged his bets by hiring Green for two weeks to write an alternative scene that could be used in place of the bridge's destruction. To his credit, Feldman was up-front with Peckinpah about it, so Sam knew about Green's task. Green's career had blossomed considerably in the years since he'd last worked on the script. By the spring of 1968, he was working as producer, director, and writer on a series of *National Geographic* specials. He was also working on preproduction for *The Hellstrom Chronicle*.

In Mexico, Green revisited his original concept of the gang's using a cable to cross the Rio Grande. To Feldman, a cable-crossing sequence seemed cheaper and more easily executed than a bridge sequence, which, among other things, would necessitate construction of the bridge. Peckinpah was fully confident in his own vision.

"I liked what I heard he was about," Green said, "a guy who gave everybody a lot of shit and stood his ground." When Green first met Sam, he was "kind of surly." Peckinpah did not respond well when Green suggested that the cable crossing was the better plan, the idea being that the cable is cut when the gang is halfway across the Rio Grande. They then are swept away into rapids before making it to shore in Mexico.

"There aren't any rapids here like in Sacramento," Peckinpah barked back at Green. Sam began running through a list of California rivers, most of which Green had never even heard of. Peckinpah then said, "I know what a river looks like and you don't." Peckinpah suggested that Green take a trip to see just what the river to be used in the picture

Wild Bunch screenwriter Walon Green turned up in Parras to write an alternate scene for the bridge explosion in case it proved unworkable. Here he speaks with William Holden. Photo by Bernie Abramson, courtesy of Tonio K.

looked like. Green did just that, using a Mexican pilot to fly him to the Río Nazas outside Torreón, which would double for the Rio Grande. Their ancient Cessna tail-dragger nearly crashed while landing, which "banged the shit out of the plane." Green thought the damage to the Cessna would anger Peckinpah. "I thought Sam would be really mad. Oddly enough, the fact that we'd nearly crashed while landing in a bad spot impressed him."

"Well," Peckinpah told Green, "you nearly killed yourself, but you know what I'm talking about, right?"[77]

The work on *The Wild Bunch* was intense for everyone involved. A small, remote town such as Parras offered little in the way of stress relief, outside of drinking. "All the wild bunch," Alfonso Arau told me, "and those were the times—all of them were drunk all the time. Everybody was drinking, all day, every day," Peckinpah's and Holden's restricted drinking notwithstanding. Arau also noted that members of the Mexican Army, arriving en masse as extras portraying federal troopers, "had the reputation in those times of being on marijuana, all the time."[78]

The stuntmen and some of the male actors gathered at a particular bar in Parras on Saturday nights, and the beer and tequila flowed nonstop. Everyone knew how the evening would end: Someone would throw a punch, then the melee would erupt. The local *policía* would arrive, haul the fiercest combatants off to jail, and send the others home to their bunks. L. Q. Jones estimated that he was jailed no fewer than a dozen times. "Those guys *became* the wild bunch," Cliff Coleman told me.[79]

The brawling among the stuntmen wasn't limited to bars. The hall that Chalo González had rented just for them, which kept them segregated from the cast and crew, became a fight zone. Soon maids refused to enter the building, with its smashed furniture and holes in the walls. In a panic, the man who owned it contacted González and said Chalo had to do something to stop the destruction. When González arrived there, he found that even windows had been broken out. He had no choice but to move the stuntmen into separate houses.[80]

In May 1968, an associate of William Holden's died in L.A., and shooting broke briefly so he could attend the funeral. L. Q. Jones returned to L.A. himself for a couple of days of rest and relaxation. He was stopped at a light on Sunset when he spied the brutal railroad boss Harrigan, actor Albert Dekker, who had completed his work on *The Wild Bunch* days earlier and returned to California. Dekker was walking alone on the sidewalk—there was no sign of the thirteen-year-old girl whom he'd passed off as his wife in Parras. Jones shouted a greeting to him, but the former California State assemblyman plodded onward, staring at the concrete below him.[81]

That night something happened—the details of it are sketchy at best—that propelled Dekker into lurid legend. The next morning, his fiancée, who'd not heard from him in three days, arrived at his apartment to check on him. She stepped inside and found Dekker dead, nude and hanging

Veteran screen and stage actor Albert Dekker became the stuff of lurid legend within days of returning to L.A. after his work was complete on *The Wild Bunch*. Photo by Paul Harper, courtesy of Nick Redman and Jeff Slater.

by a leather belt attached to the shower nozzle. An additional belt was wrapped about his torso, a makeshift blindfold made from a scarf was over his eyes, dirty hypodermic needles were stuck in his arms, his ankles were bound by rope, his hands were secured behind his back by handcuffs, and a ball gag was inserted in his mouth. Words and phrases such as *slave* and *make me suck* were written on his body in lipstick. A vagina had been drawn on his abdomen. S&M porn and sex toys were scattered around the apartment. Money and electronic equipment were missing from the apartment. However, the bathroom door was secured from the inside by a chain lock, which meant that his fiancée could only open the door a scant few inches to see his body. The door was the only exit from the bathroom—the room had no window. The coroner subsequently ruled that the demise of *The Wild Bunch*'s Harrigan was accidental, the result of what would come to be called an autoerotic fatality.

The news of Dekker's death made its way back to Mexico when *The Wild Bunch* cast and crew reassembled, but there was little time to discuss it. The focus immediately returned to the picture. Filming it was the *real world* for them.

15.

Peckinpah and his crew had their work cut out for them during their final days of shooting at Hacienda Ciénega del Carmen. Still to be filmed were the exchange of stolen rifles for gold; the torture of Angel; a pivotal encounter of two prostitutes, Pike Bishop, and the Gorch brothers; and *The Wild Bunch*'s climax, the massive gunfight that came to be called the Battle of Bloody Porch by the cast and crew. Each scene required topflight work from everyone, especially the actors, to make the ending of *The Wild Bunch* work.

The scene in which the gang members give weapons stolen from the train to Mapache and his forces in exchange for gold is superb film-making. As the last of the handovers occur, Mapache, tipped off that Jaime Sánchez's character has orchestrated the theft of a case of rifles to give to his village, confronts Angel: "He stole it." Ernest Borgnine's Dutch Engstrom is with Angel. Angel attempts to escape but is roped to the ground by Mapache's men. Suddenly the light recedes from the scene, the images soften, with clouds in the background. The look is now that of a biblical epic, Gethsemane. Mapache asks Dutch what should be done with Angel, who now seems a bit like Jesus before Pontius Pilate. Dutch, whose life Angel had saved during the train robbery, becomes a mix of Saint Peter the denier and Judas the betrayer. "Well, I'm wasting time here, adios," Dutch says, his pieces of gold literally secured to his saddle. "¿Y Angel?" Mapache says. Dutch replies, "He's a thief; you take care of him." Dutch rides away. Certainly Sam, the daily Bible reader, intended this to have religious overtones. "It was the Passion of Jesus Christ," Sánchez, who had been raised Roman Catholic in Puerto Rico, told me. "That's how I thought of it. That's how I played it. It was the torture and death of Jesus Christ."[82]

Jorge Russek (left), Jaime Sánchez, and Alfonso Arau in the scene in which Angel is tortured. "It was the Passion of Jesus Christ," Sánchez said. "That's how I thought of it. That's how I played it. It was the torture and death of Jesus Christ." Photo by Paul Harper, courtesy of Nick Redman and Jeff Slater.

Even better work was to come. The characters of Pike Bishop and Lyle and Tector Gorch finish a night spent with two women in a woebegone crib as their colleague Angel is undergoing torture in another part of town. The gang members have everything they've ever wanted, money enough for the Gorches' "opening for a new territory," Bishop's chance to "back off." They attempt to celebrate with sex and liquor. It's all in vain. The mood in the crib is more funereal than festive. Regret and self-loathing hang in the air in the dim light emanating from coal-oil lamps.

One of the women begs for more money from the Gorches. The other woman, who has spent the night with Pike, is sad. She likes Pike, almost resents his giving her money for the sex they'd had, and she recognizes his fate. In those dim rooms, Pike comes to grip with the root of his downfall. Now it is time to accept what awaits him. William Holden as Pike masterfully communicates this without stating a word. It's all in his body movements, his facial expression, and above all else, the glare in his bright blue eyes. It is the work of a master actor and also the work of a master director. Peckinpah had the courage as a filmmaker to allow this to play out without injecting any monologues. The whole tragic message of *The Wild Bunch* is conveyed by Holden's eyes and two words: "Let's go." Warren Oates's Lyle Gorch understands what Pike is saying behind his words. Lyle glances at his brother, Tector (Ben Johnson), who without a word acknowledges and accepts it himself. Lyle turns back to Pike and says, "Why not?" With that, a cloud lifts. Their former lives are finished, fading away like the dying bird on a string that Tector Gorch has been toying with.

They step out into the bright light of morning as new men, willing and ready to confront what awaits them. Ernest Borgnine's Dutch has been too filled with anguish—he betrayed Angel, the man who saved him—to partake of the women and the tequila himself. He, too, is redeemed with a glance from Pike and an exchange of smiles.

The script called for Bishop and the Gorch brothers to reunite with Dutch outside the whorehouse, arm themselves, and then go to Mapache and demand release of Angel. After they retrieved their guns from the saddlebags and scabbards on their horses, Cliff Coleman began to give orders for the next setup. The plan was to pick up at Mapache's headquarters.

Sam interrupted him. "No, no, Cliff, wait. I want to do a walk thing first."

"What do you mean, a 'walk thing'?" Coleman said.

Peckinpah muttered something Coleman couldn't make out, then lined up Holden, Borgnine, Johnson, and Oates to make a prolonged march to Mapache's headquarters. Peckinpah instructed Ballard that he wanted to shoot what came to be known as the Walk using a long lens worth tens of thousands of dollars. It had been idly sitting in reserve since *The Wild Bunch* began shooting in March, and executives in Burbank wanted it back to use on another picture. The use of photographic equipment had been an issue all along on *The Wild Bunch*. Producer Phil Feldman had dashed off a memo to cinematographer Lucien Ballard stating that a Panavision representative had informed him that *The Wild Bunch* was rapidly "approaching a world record" for use of the company's equipment.[83] A day before the long lens was to be returned, Ballard strapped it on a camera.[84]

Coleman and his colleague assistant director Jesús Marín sprang into action. Following Peckinpah's directives, they lined up drunken Mexican soldiers, still singing from the previous night's fiesta, a man shaving, another man retching from too much drink, people stepping up to see just what these crazy gringos were up to, mounted horsemen in the background, mothers with their children, and so on. Everyone possible seemed to be rounded up; Ralph Prieto was relieved from his translation duties and costumed as one of Mapache's federal soldiers. "And, all of a sudden, Jesus Christ, the music's going and the camera's rolling and these fucking guys start to walk, and everybody's going, 'Wow, it's the real thing,'" said Coleman. "Nobody knew what Sam was going to do, or what he wanted to do. Before you knew it, it built and it built and it built and it built until it became that scene. Very, very, very, very, very, very good. [Peckinpah] had those moments, and he could bring those moments out."[85]

Shooting all this with telephoto lenses emphasized one of *The Wild Bunch*'s underlying themes. These men are brothers; they stand out against everything else as they march together to accept their fate as they attempt to save Angel, who is also their brother. Peckinpah had his actors trudge through a collapsed section of a wall, the opening resembling nothing so much as a vagina. The symbolism is clear: They have been reborn.

Peckinpah knew he faced blowing up every cinematic barrier to the portrayal of violent death with the climactic upcoming scenes. Even more was at stake: Now he had to pull together all the elements of character and plot he'd been putting in place earlier in the picture. These upcoming sequences had to be the best in the movie. If not, everything he had been building up to would fall apart, as it had in *Major Dundee*. He had to be resolute in his resistance to any pressure from Phil Feldman or any of the Warners executives and follow through on his vision. He fretted about the mechanics of such a monumental undertaking. How would he stage what he had in mind? "He didn't have a fucking clue of what he was going to do," Gordon Dawson said. "It was not happening."[86] His producer, Feldman, saw that Peckinpah was stymied. A conference convened, including cast, crew, everyone who would be involved. Peckinpah, Coleman, and director of photography Lucien Ballard slowly, achingly slowly, hammered out details. It wore on Peckinpah, but he had support from cast and crew members who believed in his vision. One was Ernest Borgnine. One afternoon, Borgnine noticed Sam walking with his head low and said, "Sam, you look worried. What's the matter?"

"I'm worried."

"Worried? About what?"

"I don't know—I hesitate about getting into this next thing, you know, with all this . . ." Sam trailed off.

"Sam, what are you worried about? You've got a great picture going here." Borgnine encouraged Peckinpah to move forward heart and soul.[87]

A stuntman doubles for Jaime Sánchez during the death-of-Angel sequence, with Emilio Fernández as Mapache the killer. Photo by Bernie Abramson, courtesy of Tonio K.

The Battle of Bloody Porch commences when Pike, Dutch, and the Gorches end their march. Mapache sees them and says, *"Los gringos otra vez . . .* What you want?" Holden says they've come for Angel. "You want Angel, no? All right, I am going to give it to you . . ." Angel appears, bound, beaten, bloodied, and filthy from being dragged behind an automobile, the dreaded symbol of the twentieth century. Mapache mutters something about Angel's going free as the general cuts the binding on Angel's wrists. Then, abruptly, Mapache uses the knife to slice Angel's throat. The wild bunch opens fire on Mapache immediately after their *compañero* falls dead. After that—*nothing*. At least for a moment. Peckinpah staged it so that for an existential moment the gang is free to walk away, because the general is dead and they cared nothing about Mapache. To walk away would have meant cheating their fate. Besides, the wild bunch loves the fighting. They are at their best in the face of hell. Dutch giggles. Pike surveys the crowd, more than a hundred people, and allows his eyes to settle on one person who represents real evil in Mexico: a

Sam Peckinpah discusses a shot for the Battle of Bloody Porch with Ernest Borgnine and William Holden. Photo by Bernie Abramson, courtesy of Jeff Slater.

German officer, a man from the nation of technocrats. Pike takes careful aim, then shoots him. The next to die is the accountant, Alfonso Arau's Lieutenant Herrera, no doubt a symbolic choice on Sam's part, given his feeling about executives.

All hell breaks loose after that.

Blood flowed for day after day during the Battle of Bloody Porch. Hundreds of squibs went off. Shell casings from thousands of rounds of blank ammunition wound up scattered on the desert surrounding the ancient buildings (and they are still there at the hacienda outside Parras). The images captured by Ballard and crew were more gruesome than anything ever before staged for a Western. Lilia Castillo's character dies a particularly gruesome death—and a particularly slow one, with Pike Bishop watching her agonized demise. Special effects and makeup crew members made her up to have a particularly realistic and ugly "hole" in her from a gunshot. Once it was finished, Castillo looked down at the ersatz injury and suddenly felt nauseated—that was how genuine it looked. Peckinpah was deeply involved in the setup for that sequence, even applying stage blood himself from a squirt bottle. (The shots of Castillo's "death" eventually had to be jettisoned by Sam and his editors as they tightened the film for release.)

Peckinpah spread gore over the bodies of actors and extras because he was attempting to do the one thing that America cinema and TV had failed to do: present violent death as something real. He was coming closer to it than any American director ever had with the Battle of Bloody Porch. A double for Borgnine on the picture had served with Patton in Europe during World War II. The man broke down in tears one day because the carnage Sam was creating for the Battle of Bloody Porch was too realistic, so much so that it evoked memories of real combat. With his dozens of squibs and gallons of fake blood, Peckinpah was inventing a new vocabulary for violence in film. It would change the movies forever.

"The phrase 'Let's go'—uttered as the remaining four members of the bunch make the decision to stand up for their comrade—is not merely a call for action but also a call for moral redemption," wrote the Danish critic Kjetil Rødje. "In a familiar cinematic trope, the outlaws walk towards their deaths justified. The bunch is driven to the concluding battle by their sense of futility, and now seeks to accomplish some sense of order in the amoral universe in which they are operating. Regardless, as the scene unfolds the violence runs amok. What starts as a call for moral redemption ends in a senseless bloodbath that leaves for dead all the members of the bunch and large numbers of soldiers as well as some civilians. The resolution is, at best, partial. The final bloodbath provides no narrative closure but it still *feels* like a resolution: after the prolonged intensity of the battle, eventually it ends in a calming lull."[88]

Capturing Peckinpah's violence run amok required intense, difficult work on the part of the crew. Remembering the filming of the scene, Gordon Dawson said:

> *Five or six cameras side by side, shooting the whole master shot, with various lenses, but shooting the whole thing. And moving the entire setup five feet. And then shooting it all again. And then moving it five feet, and shooting it all again . . . All the blood hits on the wall had to be cleaned up every time. All those people who just ran in and got shot, now we're going to shoot it again, and they're going to get shot again. They've got to come back in, in clean clothes. I don't know. It was like five or six days this way. And then they say, "Okay, boys, turn it around, we're going back the other way."*[89]

Dawson and his squad functioned as a virtual costuming factory. A uniform that had been worn by an actor or extra wound up on his assembly line: washed, dried, stitched up, paint applied over damaged areas, some aging applied here and there, then back into action. Peckinpah needed daily all of those uniforms Dawson's crew were refurbishing. Peckinpah "killed" everyone available during the Battle of Bloody Porch. Stuntman and actor Billy Hart told me he was "shot" at least a half dozen times. Even Chalo González got into the act, falling "dead" while costumed as a Mexican Army officer.

The cameras rolled, capturing Peckinpah's statement on what it's really like for large numbers of people to die violently. It was miles away from any shoot-out that *Gunsmoke*'s Matt Dillon ever engaged in outside the Long Branch Saloon in Dodge City. The intent was to shock and, hopefully, induce catharsis in theater audiences. Peckinpah, perhaps recalling the brutality he witnessed in China as a marine, clearly wanted to make a statement about the effects of technology on human slaughter as well. Peckinpah had his wild bunch, armed with pump shotguns, semiautomatic pistols, and repeating rifles, situated on high ground, with relatively easy access to grenades and a machine gun. Arms of this sort were far removed from anything Billy the Kid or Wild Bill Hickok ever carried. Only four gang members were fighting dozens of Mexican soldiers, yet the wild bunch, using their high-tech weapons, as well as explosives, were able to kill Mexicans, most of whom had single-shot rifles, by the score. Finally the gang were taken down themselves, with a child killing Pike Bishop. Most of Mapache's federal troopers who die are killed by the machine gun. It presaged what would happen years later, when the technology of killing had progressed even further, when a lone killer with an assault rifle could kill dozens of unsuspecting people in moments.

After weeks of shooting, Peckinpah had the footage he wanted, all of which would be reduced to about five minutes in the released version of *The Wild Bunch*. Now came the aftermath. The bounty hunters ride into Agua Verde, whooping. "This is like a big ol' picnic!" L. Q. Jones's character, T. C., exclaims. Buzzards have descended and watch as the bounty hunters collect their booty. Deke Thornton walks sadly among the carnage until he comes across Pike's body. During the fighting, Pike had used a Colt Model 1911 semiautomatic, leaving his old-fashioned six-shooter, emblematic of the Old West, in its holster. Against the cackle of the scavenging bounty hunters, Deke lovingly retrieves Pike's six-shooter and pays no mind to the modern weapon.

Now came the sequences that would close out the film. Much of this proved difficult to stage and film, first assistant director Cliff Coleman

Top two photos, troops from the Mexican Army perform as extras during the filming of the Bloody Porch scene. Photos by Paul Harper, courtesy of Nick Redman and Jeff Slater. Bottom photo, Sam Peckinpah applies stage blood on actress Lilia Castillo. Photo courtesy of Jeff Slater.

told me, especially the material shot near sunset to get the right light effect. Wrangling buzzards presented other issues. The birds arrived in cages. Some buzzards were to be perched on buildings, surveying the bodies left over after the Battle of Bloody Porch. Tethering them didn't work, as the bird fought their bindings rather than standing still. Animal handler James Dannaldson's crew came up with a solution. Ralph Prieto's wife, working as an assistant animal handler, was assigned to glue small disks over the eyes of the buzzards, which rendered them blind, and now the birds dared not stray from their perches.[90]

Other buzzards were supposed to be filmed while in flight, but the crew discovered that as soon as they opened a buzzard's cage, the bird would rocket into the sky. How to slow down the vultures? Coleman of all people knew the answer. He jerked the huge birds from their cages and, grasping them by their feet, twirled them as if they were fat black lassos. The dizzy birds were slow to fly when they took wing, perfect for the shots Sam wanted. "I never could figure out how Coleman knew to do that," Gordon Dawson told me.[91]

With buzzards in place, the crew shot Robert Ryan as Deke sitting alone against a rock wall as dust drifts around him. The bounty hunters, the bodies of Pike, Dutch, and the Gorches stretched over saddles, ride up. "You ain't coming?" Coffer says. No, Deke's not. His old gang is dead, save for Old Man Sykes, and no one is quite sure what became of him. All Deke agreed to do was to send the wild bunch back to the United States. Deke had no reason to trust the capitalist Harrigan, who's already shown he is willing to sacrifice the lives of innocent people to protect his railroad's money from bandits. There's no guarantee that Harrigan won't send Deke back to prison. Deke has had his fill of the changing twentieth-century United States. He'll stay in Mexico. The bounty hunters depart with the bodies. They sing "Polly Wolly Doodle" as they ride away.

A sandstorm blows in from the desert. Survivors flee Agua Verde, some herding goats, some carrying furniture. The wounded limp past, leaning on shoulders. After a time, gunshots resound in the distance. Deke smiles to himself, knowing the bounty hunters have met their doom. Then Edmond O'Brien as Freddie Sykes rides in with Chano Urueta as Don José, leader of Angel's village. "Didn't expect to find you here," says Sykes.

"Why not?" Deke says. "I sent them back. That's all I said I'd do."

"They didn't get very far."

"I figured." Deke explains his plans are to drift around, try to stay out of jail.

Sykes offers him the chance to ride with him "and the boys"—men from Angel's village. The words aren't spoken that they are heading off to fight with Pancho Villa. Some of the villagers seize the machine gun and other weapons left over from the Battle of Bloody Porch. "We got some work to do." The last dialogue lines for *The Wild Bunch* had been problematic through all the drafts written by both Walon Green and Peckinpah. Now O'Brien recited the line that he had scrawled on his copy of the shooting script during rehearsals eight weeks earlier: "It ain't like it used to be. But it'll do."[92] Deke grins as he mounts up. Sykes laughs as they all ride off together. It would be used as the final footage in *The Wild Bunch*.

The middle section of the movie had yet to be shot: the train robbery; the chase of the fleeing wild bunch by soldiers and the bounty hunters; an encounter between Mapache's troops and the outlaws in canyon country; a surprise meeting with *indios* from Angel's village in a huge cave; and the bridge explosion. Finally cast and crew could say good-bye to Parras and the Hacienda Ciénega del Carmen. The filming that started in the town proper nearly two months earlier on March 25, 1968, was complete, as was all the work at the hacienda. In Parras, at the Hotel Rincón del Montero resort, they loaded into coaches provided by Ómnibus de México to travel to Torreón, leaving the hometown of Francisco Madero for good. Few, if any, of the people who worked on *The Wild Bunch* ever returned to this part of Coahuila.

16.

In Torreón, they hoped to find better food, improved lodging, and the other amenities of city life. Cast and crew soon discovered that life in Torreón had its challenges as well. Maybe no one had to worry about scorpions or tarantulas climbing into beds, but at the Hotel Río Nazas, hot running water was scarce. A bellboy who doubled as the elevator operator often overslept, leaving actors frustrated when they tried to depart for location during the early-morning hours. Air-conditioning throughout the day was unpredictable, and the hotel shut it down altogether at ten thirty each evening. There were no English-speaking telephone operators, making long-distance calls to the United States all but impossible for the Americans, and both the coffee shop and the dining room were understaffed. All the problems were duly noted in memos written by production manager Bill Faralla, though little seemed to improve.[93]

Alfonso Arau had his biggest scene in the caves and canyon country outside Dinamita in the state of Durango, about an hour's drive from Torreón. Mapache's federal troops attempt to steal the rifles and other weaponry lifted during the train robbery. The bunch had booby-trapped the guns with, well, *dinamita*. Arau had a Gold Hat–like exchange with William Holden: "I am your friend, remember? We are friends, all of us! I bring you love and affection from *el general*! . . . What bravery you have done! . . . Very smart, that's very smart for you, you damn gringos, so nobody can rob the guns . . . You blow up the guns and die or we kill you pretty soon . . . We are amigos! Please, cut the fuse, please! . . . Goddamn gringos!"

Arau was to be mounted on a horse when he delivered his lines to Holden; Holden, on a wagon. For most of the scene, Arau, Holden, and Edmond O'Brien, who was in the background but had no lines, actually sat on ladders. While filming Holden, Peckinpah instructed Arau to feed the star his lines. When it came time to film Arau, Peckinpah insisted that Holden remain on the set to provide prompts for the young Mexican actor. Arau was dumbfounded: A big star such as Holden, an Academy Award winner, performing a task most often performed by a script girl? But Holden had bought into what Peckinpah was achieving and willingly carried out the chore, all in the name of making the performances of all the actors as good as they could be.[94]

While filming outside Dinamita, Peckinpah included a sequence sure to make his original Pike Bishop, Lee Marvin, smile. The bunch tends to a wagon loaded with the guns and other arms stolen from the train. Holden is not in the scene, his character having taken off to meet with Mapache. After arguing with Ben Johnson, Edmond O'Brien wanders off the road as he lowers his breeches, intent on defecating. His bowel movement is interrupted by lit dynamite, but *The Wild Bunch* became a movie in which someone takes a shit, the very thing Marvin had called for after viewing *Lilies of the Field* five years earlier.

In the countryside around Dinamita, Jaime Sánchez had an experience that would become the stuff of legend in some quarters. Sánchez as Chino had killed Tony in *West Side Story* night after night during the play's run. The prop gun he used on Broadway was different from the real six-shooter he wore in *The Wild Bunch*. Though not familiar with pistols, he began fooling around with his gun, attempting to twirl it. Holden warned him to stop. The gun was loaded with blanks, so there was no danger of anyone's being shot, but Holden cautioned him that, in such close quarters, someone could get a powder burn or catch the shell's wad of padding in the eye. Sánchez ignored him. Then—*bam!*—the gun suddenly went off, startling and pissing off actors and crew, and spooking the horses.[95]

"I saw Sánchez come flying out that cave, with Borgnine and Holden after him," Cliff Coleman said. Coleman had disliked Sánchez from the moment he first encountered him early in the shoot—"a goddamn New York actor who thinks he knows more than anyone else." Coleman was not alone, although opinions were split about Sánchez among the *Wild Bunch* cast and crew. Some, such as Lilia Castillo, remembered him with fondness, especially times when he would strum the guitar and sing. She saw nothing of the behavior Bob Thomas reported about Sánchez in his biography of Holden: "From the outset of production, his behavior appalled the other actors and members of the crew. He lingered in his dressing room after his call to the set, keeping the rest of the cast waiting . . . He bawled out minor crew members who were afraid to talk back to him."[96] Alfonso Arau observed none of this either. He saw Sánchez as more of a victim. Arau had witnessed an ugly incident at Hacienda Ciénega del Carmen in which Ernest Borgnine lost his temper with Sánchez. Arau feared that Mexican federal soldiers, working as extras on the picture, might intervene with loaded rifles. Peckinpah stepped in to defuse the conflict before anything violent occurred.[97]

Now, at the cave outside Dinamita, the threat of fists flying seemed real. Both Holden and Borgnine were furious. Stephen Ferry, now fully ensconced in his de facto role as property master, rushed in to separate Borgnine and Sánchez before the dispute turned physical. Peckinpah soon arrived to help further defuse the situation. After some tense moments, tempers settled down. Filming progressed. In time, the incident at the cave became reputed as more than what it was. Some accounts would hold that Holden grasped Sánchez by the hair and physically forced him to apologize to the cast and crew. It was all blown out of proportion, Sánchez told me nearly a half century later: "In any other movie, it would have been forgotten long ago, but because *The Wild Bunch* is such a great movie, people still talk about it."

Another circumstance wound up being exaggerated as well. Robert Ryan and Peckinpah never got along well, even if Peckinpah was coaxing from him one of the actor's best performances in a movie. Peckinpah wanted actors to be costumed and ready to slide into character at a moment's notice. Day after day, Ryan would transform himself into Deke Thornton only to pass the hours sitting and waiting for a call to the set that never came, which angered him. Still, he did it. Time after time. He was a pro. And he was hardly alone.

(Stuntman Gary Combs doubled for Edmond O'Brien and had to undergo hours in makeup every day, often to wind up not used during the day's shooting. One day he decided enough was enough and confronted Peckinpah about it. You never knew about Sam, who could fire people on a whim but at other times respected people who defended themselves when they felt Peckinpah was wrong. He admired Combs's spunk for standing up to him. Combs became one of Peckinpah's favorite stuntmen, and Sam employed him for several pictures after *The Wild Bunch*.)

Despite stories to the contrary, Ryan never asked to be freed from the filming to allow him to go back to the United States to campaign for Robert Kennedy, who had emerged in the spring of 1968 as the favorite to win the Democratic nomination for president. Ryan still resented Kennedy's entry into the race earlier in the year because it had derailed any chance Ryan's preferred candidate, Eugene McCarthy, had of getting the nod from the Democrats. When Kennedy was assassinated on June 5, 1968, the people working on *The Wild Bunch* were, as always, absorbed by their project in Mexico. Word of Kennedy's death seemed unreal to most of them. The news reached Edmond O'Brien as he was undergoing his daily hours-long makeup routine. To him, it seemed like a dispatch from another planet. Ryan was saddened by the news and what it said about his country—two Kennedys assassinated within five years—but he felt no personal connection to the U.S. senator from New York. He did not request to be released from filming to go to the funeral.[98]

At the Durango locations, Peckinpah filmed scenes as intricate in their setup and choreography as either the opening shoot-out or the Battle of Bloody Porch, one being a battle between forces of Pancho Villa and Mapache's federal troops. It, along with sequences shot in the canyon country outside Dinamita, gave Peckinpah the chance to work in David Lean mode as the images he captured were of huge scope, fulfilling the promise of the big things he'd attempted in *Major Dundee*. The fight with the Villistas was important for developing the character of Emilio Fernández's Mapache, who is shown as being fearless, possessing the grace under pressure that great leaders exhibit. He organizes an orderly retreat, calmly walking among exploding artillery shells and whizzing bullets. His courage greatly impresses a young soldier, a very young soldier, a child—many children were soldiers in the Mexican Revolution. The federal forces flee the Villistas by a train pulled by a steam locomotive, with *soldados* and *soldaderas* clinging to the tops of the boxcars.

To shoot this scene and also the train-robbery scene, Peckinpah needed—well, a train. Production manager Bill Faralla and other Hollywood people working on the movie had no idea of how to find a vintage train in Mexico, so, early on in the picture's production, Sam had turned to Chalo González for help. González hotfooted it to Mexico City, where he made his way to the national railroad company facilities. Officials there told him, yes, they could provide *The Wild Bunch* with a train. The vintage boxcars would be no problem—plenty were still around. As for the locomotive—well, it was in pieces. They showed Chalo the various parts of the locomotive designated as NM 650. Not to worry. The workers at the rail yard would get it reassembled and running. It would be driven to the filming locations in Durango. Everything would be fine. Again, not to worry.[99]

Chalo left with a deal in place, though with a giant leap of faith on his part. Years later, he remembered those scattered pieces and his concerns about whether they could ever be assembled into a functioning

The locomotive used in *The Wild Bunch* was itself an artifact. It had been used to transport troops and arms during the Mexican Revolution. It was in pieces when Chalo González found it in a Mexican railyard, but it served *The Wild Bunch* well. Top photo from the author's collection. Bottom photo by Bernie Abramson, courtesy of Tonio K.

locomotive. But the train arrived at the filming locations in Durango, engine intact and fully functional—and more. González had no idea he'd just added a piece of history to *The Wild Bunch*.

Engine NM 650 was a 2-6-0 (the wheel arrangement also known as a Mogul) steam locomotive, built by the Baldwin Locomotive Works in Philadelphia around 1885 and placed into service in Mexico in 1901. The engine was one that likely powered the train that transported Francisco Madero from Ciudad Chihuahua to Mexico City when he assumed the presidency of Mexico in 1911. It saw heavy use throughout the Mexican Revolution, pulling cars of troops and munitions. The Mexican national railroad later used it in freight trains until it was seventy years old in 1955, when it was replaced by diesel locomotives. Then the old engine found new life in American films shot in Mexico during the 1960s, including Henry Hathaway's *The Sons of Katie Elder*, before it wound up in pieces in Mexico City at the time González came across it.[100]

NM 650 was used in *The Wild Bunch* for both the battle scene between the forces of Mapache and the Villistas and then the film's centerpiece train robbery, during which U.S. Army rifles are stolen for Mapache. In the latter, Peckinpah employed some of his finest skills as a director. The choreography of actors, stuntmen, and horses with the train went beyond what Western fans typically saw in cowboy movies of the time, beginning with Warren Oates's dropping from a small bridge abutment and Jaime Sánchez's sliding down a water chute to confront the train fireman, who is preparing to fill the engine's boiler. "Just do your work," Sánchez's Angel says, pointing a shotgun at the man.

Peckinpah also hit a high mark of verisimilitude during the robbery sequence. All those months earlier, when he was still finishing up the screenplay, Sam had told Syd Field that the robbery would be the centerpiece of *The Wild Bunch*. All the action before it would build to it; everything that came after would occur as the result of it. Because of that, it was as important as the climactic Bloody Porch shoot-out. Everything had to be just right. The look of the train itself was very un-Hollywoodlike. Cinders and smoke drifted through the air. The passenger cars were filthy and battered, as they would have been for a train running on tracks in the Chihuahuan Desert circa 1913. The actors on board were sweaty and grimy, as their characters would have been riding such a train during the Mexican Revolution. As Angel works to uncouple railcars holding bounty hunters, U.S. cavalry troopers, and their mounts from the rest of the train, his hands are caked black with grunge, his clothing wornout and rotting from filth. Angel's unhooking of the cars is as realistic as the greasy soil on his fingers, beginning with his disconnecting the air brakes before removing the pin—just the kind of things a train bandit from 1913 would have done in real life.

De facto property master Steve Ferry played Sergeant McHale and made the most of his small role, which was the most significant acting part he'd have in the movies. McHale is the NCO of a platoon of green U.S. Army cavalry troopers, most of them still boys with little training or horsemanship skills. Deke Thornton's crew of bounty hunters is on the train as well. Once the wild bunch robs the train, Thornton and the bounty hunters unload their horses from a livestock car and set off in pursuit in quick order. Not so the army troopers. They aren't even able to successfully lead their horses from the car. Those with their horses standing on the ground struggle to mount them. Their leader, McHale, who shouts orders and otherwise attempts to assert himself, is as ineffi-cient as his men. Peckinpah ordered the stirrups removed from Ferry's saddle, then filmed medium shots of Ferry's attempts to climb on his horse without benefit of a foothold. The footage made him seem incom-petent at accomplishing even the most basic of tasks—perhaps a cinematic comment from Peckinpah, the former marine, about the competency of the American military in general. Once the outlaws have unloaded the guns, ammo, and grenades they've stolen, Pike Bishop sends the locomotive and flatcars running backward to smash into the stranded passenger and stock cars. Peckinpah filmed a close-up of Ferry grimacing as the collision occurs. The horse of Billy Hart's that he'd trained to fall on its side and that had been so effective going through a window in *The Wild Bunch*'s opening shoot-out now appeared again, taking a spill inside a stock car during the wreck.[101]

A real accident happened during the train-robbery sequences. Howard Kazanjian would become a successful Hollywood producer (*The Empire Strikes Back*, *Return of the Jedi*, *Raiders of the Lost Ark*), but in 1968 he was in his midtwenties and getting a foothold in the industry. On *The Wild Bunch* he worked as one of the assistant directors reporting to Cliff Coleman. Kazanjian was on the scene when things went awry with the train:

> *Holden's in the cab of the engine, and it's hot. He's bringing the train up and stopping it, and Sam is on a crane with the camera. The train was supposed to come in and stop just about at-camera. Sam was insisting that Bill Holden drive the train himself, [even though] there was plenty of room for the real engineer to be aboard and not be seen. Ernie [Borg-nine] and Jaime Sánchez were on the rear flatcar, and Warren [Oates] was on the flatcar in front of the engine. About fifty feet beyond where the engine was supposed to stop, on a trestle, was another flatcar with our*

generator. Underneath the trestle was all of our equipment, hidden so the camera would not see it.[102]

Also under the trestle stood crew members and extras.

Peckinpah insisted on shooting take after take of the train zipping down the track and then skidding to a stop. Holden, with his daredevil instincts and love of speed, opened the old locomotive's throttle full bore to send the train flying down the track. Oates was in his position on the flatcar attached to the front of the locomotive. He later recalled, "And suddenly I'm saying to myself, 'Oh-oh, something's wrong!,' because the brakes are on and we're sliding and the sparks are flying. And up ahead is this flatcar parked on the tracks . . . I saw it approaching, and it was like slow motion. These two flatcars hit like dominoes. Somebody said I looked like I was doing a ballet. I grabbed the railing on the front of the locomotive and stepped up alongside the boiler and watched it happen 'cause it was something to behold!"[103]

Gordon Dawson was on the scene and watched as the flatcars smashed into each other, sending the generator flying. Dawson, like others on the set, immediately feared that the locomotive's boiler would explode, so he took off running. He was young and fast, outrunning fleeing actors and crew members who scampered up a hill toward safety. Suddenly he noticed someone speeding past him. It was Oates, who had run down the flatcar, vaulted himself onto the trestle, leaped to the ravine below, then raced up the hill. Oates, who had suffered through near-death experiences in the marines and at other times in his life, was shouting, "I beat it again! I beat it again!"[104] But the boiler never blew, no one was injured, and filming proceeded.

Finally, Peckinpah was ready to shoot the bridge explosion, which would be the climax of the robbery scene and the most important part of *The Wild Bunch*'s centerpiece section. When the bridge explodes, the outlaws are home free back in Mexico. It was the last major scene of *The Wild Bunch* to be filmed. True to his word, Peckinpah ignored the alternative scene Walon Green had written, with a cable crossing. A Mexican construction crew had built the bridge to Sam's liking over the Río Nazas, just a short distance outside Torreón. The relatively uncomplicated foundation structure had a cable-supported platform of sturdy wood that could drop like the trap on a gallows when triggered to do so. Though the bridge-explosion sequence would become something of a special effects legend, it was, as first assistant director Cliff Coleman told me, a simple platform drop with horses and men falling into the river as

Mexican contractors present a model for the bridge to be blown up following the gang's robbery of rifles and other arms from an American train. Photo by Bernie Abramson, courtesy of Tonio K.

dynamite goes off, nothing particularly sophisticated.[105] But it was certainly dangerous, very dangerous, given the dynamite and the conditions of the river.

Around that plain platform, the local crew had built an elaborate structure, mostly of balsa wood. It looked very much like a truss bridge from the early 1900s. The project had its share of controversy. Buck Holland said he heard that Warner Bros.-Seven Arts had budgeted $80,000 for its construction, but Peckinpah had gotten it built for half that much and pocketed the difference—the rumor held that a driver sped the cash to Laredo, Texas, to be deposited in a bank account in Sam's name. There was in fact no subterfuge. *El mil usos*, Chalo González, found a Mexican crew to build the bridge, and it cost around $40,000, not the $80,000 budgeted. It all wound up recorded in Warner Bros. documents. If a driver transported cash related to the bridge from Torreón to Laredo, it was to deposit money in a Warners account, not one controlled by Sam.[106]

In earlier times, *indios* in the area referred to the Río Nazas as "the devil," with good reason. The deceptive and dangerous river was known for its strong and unpredictable currents. On Saturday, June 29, 1968, the river was flowing hard and fast, and a stout wind blew up the Nazas valley, at times dislodging some of the balsa trappings on the bridge.

Sam Peckinpah and crew on a barge fashioned from fifty-five gallon drums and wood prepare to film the bridge explosion. The Río Nazas had stronger-than-normal currents on the day of the shoot, and the wind blowing down the river valley was stout. Photo by Paul Harper, courtesy of Nick Redman and Jeff Slater.

Crew members stayed busy attempting to keep everything together as special effects director Bud Hulburd and his hands set up the dynamite that Chalo González had procured from the Mexican Army for the explosion scene.

Hulburd had three decades of experience working on special effects in movies, but many members of his mostly Mexican team had no experience rigging explosives. The Canutt brothers, Tap and Joe, raised their hackles when they realized the level of ignorance some of the workers had with dynamite, especially after they saw one local—still a kid—using a hammer to attempt to drive a stick of dynamite into the riverbed.[107] Joe Canutt began to wonder if Hulburd had any idea what he was doing. Canutt checked some of the rigging and saw enough explosives to "blow us clean onto dry land. My mother didn't have any stupid children. I told him if he didn't cut those charges, they'd have to find somebody else to do the stunt. Well, he eventually did, and I rode the stunt. But I told that son of bitch Peckinpah that I'd never work for [Peckinpah] again."[108]

Peckinpah maddened nearly everyone as he delayed and delayed filming the explosion. He ordered close-up after close-up of burning fuses, chewing up hour after hour of precious daylight. Edward Carrere was going crazy as he fretted about the balsa blowing away in the strengthening wind. Others on the crew were equally exasperated. Time after time stuntmen were ordered onto the bridge with their horses, only to sit and sit and sit. Then Sam would order everyone off the bridge. Then he would order everyone back again. It almost seemed as if he was reluctant to pull the trigger on this final major sequence of the picture. At last, the light faded, and it was too dark to shoot. Everyone broke for the day to attend what was supposed to be the picture's wrap party at Torreón's Apolo Palacio Restaurant, never mind that a sequence was still to be shot.

The next day, a Sunday, Joe Canutt still worried about how well Hulburd would be able to execute the explosion. He convinced Gordon Dawson to step in as a safety valve. Canutt armed Dawson with a club and instructed him to knock Hulburd over the head if anything seemed not right, anything that could cause one of the stuntmen to plunge into the drink before Hulburd had a chance to set off the final charge. With that, Canutt and his brother, Tap, along with stuntmen Bill Shannon, Jim Sheppard, and Billy Hart, rode their horses onto the bridge. Hart was still recovering from the broken ankle he'd suffered when rescuing Peckinpah from the bar fight, so a costume-crew member had to saw off Hart's cast before he could do the stunt. Now he was up on the horse on the bridge, "and we really had no idea what was going to happen," he said. "Like we do with most of our stunts, we pray, then we go for it. And that's what happened that day."[109] But nothing occurred quickly. Hart and others waited an hour on the bridge as Sam readied everything below. Just before the charges went off, Hart sensed that everyone and everything was in just the right place to make the stunt work.

He was right. Peckinpah had six cameras situated on barges in the river, on the riverbanks, and up on a hill overlooking the valley. Rescue boats were in the water upstream, ready to move into the area below the bridge in an instant to pluck stuntmen from the water. Cables were strung across the river for stuntmen to grasp if they felt as if they were being swept away. Wranglers with ropes were stationed on each side of the river to retrieve horses. "The horses were nervous, one's backing up, one's moving forward, the others are doing this and that," Hart said. "But I've never seen anything just like it, where everything happened just like it was supposed to. I don't know how Sam did that. I mean, that guy was fantastic. Sam Peckinpah was *fantastic*." The charges exploded, fountains of river water shot into the air, the bridge fell open like a trapdoor, and the riders and horses hit the water.

Actor Paul Harper captured the bridge explosion as it occurred. Top photo, with actors and horses in place; middle photo, the explosives discharge; bottom photo, horses and stuntmen swim toward shore. Photos by Paul Harper, courtesy of Nick Redman and Jeff Slater.

Hart, ears ringing from the explosion, looked over at his friend Sheppard, who was in the river near him, and shouted, "This was pretty easy!"

Sheppard shouted back, "Yes, it was!"[110]

But at that moment, the swift water of the Nazas swept Hart under one of the rescue cables. The river was flowing so fast and so hard that Hart couldn't free himself. After a scary few moments, men in a boat rescued him. He was able to see that other stuntmen were not quite as fortunate as he and Sheppard. The concussion of the blast had knocked out Shannon. The rescuers were able to fish his lower body out of the water, but the strong current kept his head submerged for what seemed like forever before he was completely in a boat. The panicked horses were trying to reach firm ground, their legs thrashing furiously in the river current. One of the desperate horses swam over one of the Canutt brothers, beating him all but senseless with its hooves. The wranglers nearly lost two horses, but in the end, all were safely hauled out of the river. None drowned, never mind later rumors to the contrary. Hart had his broken ankle recast once he was back on firm ground, and he pulled splinters from his skin for a while afterward, but, he said, no one wound up seriously injured in what would become one of the most famous stunts in movie history. After witnessing the explosion, Hulburd said, "I've just had the opportunity to hang a Rembrandt. It will probably never happen to me again."[111]

Now principal photography on *The Wild Bunch* was all but complete—just one more day of shooting pickup shots at a studio in Mexico City remained. The crew broke down the final location set. People commenced saying good-byes to one another. Sam searched out Ralph Prieto Sr., the patriarch of the destitute and stranded Mexican American family who had worked different jobs on the picture ever since the days when Sam filmed the Angel's-village scene early in the production. Sam pulled $2,500 in cash from his Levi's pocket and asked Prieto if that would be enough money to get his family back into the United States and settled. Twenty-five hundred dollars went a long way in 1968, and a shocked yet grateful Prieto said yes, thank you, it would be more than enough.[112]

Peckinpah and a few of the actors flew to Mexico City to complete the pickup shots needed for *The Wild Bunch*. After they worked for a day at Churubusco Studios, all the filming was complete, after more than eighty days of production. Sam wandered off by himself to an isolated corner of a soundstage at Churubusco and wept.[113]

PART VI

"It Ain't Like It Used to Be. But It'll Do"

1.

S am Peckinpah and Lou Lombardo remained in Mexico for the next three months to work on editing the footage into a movie. Torreón was far removed from Burbank and the prying eyes of Warners executives. Peckinpah had shot some 330,000 feet of film, nearly 50 percent more than Warner Bros.-Seven Arts had budgeted for *The Wild Bunch*. Sam ordered nearly all of it to be printed to give Lombardo and himself, as well as another editor, Robert Wolfe, as much raw material as possible to work with. Wolfe was yet another emerging Hollywood talent who had cut his teeth not in the traditional studio system but in television. He, like Lombardo, had his work cut out for him. He wound up editing the Battle of Bloody Porch sequences.

As a young man, Peckinpah had worked briefly as an assistant film editor at CBS. The job had introduced him to the tools and concepts of film editing. He absorbed an astonishing understanding of the art of cutting. His prowess in the cutting room only grew with the years. He served as something of a mentor to Lombardo and Wolfe as they worked on *The Wild Bunch*, though both editors were well experienced when they came to work for Sam. He led them to making the most minuscule of edits: one frame less here, two more frames there. "I don't think anyone was as careful with detail as Sam was," said Phil Feldman, who considered *The Wild Bunch* the most meticulously edited and dubbed movie ever made.[1]

As a reward to Gordon Dawson for coming on board as *The Wild Bunch*'s wardrobe supervisor, Peckinpah had agreed to help Dawson do a rewrite on Sam's next picture, a Western called *The Ballad of Cable Hogue*. In spite of all the hours he was putting in editing *The Wild Bunch*, Peckinpah squeezed in time to work on the script with Dawson. Warners approved *Cable Hogue* for production. This meant Sam and his editors had to abandon their lair in Torreón to return to L.A. Peckinpah brought with him a three-hour, forty-five-minute cut of *The Wild Bunch*. That was still more than an hour too long for the Warners brass, so plenty of editing remained, not to mention looping, adding a musical score, and a thousand other lesser tasks. Yet Sam had to head to Nevada to film exteriors for *The Ballad of Cable Hogue* at the Valley of Fire State Park, with his film company basing itself at the hotel at Echo Bay on Lake Mead.

Everything should have been easy on *The Ballad of Cable Hogue*. Sam himself was the producer. He and Phil Feldman had had their spats in Mexico, but Peckinpah had had a more positive relationship with him than with previous big-screen producers; Feldman was on board as executive producer for *Cable Hogue*. Actors Peckinpah had worked with before (Jason Robards, L. Q. Jones, Slim Pickens, Strother Martin, R. G. Armstrong) were in the cast. Lucien Ballard was again behind the camera; Cliff Coleman returned as first assistant director. The budget was small; the shooting schedule, tight. The location was in the United States, just an hour's drive outside Las Vegas. The script was well polished.

In the story, a desert rat, after being abandoned to die in the heat by his companions, survives: Peckinpah described is as a movie "about a man who found water where it wasn't, about love . . . it's also about God." With fast-motion sequences, winking dollar bills, and a completely unrealistic pairing of the aging and ugly, dirt-encrusted title character (Robards) and a gorgeous blonde (Stella Stevens in the best role of her career), the film as released would be a comic fantasy built on an underpinning of serious themes, with little violence. Today it plays best as the extended hallucination of a man dying of thirst, an early entry in the Acid Western genre.[2] Film scholars would come to number the film as among the best revisionist Westerns ever made, and Sam would say that *The Ballad of Cable Hogue* was his favorite among his movies. Getting it made damn near killed him—and just about everyone else who worked on it. Slim Pickens battled pneumonia during the shoot. Peckinpah's friend Max Evans, who had a small role in *Cable Hogue*, fretted throughout the shoot about the health of the cowboy actor with the distinctive drawl.

Conditions were not at all good for anyone suffering a respiratory ailment. After the *Cable Hogue* cast and crew decamped to the Nevada desert, the skies opened. Rain fell in torrents on one of the driest areas of the continental United States—and it continued for day after day. Everyone on location was forced to hole up in the Echo Bay hotel, hoping against hope that the weather would let up. If Sam had placed restraints on his drinking in Mexico, he now kicked loose the shackles. Others working on the picture followed his lead. Bar bills climbed to staggering levels, with the inevitable problems that follow that kind of boozing. Some bored and drunk men working on the picture found it easy to let down their guard when a couple of theretofore unknown women showed up at the hotel and joined the partying, which extended for weeks. Soon, an outbreak of gonorrhea added to *Cable Hogue*'s production woes.

Peckinpah never showed much tolerance toward anyone who was slacking at his or her job. This became especially true as his frustration mounted in the Valley of Fire. He readily fired people from *Cable Hogue* for not doing their jobs to his standards—the firings would become the stuff of legend, and the actual number of people put on the bus became exaggerated over the years. But Peckinpah carried such a heavy work burden at the time that he could have no bandwidth for incompetence by people hired to do a job. For all the difficulties and distractions, Peckinpah moved forward with *Cable Hogue* while continuing to edit *The Wild Bunch*. A laundry room at the Echo Bay hotel had been refurbished to serve as a screening room. Lombardo showed up on weekends for Sam to review Lombardo's work on *The Wild Bunch*. Still more footage had to be excised from the movie. It was tough going now. All the chaff was long gone. Now every cut meant ditching gold.

The Wild Bunch was far from being in final form, yet the time had come to begin sharing it with the outside world. Film students at both UCLA and USC were shown the film, then Peckinpah arranged for an exhibition at the Fox Theatre in Phoenix, where the *Cable Hogue* cast and crew had relocated to shoot interiors. Lights went down at the Fox at nine A.M. Though without a score and with sound effects incomplete, *The Wild Bunch* had an immediate and powerful impact. Lombardo had flown in for the showing, and he was blown away by the crowd's reaction: "People cheered and applauded and just went crazy."[3]

2.

To compose the score for *The Wild Bunch*, Peckinpah recruited Jerry Fielding, the onetime blacklisted composer with whom Sam had first worked on "Noon Wine" a couple of years earlier. Phil Feldman and the brass at Warner Bros.-Seven Arts pushed back: Fielding was a TV composer, not a big-screen guy, never mind that he'd scored *Advise & Consent* for Otto Preminger a half dozen years earlier. Since then his work had been confined to television, with the exception of two quickie *McHale's Navy* farces released to cinemas to cash in on that TV franchise. It was not nearly enough to push him to the front of the line of movie composers.

Peckinpah still loved the understated score Fielding had composed for "Noon Wine." Peckinpah had in mind something similar for *The Wild Bunch*, maybe limited to just gut-string guitars and a handful of other instruments. He didn't want anything overly wrought—no splashy Elmer Bernstein score for his picture. He certainly didn't want a song to emerge from his film, nothing like the theme from *The Magnificent Seven*, which was now turning up in TV commercials. No, it should be sophisticated, artistic, and minimalist, enhancing the story, not distracting from it. He believed Fielding could pull it off. Peckinpah dug in his heels. Feldman and the others caved.

Peckinpah had brought Fielding to Mexico during filming of *The Wild Bunch* so that the composer could get a feel for the land and the people—and the music of the people. Fielding, a musical sponge, traveled around the country absorbing the work of mariachis, pop *grupos*, solitary guitarists, and *orquestas*, as well as everyday people singing as they went about their business in *mercados*. He heard *corridos* about Pancho Villa and other Mexican Revolution leaders. He listened to songs that had taken on great resonance for Mexican people during the revolution:

"Las Golondrinas," but also "Jesusita en Chihuahua," "La Adelita," and "Santa Amalia," among many others.

The music he heard was very much the music of Mexico during the late 1960s, not the 1910s. The *científicos* and other followers of Díaz, in their attempt to emulate Germans of the imperial period, eschewed indigenous music altogether, preferring military music and symphonies by European composers. In the music of *la gente*, mariachis were dominated by stringed instruments, with violins at the forefront. Brass instruments, if used at all, were primarily in the background. Trumpets did not become dominate in *música son* until the 1930s. Accordions were still relatively rare in Mexico and were considered something of a low-class instrument. In the 1910s, as in the 1960s, use of an accordion in mariachi music was considered improper. Those distinctions did not seem to register with Fielding as he did his sonic research—or if they did, he ignored them. A sound was coalescing in his head that would draw on everything he'd heard in Mexico but would be a highly personalized musical statement.

Back in the States after the filming of *The Wild Bunch* wrapped, producer and director gave Fielding the okay to proceed. Peckinpah did impose one requirement on Fielding: Sam insisted that the composer use Sam's longtime friend and traveling companion Julio Corona on guitar during the recordings. That was problematic: No one knew where Julito was. It fell to Chalo González to head back to Mexico. González cut a wide swath across the northern tier of states, hitting bars, restaurants, and whorehouses in his search for the guitarist. Chalo couldn't find him anywhere. Defeated, González headed back toward the United States. He stopped at a cantina in Tijuana for a final drink before crossing the border, where he knew he'd have to face an angry Peckinpah. But there in the bar—miracle of miracles—was Julito, performing his finger magic on the fretboard for drunken bar patrons. González took him to L.A. for the sessions.[4]

Fielding would have to hustle for a living his whole life, ping-ponging from one writing gig to the next, earning just enough money to cover the expenses of his family. In the mid-1960s, he'd purchased a multilevel house in the Hollywood Hills for $60,000, an outrageously high sum of money to Fielding's eyes. He fretted constantly about keeping the mortgage covered and paying the property taxes. As a result, he worked outrageously long days, fueled by caffeine and nicotine; sometimes, like many other people in the 1960s, he also added a little amphetamine, legal at the time as "pep pills" with a doctor's prescription, to give him a boost. He ensconced himself at the piano in the lower level of his house and through a haze of cigarette smoke composed the score of *The Wild Bunch*, assisted by orchestrators Greig McRitchie, Al Woodbury, and Art Beck, all of whom were well experienced at doing intricate work at high speed.

Peckinpah and his associates felt that a film score should be like a man in a green suit walking in a forest, as Gordon Dawson put it.[5] The music should support the story, acting, and photography, not rise above it. The audience should respond to the music, but not be aware of it. Fielding subscribed to this notion. "If the director feels an emotional ingredient he wanted to capture on film is missing," Fielding said, "then he is going to push the composer to try to do what he failed to do. Consequently, there has to be an emotional rapport between the composer and the director before the composer will be able to understand what was missed." But Fielding added that, as a film composer, "you ought not ever let your ego, your ambition, and your wish to show off" become the primary aim when composing. He would come to dislike Burt Bacharach's score for *Butch Cassidy and the Sundance Kid*. Paul Newman and Katharine Ross riding a bicycle in the rain to music was an example of "violating the gospel" of how a movie score should work.[6]

Fielding viewed final cuts of *The Wild Bunch* and decided it was "possibly, in my view, one of the few almost perfect pictures ever made. I could look at it every day and never get tired of it."[7] He viewed it as a love story about Pike Bishop and Dutch Engstrom, with the jilted lover Deke Thornton adding complications. "It was not," Fielding said, "gunshots and open wounds and children getting shot. Even the battle was a ballet." Fielding set about to make a "poetic statement" with his music.[8] He made some recordings of his preliminary work with a six-member combo. Feldman liked what he heard when he played the tapes and dispatched them to Peckinpah, who was still in Nevada working on *The Ballad of Cable Hogue*. Sam listened to them in the converted laundry room used for screenings. He hated what he heard. He thought Fielding's music ran counter to everything he was attempting to accomplish with *The Wild Bunch*: "I wanted Mexico—what did I get, Vienna?" Peckinpah wrote in a memo to Fielding.[9]

Fielding was bummed out by Sam's memo. At Phil Feldman's urging, Fielding boarded a plane for Phoenix, where Sam was continuing to shoot interiors for *Cable Hogue*. Fielding caught up with him at a theater where Peckinpah had been viewing dailies. Fielding, as soon as he saw Peckinpah, lit into him: "You fucking two-bit Toscanini, you twerp!

How dare you send me that letter, what do you know about anything?" Sam slumped into a chair and hid behind his hat.[10] Peckinpah agreed to listen to the tapes again after Fielding explained his ideas about the score. Sam eventually bought into Fielding's concepts, and Fielding moved ahead.

Recording of the score occurred between January and April 1969 at the Warner Bros. scoring stage in Burbank. Fielding happily met one of Peckinpah's demands—employing Julito Corona to play guitar. Fielding tended to have little respect for musicians who could not read music and who were otherwise unschooled in the formalities of the art. Julito was different; he lived and breathed music, had absorbed the finer points of performance and theory without knowing he'd done so, and was an absolute master of the guitar. "He was Sam's troubadour," Fielding said. "Sweet little guy. Alcoholic. He played all those Mexican songs, those *rancheras*, those cry-in-your-beer things. He knew 'em all. He was, like, born with his fingers on a guitar, nobody ever taught him, he just did it. Julio was two hundred percent Mexican and a very sad man. He used to say, 'It's time for gasoline,' and you'd give him some tequila. He couldn't read music and he had a hell of a time with the parts on the five-guitar sections, but when he played, it was not a studio musician trying to be a Mexican imitation."[11]

The rest of the musicians numbered among L.A.'s finest. At Fielding's command were first-rate classical musicians playing violin, viola, cello, and bass. They were augmented by the top pop and rock studio musicians in the city: guitarist Tommy Tedesco had played on Elvis Presley's '68 *Comeback Special*, Richard Harris's recording of "MacArthur Park," and the Beach Boys' seminal *Pet Sounds*; accordionist Carl Fortina and harmonicist Tommy Morgan had also performed on *Pet Sounds*. The other musicians had equally impressive credits.

When Fielding was finished, he had created a remarkable score to complement "one of the few almost perfect movies."[12]

3.

The fine cut of *The Wild Bunch* ran about two and a half hours when Warner Bros.-Seven Arts previewed it in Kansas City at the Royal Theatre on May 1, 1969. Fielding may have figured out that the movie was a love story, but the relationships among Bishop, Engstrom, and Thornton were by and large lost on the thousand or so normally stolid Midwesterners who packed the Royal. They mostly reacted to the violence in the balletlike shoot-outs that bookended the picture. A number fled in horror, some stopping to puke in the alley. *It seemed so real* . . . Peckinpah would later say he hoped that the violence in *The Wild Bunch* would have a cathartic effect on Americans who viewed it during the age of Vietnam and great civil strife. It certainly struck a nerve, but whether any moviegoers actually underwent catharsis that night was unclear. (Seven years later Peckinpah would say in an interview on the BBC while discussing *The Wild Bunch*, "'Bloody Sam' was merely a changeover from dishonesty to at least looking at the fact that people do bleed and are hurt. But I am not responsible for the *Chainsaw*, whatever its name is, or any of the other trash that has been put forth. I deal in violence in terms of very sad poetry . . . I made *The Wild Bunch* because I still believed in the Greek theory of catharsis, that by seeing this movie, [it] purged by pity and fear and [got] this out of our system. I was wrong.")[13]

A group of nuns who saw the film at the next preview, which was in Peckinpah's hometown, Fresno, stormed out after the opening shoot-out. Apparently none of them went through catharsis. A final preview occurred at Long Beach, California. The combined audience-reaction cards from the three previews suggested that the majority of the viewers did not like *The Wild Bunch*. The people who watched it were so overwhelmed by the violence that they failed to notice that they'd just seen a masterpiece.

But clearly, no one in the theaters had been bored by it. Everyone seemed to react in some way, be it negative or positive. That made Feldman and others at Warners feel confident that the film would do good business, regardless of any controversy that might surround it. Warner Bros.-Seven Arts production head Ken Hyman was convinced it was a great picture. He'd attended the Fresno preview and had witnessed himself the audience getting into *The Wild Bunch*. He was enthusiastic about releasing the movie. A woman who'd seen *The Wild Bunch* in Kansas City had complained about it to her congressman in a letter. The congressman contacted Motion Picture Association of America president Jack Valenti about his constituent's concerns. Valenti, who often seemed at odds with the New Hollywood, stepped up and defended Peckinpah's work on First Amendment grounds.

The Wild Bunch was slated to premiere in L.A. on June 18, 1969, with an opening in New York scheduled for a week later. It was a remarkable year for movies. Worldwide, more than three thousand pictures hit cinemas that year. Movie patrons had many titles to choose from in the United States, and the variety was astonishing: Paul Mazursky's *Bob & Carol & Ted & Alice*, Peter Hunt's *On Her Majesty's Secret Service*, Costa-Gavras's *Z*, Gene Kelly's *Hello, Dolly!*, Ronald Neame's *The Prime of Miss Jean Brodie*, Jacques Deray's *The Swimming Pool*, Federico Fellini's *Fellini's Satyricon*, Sydney Pollack's *They Shoot Horses, Don't They?*, Charles Jarrott's *Anne of the Thousand Days*, Ken Russell's *Women in Love*, Alfred Hitchcock's *Topaz*, Joseph McGrath's *The Magic Christian*, Bob Fosse's *Sweet Charity*, Michael Ritchie's *Downhill Racer*, Woody Allen's *Take the Money and Run*, Francis Ford Coppola's *The Rain People*, Haskell Wexler's *Medium Cool*, Andy Warhol's *Blue Movie*, Elia Kazan's *The Arrangement*, Arthur Penn's *Alice's Restaurant*, Gordon Parks's *The Learning Tree*, Peter Yates's *John and Mary*, Robert Altman's *That Cold Day in the Park*.

Westerns and the other cowboy-themed movies were the real standouts of the films released that year. Henry Hathaway's *True Grit* was a watered-down version of Charles Portis's revisionist Western novel, but John Wayne delivered one of his most memorable performances, although it was not nearly as effective as what he had done in *The Searchers*. Soon after *True Grit*'s release in early June 1969, Oscar buzz began for Wayne as Best Actor. The picture also featured Strother Martin and Dennis Hopper in supporting roles, and the director of photography was Lucien Ballard. Sergio Leone's *Once Upon a Time in the West* opened in New York about a week before *The Wild Bunch*'s L.A. premiere. Critics and American audiences were by and large cool to Leone's film at the time, though film scholars would come to consider it a more important film than any entry in his Man with No Name trilogy. Coming later in the year were *Butch Cassidy and the Sundance Kid* and *Tell Them Willie Boy Is Here*, both with heartthrob Robert Redford.

Roughly a month before *The Wild Bunch*'s premiere, John Schlesinger's *Midnight Cowboy* opened, and it stunned audiences as much as *The Wild Bunch* had shocked the crowd in Kansas City. It wasn't violence that upset people. Instead it was the gritty depiction of the lives of street hustlers, including a male-on-male oral-sex sequence. The MPAA had slapped an X rating on the picture, but ticket sales were good (the picture eventually earned more than ten times its cost), and the image of Jon Voight attired in fringed buckskin, Western hat, and cowboy boots with a background of New York City streets and buildings was on its way to becoming an icon of American cinema. More Oscar buzz surrounded *Midnight Cowboy* than any picture released in early 1969.

Also in May 1969, *Easy Rider*, Dennis Hopper's tale of Old West outlaws reimagined as 1960s bikers, became the surprise hit of the 22nd Cannes Film Festival, winning for Hopper the festival award for best first director. The film grew out of the biker flicks of the mid-1960s, quickies inspired by Brando's *The Wild One* that were dumped into

Sam Peckinpah and William Holden missed out on Oscars for their work on *The Wild Bunch*, but the movie reenergized both of their careers. Photo by Paul Harper, courtesy of Nick Redman and Jeff Slater.

drive-in theaters to cash in on the teen market. Producers spent next to nothing on screenplays, actors, sets, or experienced crew members, but *Easy Rider* turned out far different from *The Glory Stompers*, *Motorpsycho*, or *Hells Angels on Wheels*, as the Cannes award indicated. *Easy Rider* was an art picture, albeit one with an obvious, heavy-handed story line. Peter Fonda's performance as Wyatt, aka Captain America, was nowhere in a league with the high level of acting in *The Wild Bunch*, but it was much better than anything he'd previously done. Hopper as Billy, Karen Black, Toni Basil, Luke Askew, and Warren Finnerty all turned in first-rate performances; better still were the non-actors Hopper found in Louisiana who were chilling as a group of murderous peckerwoods. The movie would make Jack Nicholson a star. Best of all was László Kovács's sublime cinematography. *Easy Rider* was set to open in the United States a month after *The Wild Bunch*. In the late spring of 1969, few people could have suspected *Easy Rider* would have the impact it eventually did on American filmmaking, let alone achieve an iconic status, but it, too, was a movie with buzz surrounding it before it hit theaters in America.

Shortly before *The Wild Bunch*'s release, Warner Bros.-Seven Arts set up a press junket to Grand Bahama Island to give reviewers a chance to see six pictures the studio would be releasing in upcoming months. *The Wild Bunch* was the last picture exhibited. After its showing, a press conference was scheduled with Peckinpah and some of the stars. Some of the critics—critics! People paid to review movies!—walked out during the film. The lights went up to a mixture of applause and boos and hisses. Roger Ebert, just twenty-seven years old but already writing striking reviews for the *Chicago Sun-Times*, was in the audience. As he stood to leave for the press conference, a woman said to him in outrage, "I never thought that I'd live long enough to see William Holden shoot a woman."[14] She was referring to a sequence in the final shoot-out in which Holden's Pike Bishop shotguns Yolanda Ponce's character, Yolis. The woman was hardly the only upset person.

Many of the critics unsheathed their knives at the ensuing panel made up of the film's stars and Peckinpah. "I have only one question to ask," said an enraged Virginia Kelly, who wrote for *Reader's Digest*, the popular magazine that more than any other represented the pedestrian views of newly inaugurated president Richard M. Nixon's supporters: "Why was this film made?" Holden stared sheepishly at the table before him. Panelist Ernest Borgnine was outraged. How dare someone ask why a work of art was created? Another critic demanded to know why there was so much blood in the movie. Borgnine, the World War II vet, had had enough: "Lady, did you ever see anyone shot by a gun without bleeding?"[15]

Holden was now irritated, too: "I just can't get over the reaction here. Are people surprised that violence really exists in the world? Just turn on your TV set any night. The viewer sees the Vietnam War, cities burning, campus riots. He sees plenty of violence."

Borgnine said, "When I was handed the script, to be quite honest with you, I did not read into it all the controversy it seems to have stirred up. I had made violent films before, of course; Westerns and war pictures. This is a script about people who have outlived their time, who have anachronisms. I accepted it on those terms. When we were actually shooting, we were all repulsed at times. There were nights when we'd finish shooting and I'd say, 'My God, my God!' But I was always back the next morning, because I sincerely believed we were achieving something."[16]

Peckinpah was asked if he felt he had crossed a line with *The Wild Bunch*'s depiction of bloodshed, particularly when Mapache slits Angel's throat. "I know what you mean," Peckinpah said. "There is a very, very thin line, and I think we operated as close to it as we dared. We hope that, for most audiences, we stayed on this side of the line. But I am willing to admit that we may have passed over it at some point. We feel the violence is a catharsis, a release, but sometimes the line is hard to find. To tell you the truth, I really cannot stand to see the film myself anymore. It is too much an emotional thing. I saw it last night, but I do not want to see it again for perhaps five years."[17]

Ebert pronounced, "I suppose all of you up there are getting the impression that this film has no defenders. That's not true. A lot of us think *The Wild Bunch* is a great film. It's hard to ask questions about a film you like, easy about one you hate. I just wanted it said: To a lot of people, this film is a masterpiece."[18]

The critical reaction Peckinpah faced in the Bahamas set the pace for much of the reaction to *The Wild Bunch*. A private showing of the film took place in New York for *Time* critic Jay Cocks and up-and-coming director Martin Scorsese, who both thought Sam's picture was a tour de force. "We were mesmerized by it; it was obviously a masterpiece. It was real filmmaking, using film in such a way that no other form could do it; it couldn't be done any other way. To see that in an American film-maker was so exciting," Scorsese would remember. Cocks and Scorsese turned to look at each other after the conclusion of the final shoot-out.

"We were both looking at each other, shaking our heads, like we had just come out of a shared fever dream," Cocks said.[19]

But critics of the likes of Judith Crist, who wrote for *New York* magazine and delivered reviews on the *Today* show, and Rex Reed, who wrote for *Holiday* magazine, were hostile to the film; in the Bahamas, Reed had been among those demanding to know why the film was even made. Unsurprisingly, they damned it in their reviews. Reed called it a "phony, pretentious piece of throat-slashing slobber . . . which goes around announcing good anti-violent intentions while exploiting and glorifying violence to the happy jingle of box office coins." Reed determined that Peckinpah was a nihilist who viewed humanity as having no redeeming virtues and, therefore, should be blown away. "He's a man to be pitied, not admired."[20] Crist complained of buckets of blood and incoherent narrative and described *The Wild Bunch* as "undoubtedly the worst movie of 1969."[21] Reed and Crist were hardly alone. Arthur Knight, who taught at Sam's grad school alma mater, USC, wrote in the *Saturday Review* that he doubted that "anyone who was not totally honest in his wrongheadedness could even come up with a picture as wholly revolting as this film." Knight confided to colleagues and students that *The Wild Bunch* would have been a much better movie had his friend Richard Brooks directed it, never mind that Brooks would deliver an absolute snoozefest of a film in 1969 called *The Happy Ending*.[22] The influential New York art weekly *Cue*'s critic William Wolf damned *The Wild Bunch* as an "ugly, pointless, disgustingly blood film."[23]

The negative reviews were offset by those written by critics who understood what Peckinpah was up to with *The Wild Bunch*—and were sensitive to the seismic shifts occurring in American culture in the late 1960s. The anonymous review appearing in *Time* (written by Cocks) referred to Peckinpah as being, along with Stanley Kubrick and Arthur Penn, the best of a new generation of filmmakers; it called *The Wild Bunch* "a triumph."[24] In the *New York Times*, Vincent Canby called it "beautiful and the first truly interesting American-made Western in years . . . After years of giving bored performances in boring movies, [star] Holden comes back gallantly in *The Wild Bunch*." Canby had some reservations but called *The Wild Bunch* "a fascinating movie."[25] Writing for *Life* magazine, Richard Schickel proclaimed *The Wild Bunch* "the first masterpiece in the new tradition of what should be called the dirty Western." Schickel was one of the first critics to associate *The Wild Bunch* with the war in Vietnam and a rising underclass in America. It rent asunder notions of the "fake frontier" portrayed in traditional Westerns. It already was, he wrote, "one of the most important American films of the era."[26]

Andrew Sarris, defender of the auteur theory, had issues with the "warts" and other flaws he detected in *The Wild Bunch*, but he said in his *Village Voice* review that Peckinpah was "a distinctive talent": "Even when he is most awkward and wrong-headed, Peckinpah is wildly original and individualistic."[27] At the time of its release, Pauline Kael considered *The Wild Bunch* to be a failed attempt at an antiviolence movie that, nevertheless, was brilliantly directed and photographed. Several years later, she said that *The Wild Bunch* was comparable to Kurosawa's best work, "a traumatic poem of violence, with imagery as ambivalent as Goya's." She added Peckinpah had poured "new wine into the bottle of the Western" and "explodes the bottle": "And it's no accident that you feel a sense of loss for each killer of the Bunch: Peckinpah has made them seem heroically, mythically alive on the screen."[28]

Stanley Kauffmann, the film critic of the *New Republic*, gave *The Wild Bunch* its most perceptive review. He was one of the few critics of the time to look beyond the violence in *The Wild Bunch*: "the ballet, not the bullet." He considered it a landmark movie, "a Western that enlarged the form aesthetically, thematically, and demonically," especially in its use of slow motion, which draws the viewer's "attention to the film as such; second, because Peckinpah is right—right to remind us that more than one prism of vision is possible at every moment of life and that this prism at this moment magnifies the enjoyment of killing."[29] Later, Kauffmann would say in an interview that *The Wild Bunch* "calls to mind the writings on violence of Antonin Artaud, who sees in certain kinds of theatrical violence a refuge and hope. I don't say that is exactly what I feel about Peckinpah's work, but at least it's possible to entertain such a thought when you see his film."[30]

The film stirred interest among critics beyond the entertainment centers of New York and Los Angeles. In central North Carolina, Robert Marks, a reporter on the *High Point Enterprise*, wrote one of the most insightful of all the *Wild Bunch* reviews: "*The Wild Bunch* is a beautiful film. No other word will do to describe this movie now playing at the Towne Theater. It is beautiful for its unity, for the completeness of its structure from beginning to end, for the feeling it has for a particular group of men in a particular time and place, and for the forces that have ravaged both the men and the land in which they move." Marks was one of the first writers to pick up on the paradox of Peckinpah's presentation of violence both in sickening realism and with "the grace and beauty of ballet."[31]

The film also affected would-be filmmakers. George Lucas had come of age in the rough-and-tumble world of California automobile racing, but he also attended showings of foreign art films at the Bay Area's Canyon Cinema. He moved to L.A. to enroll in the University of California's School of Cinematic Arts. He fell in with a group of young Turks studying film who would eventually be called the Dirty Dozen, among them John Milius, a future screenwriter and director, and Howard Kazanjian, who worked as an assistant director on *The Wild Bunch* and later became a producer. Lucas also befriended Steven Spielberg, a film prodigy who had applied to USC but who had been rejected because of his low high-school GPA. The week *The Wild Bunch* opened in L.A., Lucas saw it and was astonished. He spread the word to his friends. "This is the best movie ever made!" the future creator of the *Star Wars* franchise told Milius. "It's better than *The Searchers*. It's better than anything. You all have to go see it."[32]

Milius was likewise impressed by *The Wild Bunch*, as well as by Peckinpah's earlier work. More than four decades later, I visited Milius at his Westwood condo. He was now an old Hollywood lion who had written and directed many films. He had suffered a stroke a few years earlier and had difficulty speaking, but he told me clearly who his biggest cinematic influences were: "John Ford, Kurosawa, Sam Peckinpah."[33]

In the summer of 1969, Ron Shelton was playing baseball in the AA Texas League. While on the road, he took in movies every chance he had; a professor had introduced Shelton to foreign films when he was a college student, and Shelton, who had been prohibited from seeing movies as a kid by his Baptist parents, was completely taken by the art form. He saw the truncated version of *The Wild Bunch* while he was in Little Rock, Arkansas, for a three-game series. He went back the next day. And the day after. "Something was different about this movie, and I took a bunch of the ballplayers to see it and they just thought it was another shoot-'em-up," said Shelton, who went on to become a much-respected screenwriter and director, with such films as *Under Fire, Bull Durham, Tin Cup, Blaze, White Men Can't Jump,* and *Cobb* to his credit. "I tried to explain that it was more than that, but I couldn't figure out what to say. So I've been trying to answer that question ever since. And the movie grows in stature for me." To Shelton, *The Wild Bunch* remains among the best pictures ever made.[34]

A few years later, Kathryn Bigelow, who had studied at the San Francisco Art Institute, moved to New York, enrolling in Columbia University's master's program in film criticism. On a double bill, she saw Scorsese's *Mean Streets* with *The Wild Bunch*. "It took all my semiotic Lacanian deconstructivist saturation and torqued it," said the future director of *Near Dark*, *Point Break*, and *The Hurt Locker*. It represented a paradigm shift for her, made her want to get into movies. "I realized that there's a more muscular approach to filmmaking that I found very inspiring."[35] She, too, became a supporter of Peckinpah's and his greatest movie, as did younger directors such as Quentin Tarantino, who would say, "The final shoot-out sequence of *The Wild Bunch* is a masterpiece beyond compare."[36]

Most of the discourse about *The Wild Bunch* during the summer of 1969 focused on its bloodshed. The movie was condemned in pulpits and on editorial pages. Violence seemed to be on everyone's mind that summer as the Vietnam War raged on, with America's new president, Richard Nixon, planning to increase the scope of the carnage to force North Vietnam to a peace negotiating table. Violent crime continued in the cities, prompting Nixon to promise crackdowns in the name of law and order.

Hollywood had no immunity from America's domestic violence. Two days before Robert Marks's column appeared in the *High Point Enterprise*, followers of Charles Manson murdered film actress Sharon Tate and Jay Sebring, hairstylist to the stars, along with a coffee heiress, a grounds-keeper, and a Polish friend of Tate's movie director husband, Roman Polanski. The murders occurred at a house in L.A. that Polanski and Tate had rented. It was familiar to many in the film community—Lillian Gish, Henry Fonda, Samantha Eggar, Olivia Hussey, Cary Grant, Dyan Cannon, Candice Bergen, and Doris Day's son had all once called it home over the years.

The murders shocked the nation, but they created a sense of terror within the Hollywood community. A week to the day after the Tate killings, the relatively peaceful Woodstock Music & Art Fair, with its audience of nearly half a million, got under way in upstate New York. It ultimately was an aberration. The murder, bad acid, and general mayhem of the Rolling Stones' Altamont Speedway Free Festival was much more representative of the times. No one was stardust there; no one was golden.

Roger Ebert predicted that *The Wild Bunch* would wind up doing the best box office of 1969. In places, especially L.A. and New York, it indeed played well. Jaime Sánchez, working live theater in New York, felt both excitement and pride when he saw a line of people extending down the block from the ticket booth at a cinema in Midtown Manhattan to see

The Wild Bunch, the movie he played such an important role in. In Europe, where it received excellent notices, *The Wild Bunch* opened as a road show, replete with intermission. Exhibitors in the United States persuaded Warners that the movie was just another Western, not unlike a typical John Wayne Western of the midsixties that had been shot in Mexico. Over objections from producer Phil Feldman, the studio followed the distribution model of a Wayne Western, giving *The Wild Bunch* mass bookings in Texas and across the Southwest. Then Warners brought it north for saturation bookings. In retrospect, the film would clearly have been better served with a distribution model more akin to that used by United Artists for *Midnight Cowboy*. That film opened in select theaters in just a few large cities to allow word of mouth to build before giving it wide release. It worked for *Midnight Cowboy*, which became a box office smash.

The acquisition of Warner Bros.-Seven Arts by Kinney National Company was a fait accompli in 1969. Peckinpah's patron, Ken Hyman, was out as the studio's head of production. Hyman might have taken steps to protect Sam's film, but the regime of new Warner Bros. president Ted Ashley was more focused on dollars and cents than artistic achievement. Distribution chief Ben Kalmenson had already called on Peckinpah and Feldman to cut a minute and a half of *The Wild Bunch*. American exhibitors complained that the film still ran too long and requested further cuts to allow theaters to squeeze in one more showing per day. Ashley and Kalmenson acceded to their demands. With Peckinpah in Hawaii, Feldman determined which cuts should be made. He didn't notify Sam about what he was doing until it was a done deal, too late to reverse. So, on July 3, 1969, the directive went out by telegram from Warners' head of distribution, Morey "Razz" Goldstein, to all branch and division managers: "It has been decided to make immediately five direct positive cuts in all the prints of *The Wild Bunch* as follows reel 2AB cut from key number 2B 312 feet plus 7 frames . . ." Around nine minutes disappeared from *The Wild Bunch*—all the flashbacks, some dialogue, and the battle scene between Mapache's forces and Villistas. For the rest of his life, Peckinpah held these cuts against Feldman; not long before his death, he said he'd like to see someone take the cuts "and shove 'em up Feldman's butt!" Feldman's actions had irreparably damaged the effectiveness of *The Wild Bunch*, Sam said.[37] The cuts added an element of the absurd to the picture for those fans who paid close attention to the credits: Elsa Cárdenas remained billed as "Elsa" and Aurora Clavel as "Aurora," though their scenes had been hacked away.

The Mexican and Mexican American actors who performed in *The Wild Bunch* were by and large happy with it. Alfonso Arau listed it at the top of the films he had worked on. In his eyes the only Western that came close to *The Wild Bunch* was *El Topo*, the 1970 Mexican Acid Western directed, scored, and written by, as well as starring, Chilean filmmaker Alejandro Jodorowsky. Arau's friendship with Peckinpah lasted until Sam's death. Those early lessons Arau learned about directing from Peckinpah paid off over time. His movie *Like Water for Chocolate* won the Golden Globe Award for Best Foreign Language Film in 1992 and also received the Ariel Award for Best Picture.

Sonia Amelio told me she enjoyed working with Peckinpah and others on the production, especially Jaime Sánchez, and regretted that her life of touring did not permit her to stay in touch with them. She was proud of her work in *The Wild Bunch* and of the movie. "*The Wild Bunch* was very important to my career," she said. "Peckinpah was a great person and an extraordinary director."[38]

The Wild Bunch was largely ignored in Mexico itself—and remains so a half century after its release. In the United States, it was controversial among Latino moviegoers from the moment of its release. It was one of the movies that prompted the formation of a protest organization called Justicia—Justice for Chicanos in the Motion Picture and Television Industry. Justicia listed *The Wild Bunch* along with *100 Rifles*, *Butch Cassidy and the Sundance Kid*, and *El Condor* as offensive, especially in showing vastly outnumbered Anglos gunning down whole armies of Mexicans or other Latin Americans. Justicia's chair, Ray Andrade, a former Green Beret who eventually became a TV producer, alleged Hollywood had for too long portrayed Mexicans and other Latinos as "objects of filth, chicanery, and sexual perversion." Just before meeting with Screen Actors Guild president Charlton Heston, Andrade demanded to know why SAG had been "sanctioning racist movies such as these for so long." Heston was receptive to Andrade's complaints. After meeting with him, Heston said, "We've got to go along with them. I don't see how we can challenge the charges."[39]

Suave leading man Ricardo Montalbán, who'd been born in Mexico City and grown up Torreón, headed up his own organization, Nosotros, which also strived to improve the image of Latinos in American films. He complained that a Spanish-speaking American child who watches *The Wild Bunch* sees four Anglos "annihilate the Mexican Army. It's only natural for him to say, 'Gee, I wish I were an Anglo.'" Something had to be done to improve the image of Latinos, Montalbán said.[40] Peckinpah may have loved Mexico and the Mexican people, and he may have been attempting to confront clichés to make them fresh or to destroy them in *The Wild Bunch*, but it would remain challenging for many Latinos for years to come.

"Regarding *The Wild Bunch*," said one Latino filmmaker about his own contradictory feelings about Peckinpah's movie, "yes, I've seen the film. A few times. As with most of these classic yet truly problematic border films, I view them two ways, as a Chicano and through a formal, more 'filmmaker' lens. The movie is amazing in terms of its use of slow motion, the then-radical use of violence as cinematic technique, et cetera, et cetera. But its depictions of some of the Mexican stereotypes are pretty bad. And yet some of them are given real agency—rare both then and now. Man, don't get me started on this movie. In fact, I was introduced to the film in college by my [Chicano friend] from Raymondville, Texas. It was his favorite movie. There's something about Chicanos and their Westerns!"[41]

During its theatrical run through the summer and into the early fall of 1969, *The Wild Bunch* was one of the most widely discussed movies in America. It performed respectably at the box office, earning Warner Bros.-Seven Arts a solid return on its investment.[42] But it fell far short of blockbuster status. *Midnight Cowboy*, *Hello, Dolly!*, *Bob & Carol & Ted & Alice*, *True Grit*, *Cactus Flower*, and *On Her Majesty's Secret Service* all made more money. From a financial perspective, *Easy Rider* was the attention getter. It ranked third in box office receipts, earning tens of millions of dollars. Its budget had been less than $400,000. The big winner was *Butch Cassidy and the Sundance Kid*. It was glossy, well put together, and well acted, with Paul Newman, Robert Redford, and Katharine Ross looking gorgeous in every frame. Newman and Redford had glib chemistry—Hope and Crosby updated to the Age of Aquarius—and nothing in the movie, not even its somewhat downbeat ending, could cause anyone much despair or even to think about anything very much (except, perhaps, why the bicycle-in-the-rain sequence was included). This great popcorn-munching movie put asses in the seats night after night. The dollars piled up for Twentieth Century-Fox.

When Academy Award nominations were announced, *The Wild Bunch* received two: Peckinpah, Walon Green, and Roy Sickner for best original story and screenplay; and Jerry Fielding for best score. *Butch Cassidy and the Sundance Kid* wound up winning both categories. It and *Midnight Cowboy* were the big winners on Oscar night, April 7, 1970. John Wayne took home the award for Best Actor for *True Grit*. Holden as Pike Bishop was never even considered.

4.

*T*he *Wild Bunch* never went away, not in the way other 1969 pictures were chopped up and neutered for television, then largely forgotten. A cult grew around it. *The Wild Bunch* showed up in theaters around Los Angeles with regularity through the 1970s. "The screening may be some neighborhood theater," Strother Martin said, "but somebody says, '*The Wild Bunch* is showing!,' and word spreads like wildfire. Sam had a screening three years ago at the Beverly Canon. The whole theater was *filled* with friends of that film. When I say 'friends,' I mean some of them are PhDs in film, some of them are Hells Angels type of guys. And you run into people that say, I've seen it thirty-two times, man. Greatest Western ever made! . . . I've seen it seven times, and every time, I see something new."[43]

In 1969, Jim Kitses of the British Film Institute published *Horizons West*, a book-length study of the Westerns of Anthony Mann, Budd Boetticher, and Sam Peckinpah. It was the first extended study of Peckinpah. Although *The Wild Bunch* had been released just months earlier, Kitses already understood it was an "extraordinary work . . . this great work . . . we must see in it another chapter in Peckinpah's deeply troubled commentary on his country. *The Wild Bunch* is America."[44]

More books followed, with three becoming standard works on Peckinpah. In 1980, Paul Seydor's seminal *Peckinpah: The Western Films* appeared from the University of Illinois Press; it became a classic of film scholarship, especially as revised, expanded, and rereleased as *Peckinpah: The Western Films: A Reconsideration*. In 1982, Garner Simmons published his *Peckinpah: A Portrait in Montage*, which took an oral-history approach to Peckinpah's life and work. David Weddle's comprehensive Peckinpah biography, *If They Move . . . Kill 'Em!*, hit bookstores in 1994; it was the first book to go into depth on the making of *The Wild Bunch*.

The Wild Bunch made Peckinpah a well-known director. His very name would become associated with action pictures in which violence was unleashed and blood flowed: *It's a Peckinpah kind of movie.* Peckinpah would come to feel trapped by his reputation. His dramatic hero might have been Tennessee Williams, but producers wanted him for action-adventure flicks with car wrecks and hemorrhaging aplenty. He had little opportunity to develop work he really wanted to do. He would liken himself to "a good whore." "I go where I'm kicked," Peckinpah said.[45]

Still, in the 1960s and '70s, he was able to create a cycle of remarkable films: *Ride the High Country, Major Dundee,* the made-for-TV "Noon Wine," *The Wild Bunch, The Ballad of Cable Hogue, Straw Dogs,* the overlooked *Junior Bonner,* the underappreciated contemporary Western *The Getaway, Pat Garrett and Billy the Kid,* and, finally, the dark masterwork *Bring Me the Head of Alfredo Garcia.* He used and reused the same actors and crew members, so the cycle developed a cohesive look. He revisited the same themes: men struggling to live outside their time, the bonds between men, betrayal, failure to live up to codes of ethics, the dehumanizing evils of the technologically driven modern world, self-loathing, the hypocrisy of social mores, failed relationships between men and women, and, finally, the potential for violence that resides in the heart of us all. *The Wild Bunch* stands at the apex of these films.

Through the latter half of the 1970s and into the 1980s, Peckinpah struggled with worsening alcoholism and addiction to cocaine. His work suffered—and the American film industry was moving away from the kind of movies he was best at making—though he managed a return to form with *Cross of Iron,* a World War II drama filmed in Yugoslavia. It received critical raves in Europe, where it was a box office smash. In the United States, however, critics ignored it, and few people saw it in theaters, never mind that Orson Welles told Peckinpah that *Cross of Iron* was the best war movie from an enlisted man's point of view to be made since Lewis Milestone's *All Quiet on the Western Front.*

Peckinpah suffered a heart attack in December 1984 while visiting his ex-wife Begoña Palacios in Mexico. He survived a flight back to Los Angeles but died three days after Christmas. A few months before, he had made his last public appearance at a retrospective held at Rice University in Houston. At the time, he was dating Carol O'Connor, whom he'd met when she worked as a Malibu hairstylist. It was a frustrating period for Peckinpah as he tried without success to find directing jobs, but it was also one of relative peace. He was sober and was trying to live a healthier life. *The Wild Bunch* and *The Ballad of Cable Hogue* were slated to be shown at Rice. He put O'Connor to work researching chemical reactions in the brain during times of stress and how they affected perceptions of time so he could answer questions about his use of slow motion in *The Wild Bunch*.[46] They traveled together to Houston, where no one asked him about slow motion per se.

The hall was packed, and plenty of questions came his way. His friend Jerry Holt, a professor from Oklahoma, moderated as Peckinpah, looking relaxed, provided answers. "*The Wild Bunch* . . . I wrote it. And I wrote it as I do all the work I do, as something *I* want to see from the story I was given. I didn't write it to shock the audience. I wrote it as a picture I would pay money to see. I make pictures for myself. I am the audience. Do I like seeing people shot? No. No one's asked me to make *South Pacific* or anything else. I think *The Wild Bunch* is a good story. These things were happening in Mexico at that time."[47]

These things have actually been happening everywhere throughout all time. Sam did not live long enough to fully appreciate the home-video revolution and widespread cable and satellite-television availability. Combined, they opened doors for millions of people around the world to watch his movies. *The Wild Bunch*, in particular, grew in stature, becoming in the minds of many a classic American picture. Fans watched it over and over. Like Strother Martin, they saw something new each time they did. Producer and writer Rob Word described it as "the Bible," with fans quoting lines from it at every turn.[48]

In its early days, *The Wild Bunch* drew the most attention for the way it portrayed bloodshed. It was quickly trumped by other movies in savagery. Now it seems somewhat tame in terms of how many gallons of plasma wind up spread on the viewing screen. *The Wild Bunch*'s carnage still disturbs because of the psychology behind it. Peckinpah opened a window into the minds of men who live violent lives and thrive on it. Because of that, it resonates in an America where gun violence continues to be a significant issue.

There is much more to *The Wild Bunch*. It is a Western, in most ways the *last* Western. With it, Peckinpah destroyed all the standard stereotypes that made up cowboy pictures that came before it. Peckinpah's West was a dirty, often vile place, very much like how the Old West was. When *The Wild Bunch* was released, it placed a tombstone on the head of the grave of the old-fashioned John Wayne Western. It changed all the rules.

It also accurately presented a preview of the technological dystopia that would overtake the world during the twentieth century. Codes of honor destroyed, human value diminished. The love and respect people have between each other is obliterated in the name of the machine. Without becoming didactic about it, *The Wild Bunch* howls against what has happened to mankind during modern times.

The Wild Bunch is art. William Holden, Robert Ryan, Ernest Borgnine, Warren Oates, and Edmond O'Brien all did their best work in the picture, as did cinematographer Lucien Ballard. Oates said the credit went to Peckinpah: "He made that picture. He carved that picture out of stone, with his own historical interest in Mexico. And his sense of imagination, his strong images, that conveyed the horror of war and desperate people . . . So I don't know, but the whole thing about *The Wild Bunch* is it's a dynamic film. It changed the way people thought about films."[49]

As a work of art, *The Wild Bunch* deals with major themes: honor, betrayal, love, death and dying, the end of the American West, revolution, repression, people who have outlived their times, the dread of living in the age of technology. It ranks with the great movies of all time: *The Rules of the Game, Battleship Potemkin, La Strada, The 400 Blows, The Searchers* and *The Grapes of Wrath, The Bicycle Thief, Rashomon, L'Avventura,* and, of course, *Citizen Kane* and *Touch of Evil. The Wild Bunch* is totally engaging. On a cold autumn night outside Denver a couple of years ago, I streamed it on my iPad. Even in that small format, *The Wild Bunch* played beautifully. All too soon, it was over. Edmond O'Brien appears and utters, "It ain't like it used to be. But it'll do," followed by laughter and the strains of "Las Golondrinas," the song that I've requested be played at my own memorial service.

I've never seen a better movie.

ACKNOWLEDGMENTS

Though one person usually winds up listed as author, book writing is a cooperative undertaking. *The Wild Bunch* is no exception. I must first mention two names: Paul Seydor and David Weddle. Seydor is *the* Peckinpah scholar; Pauline Kael essentially described him as such, and his books, *Peckinpah: The Western Films: A Reconsideration* and *The Authentic Death and Contentious Afterlife of Pat Garrett and Billy the Kid: The Untold Story of Peckinpah's Last Western Film*, as well as his critical essays, prove this. Weddle is the author of the authoritative biography *If They Move . . . Kill 'Em!: The Life and Times of Sam Peckinpah*. Both Paul and David have become my friends, and both have generously supported this project from the beginning, including giving me access to their research materials. I asked them both to read a bloated, rickety draft of the manuscript, and their suggestions proved invaluable. In fact, they prevented me from making numerous boneheaded errors and misreads. These guys amaze me: Paul made his edits while on a family ski vacation. David performed a virtual line edit while he was simultaneously producing a TV series. I cannot thank them enough for all they've done for me.

Paul and David along with Garner Simmons and Nick Redman form a foursome known as the Dog Brothers. They've provided the expert commentary for the best DVD and Blu-ray releases of Peckinpah's films. When I started sending out feelers about this project, Nick immediately called me to welcome me aboard. In 1996, Nick and Paul produced the Oscar-nominated documentary *The Wild Bunch: An Album in Montage*, which had a significant bearing on my book. Nick's passion is film scores, and he provided me with much insight into Jerry Fielding and has been a consistent cheerleader for my project. In 1982, the University of Texas Press published Garner's *Peckinpah: A Portrait in Montage*. About a year later, I found a copy at a used bookstore in Stillwater, Oklahoma, and read it in one setting. Garner's book stoked my interest in Peckinpah the artist. He has supported me throughout this undertaking, for which I am grateful.

This book simply could not have been written without the help of my good friend John Schulian. During my research journeys to Los Angeles, John time and again provided me lodging at his house in Pasadena, not far from the suicide bridge where a young William Holden used to cheat death. Moreover, John is an excellent writer with a long history of success in Hollywood. His counsel and encouragement helped me tremendously. He also had great suggestions for how to navigate L.A. traffic, which saved me many hours and helped me get to know many of the city's neighborhoods.

My longtime friend Kelly Lyons is an entrepreneur, first-rate horsewoman, amazing hairstylist, and Reiki master. One day after a haircut, she performed a Reiki session with me and told me she'd picked up on images of old-time soldiers (after the Civil War, but not modern) who were angry and violent. Did it mean anything to me at the time? No. But a week or two later, my mind drifted to the opening shoot-out in *The Wild Bunch*, which aligns very much with what Kelly "saw" during the session. Thus began this book.

Not long afterward, I was visiting my friend Eddie Wilson, who has contributed much to Austin, Texas, culture over the years. When I mentioned I was thinking about a Sam Peckinpah book, Eddie said, "Don Hyde." Within a day, I was communicating with Don, who was living in Italy. Back in the day, Don became one of the architects of the Austin live-music scene when he was the principal founder of the Vulcan Gas Company venue in 1967. Run out of town by Austin police within a couple of years, Hyde landed on the West Coast, where he became a cinema owner and video editor as well as a fixture in the Bay Area music scene. He befriended Peckinpah within a few years and has remained a Sam loyalist since. Don has been extremely important to my *Wild Bunch* project, giving suggestions, introducing me to people who've acted as sources, and always shouting encouragement all the way from Florence. He's also lent me a number of videos and documents. Don connected me with the fabulous Tonio K, the rock star and musician who owns a huge archive of *Wild Bunch* photographs and other material related to the movie. My thanks to Tonio for his generosity.

Likewise, I'm indebted to my friend from the UK, Jeff Slater. Jeff is the preeminent collector of all things Peckinpah. His book, *Entered His House Justified: The Making of the Films of Sam Peckinpah*, is difficult to find, but I'm delighted that one came into my possession: It was essential for the success of my book. No one I know has more passion for Sam's work than Jeff. I'm deeply indebted to him and, again, to Nick Redman for allowing access to the very rarely seen Paul Harper photographs taken on location in Mexico, some of which I've used in my book. The interviews included in Mike Siegel's *Passion & Poetry* series of videos are essential to any student of the life and movies of Peckinpah, and I profited from watching and rewatching them. Mike has also done me some important favors, including preventing me from making mistakes. He was kind enough to introduce me to the *Wild Bunch* actress Lilia Castillo. These days she lives in Southern California, far removed from the film industry, under the name Lily Richards Gagliardotto. Lily has become a friend; she's a class act all the way around.

I want to give a special shout out to Alfonso Arau, Elsa Cárdenas, and Sonia Amelio. My early interviews with them gave me insight into the indispensable contributions to *The Wild Bunch* made by Mexican and Mexican American film professionals, which, sadly, has been largely overlooked. I especially treasure my conversations with Arau and Cárdenas, which I conducted with them from their homes in Mexico City via telephone and Skype. Amelio went out of her way to make our interview work, in spite of her limited English and my poor Spanish. She is an amazing talent, and I'm grateful she took time away from her busy touring schedule to communicate with me. Likewise, I want to thank Ralph Prieto Jr., who shared his family's adventures while working on Peckinpah's masterpiece as well as rare family photographs. Edgar Pablos provided a connection to Chalo González and also graciously allowed me to view his documentary about Chalo while it was still being edited. Thank you, Edgar.

My thanks to Cecilia Ballí for informative conversations about border issues and the portrayal of Mexican and Mexican American women in Hollywood movies, as well as for books and articles to which she referred me. My longtime friend Tamara Cryar de Ramirez helped me with the nuances of Teresa's speech during her encounter with Angel at Agua Verde. My buddy Tom Russell is one of America's great Renaissance men, an extraordinary singer/songwriter but also a first-rate painter and essayist—and fan of Peckinpah's movies. Tom has championed my work at his concerts and has provided me with introductions and other aid that made this book a possibility. Tom and I hit on so many of the same cylinders in terms of our interests that I sometimes think of him as a long-lost big brother. *Mil gracias, hermano.*

Mil gracias also to Melissa del Bosque and Eugenio del Bosque, both for their support and hospitality. Eugenio, past director of the Cine las Americas International Film Festival as well as a documentary filmmaker himself, helped me understand more about Peckinpah and his relationship with Mexican filmmakers. My friend Callie Jones has been with me through thick and thin on different writing projects, and I'm deeply thankful for her help on *The Wild Bunch*. My gratitude, too, to Andrés Tijerina, the eminent Tejano historian. I talked my way through much of this book with Andrés during drives from Austin to Dallas and back. The backing I've received from him and his lovely wife, Juanita, has meant much to me.

One of the things this book has done is bring me back into contact with the great Jerry Holt, who was a legend in Oklahoma for his support of writing and filmmaking back in the day. Jerry, who was the moderator of Peckinpah's last public appearance, the retrospective at Rice University, sent me a box containing VHS tapes of the Rice event, other documents, and even his doctoral dissertation. Jerry's a terrific guy, a friend of Sam's who continues to teach students about Peckinpah's great achievements in cinema. I'm glad we're reconnected and thankful for all he's done for me. Going back to the old days in Oklahoma, Michael Kennedy and the late Frank Parman encouraged me to start watching Peckinpah's films anew in the mid-1980s. I also want to mention John Pickard, an eccentric humanities prof at good ol' CSU (now the University of Central Oklahoma) who taught me that film could be art way back when. I learned a lot from John.

This book would not have been possible without the availability of the Peckinpah archives at the Margaret Herrick Library of the Academy of Motion Picture Arts and Sciences. I'm deeply indebted to the library staff for its help with *The Wild Bunch*. I found additional useful information in collections housed at UCLA, USC, SMU, the El Paso Public Library, the University of Texas at El Paso library, the Wittliff Collections at Texas State University, the Harry Ransom Center at the University of Texas, the Dolph Briscoe Center for American History at the University of Texas, Centro de Artes, the Guadalupe Cultural Arts Center, El Museo del Ferrocarril de México, and Museo de la Revolucion en La Frontera. I'm grateful to them and their staffs. I want to especially recognize Jeremy D. Moore at the Wittliff Collections for his photo recovery expertise. I'm grateful to my friends and colleagues at the Mayborn Literary Nonfiction Conference, especially director emeritus George Getschow, to whom I owe much.

I tend to undertake major projects such as this one at just the right time to correspond to crises in my life, both professional and personal. I want to thank my family and some very close friends (you know who you are) for their support during trying times. I'd be lost without a group of longtime buddies known in some quarters as Los Knuckleheads: Christopher Cook, Steve Davis, Ron Querry, Jan Reid, Jesse Sublett, David Wilkinson, the aforementioned Eddie Wilson, and Tom Zigal, all of whom have helped me with *The Wild Bunch*. Steve Davis has been an especially important sounding board, as have my good friends Sergio Troncoso, Stephen Harrigan, and Elizabeth Crook. Special thanks go to Luís Alberto Urrea. I also appreciate the support and railroad research provided by my longtime buddy H. Mark Belanger. Thanks to Jason Culp for insight into his father's relationship with Sam and Peckinpah family life in Malibu. Thanks also to Manny Alfaro and Manuel Herrera at New York's HOLA (Hispanic Oragnization of Latin Actors).

I'm so happy to be at Bloomsbury Publishing, where executive editor Anton Mueller has been a deft guide as I've worked on *The Wild Bunch*. Grace McNamee has been diligent in pulling together all the loose ends, and Jenna Dutton's work on the book has improved it immeasurably. *¡Me quitaría el sombrero ante tí, Jenna!* Bloomsbury enlisted copy editor Steve Boldt to work on my book, and he corrected errors by the dozen plus performed a first-rate fact-checking job. Thank you, Steve. Thanks as well to David Chesanow, an excellent editor and fan of *The Wild Bunch*, for a deft proofreading job on the manuscript. I also want to recognize my longtime agent David McCormick for all he has done for my career, not the least of which is landing *The Wild Bunch* at Bloomsbury.

Finally, I want to thank the following people for consenting to be interviewed (both for direct quotes and for background material) as well as for suggestions, introductions and connections, tidbits of information, and other help and encouragement: Rico Ainslie, Terry Allen, Carroll Ballard, Gregg Barrios, Sarah Bird, Michael Bliss, Mary Bones, Adra Brown, Cliff Coleman, Pamela Colloff, Susan Compo, Gordon Dawson, Francisco de la Cabada, James Donovan, Max Evans, Emily Ferry, Stephen Ferry, Darrell Fetty, Robert Flynn, Glenn Frankel, Hector Galan, Mark Lee Gardner, Chalo González, Don Graham, Walon Green, Katy Haber, the late Billy Hart, Monte Hellman, Lance Henson, the late Buck Holland, Richard Holland, Connie Hoy, Kathryn Jones, L. Q. Jones, C. Courtney Joyner, Glenn Justice, Kathleen Keen, Robert Earl Keen, Paul Knight, Kathryn Lane, Manuel Luis Martinez,

C. M. Mayo, Michael Meredith, John Milius, David Moorman, Nancy Novack, Brendan O'Brien, Carol O'Conner, William O'Hara, ZZ Packer, Deneen Peckinpah, Lupita Peckinpah, Stephen Prince, David Rawlins, Lex Rawlins, Clay Reynolds, David Richards, B. J. Robbins, Jeb Rosebrook, Stuart Rosebrook, Antonio Ruiz-Camacho, Cheyney Ryan, Michael Sragow, Jaime Sánchez, Ron Shelton, Bill Sibley, Jim Silke, Jake Silverstein, Morgan Smith, Dianne Solis, John Spong, Deeanne Stillman, Brian Sweany, Carmen Tafolla, Lonn Taylor, Juan Tejeda, Bob "Daddy-O" Wade, my old teacher and great friend Kenny Walter, Cary White, Jeff Wilson, Bill Wittliff, Sally Wittliff, and Rob Word.

WKS
July 1, 2018

SOURCES

Periodicals

Action!, American Studies in Scandanavia, Billboard, Chicago Sun-Times, Cinema, Cinema Retro, Denver Post, Esquire, Film Comment, Film Quarterly, Gettysburg (PA) Times, Guardian, High Point (NC) Enterprise, Entertainment World, Literature/Film Quarterly, Los Angeles Times, Mosaic: A Journal for the Interdisciplinary Study of Literature, Life, New Republic, New York, New York Times, New Yorker, Playboy, Readers Digest, Rolling Stone, Shock Cinema, South Dakota Review, Sight and Sound, Soundtrack, Southwest Review, Variety, Village Voice, Time, Soundtrack, Washington Post, Wide Angle

Video

Ben Johnson: Third Cowboy on the Right. FBN Productions, 1996.
A Justified Life: Sam Peckinpah and the High Country. Turner Entertainment, 2006.
The Lost Reels of Pancho Villa, Archiva, 2003.
Pat Garrett & Billy the Kid: One Foot in the Groove. Warner Bros., 2006.
Passion & Poetry: The Ballad of Sam Peckinpah. El Dorado Productions, 2005.
Sam Peckinpah's West Legacy of a Hollywood Renegade. FBN Productions, 2004.
Sam Peckinpah: Man of Iron. Lucida Films, BBC, A&E Television Networks, 1993.
Warren Oates: Across the Border. FBN Productions, 1993.
The Wild Bunch: An Album in Montage. Tyrus Entertainment, 1996.

Radio

Sam Peckinpah's West: A Study of the Filmmaker. KPFK, 1969.

Soundtrack

The Wild Bunch: End of the Line Edition. Complete score plus extras. Liner notes by John Takis and Lukas Kendall. FSM Silver Age Classics, 2013.

Books

Alonzo, Juan J. *Badmen, Bandits, and Folk Heroes.* Tucson: University of Arizona Press, 2009.
Berg, Charles Ramirez. *Cinema of Solitude.* Austin, TX: University of Texas Press, 1992.

——. *The Classical Mexican Cinema*. Austin: University of Texas Press, 2015.

Biskind, Peter. *Easy Riders, Raging Bulls: How the Sex-Drugs-and-Rock 'n' Roll Generation Saved Hollywood*. New York: Simon & Schuster, 1998.

Bliss, Michael (ed). *Doing It Right: The Best Criticism on Sam Peckinpah's* The Wild Bunch. Carbondale, IL: Southern Illinois University Press, 1994.

——. *Justified Lives*. Carbondale, IL: Southern Illinois University Press, 1993.

—— (ed). *Peckinpah Today*. Carbondale, IL: Southern Illinois University Press, 2012.

Bouzereau, Laurent. *Ultra Violent Movies*. New York: Citadel Press, 1996, 2000.

Butler, Terrence. *Crucified Heroes: Films of Sam Peckinpah*. London: Gordon Fraser, 1979.

Cano, Tony and Ann Sochat. *Bandido: The True Story of Chico Cano, the Last Western Bandit*. Canutillo, TX: Reata Publishing Company, 1997.

Canutt, Yakima, with Oliver Drake. *Stunt Man*. Norman, OK: University of Oklahoma Press, 1997.

Carter, Matthew, and Andrew Patrick Nelson (eds). *ReFocus: The Films of Delmer Daves*. Edinburgh, UK: Edinburgh University Press, 2016.

Cary, Diana Serra. *The Hollywood Posse*. Norman, OK: University of Oklahoma Press, 1975, 1995.

Champlin, Charles. *Hollywood's Revolutionary Decade*. Santa Barbara, CA: John Daniel and Company, 1998.

Compo, Susan A. *Warren Oates: A Wild Life*. Lexington, KY: University of Kentucky Press, 2010.

Crumley, James. *Whores*. Missoula, MT: Dennis McMillan Publications, 1989.

de Orellana, Margarita. *Filming Pancho Villa: How Hollywood Shaped the Mexican Revolution*. London: Verso, 2009.

Dukore, Bernard F. *Sam Peckinpah's Feature Films*. Urbana, IL: University of Illinois Press, 1999.

Engel, Leonard (ed). *Sam Peckinpah's West*. Salt Lake City, UT: University of Utah Press, 2003.

Epstein, Dwayne. *Lee Marvin: Point Blank*. Tucscon: Schaffner Press Inc., 2013.

Evans, Max. *Hi-Lo to Hollywood: A Max Evans Reader*. Lubbock: Texas Tech University Press, 1998.

——. *Sam Peckinpah, Master of Violence: Being the Account of the Making of a Movie and Other Sundry Things*. Vermillion, SD: Dakota Press, 1972.

—— with Robert Nott. *Goin' Crazy with Sam Peckinpah and All Our Friends*. Albuquerque: University of New Mexico Press, 2014.

Feldman, Edward S. *Tell Me How You Love the Picture*. New York: St. Martin's Press, 2005.

Field, Syd. *Going to the Movies*. New York: Delta, 2001.

Fiedler, Leslie A. *Love and Death in the American Novel*. New York: Criterion Books, 1960.

——. *The Return of the Vanishing American*. New York: Stein and Day, 1968.

Fine, Marshall. *Bloody Sam: The Life and Films of Sam Peckinpah*. New York: Donald I. Fine Inc., 1991.

Firestone, Ross (ed). *El Topo*. New York: Douglas Book Corporation, 1971.

Frayling, Christopher. *Sergio Leone: Something to Do with Death*. Minneapolis: University of Minnesota Press, 2012.

French, Peter A. *Cowboy Metaphysics*. Lanham, MD: Rowman & Littlefield Publishers, Inc., 1997.

Fulwood, Neil. *The Films of Sam Peckinpah*. London: Batsford Books, 2003.

Ganzo, Fernando (ed). *Sam Peckinpah*. Paris: Capricci, 2015.

Gifford, Barry. *Brando Rides Alone*. Berkeley, CA: North Atlantic Books, 2004.

González, Jovita. *Life Along the Border*. College Station, TX: Texas A&M University Press, 2006.

Hayes, Kevin, J. (ed). *Sam Peckinpah Interviews*. Jackson, MS: University of Mississippi Press, 2008.

Horton, Andrew. *The Films of George Roy Hill*. New York: Columbia University Press, 1984.

Irwin, Robert McKee, and Maricruz Castro Ricalde et al. *Global Mexican Cinema: Its Golden Age*. New York: British Film Institute/Palgrave Macmillan, 2013.

Jarlett, Franklin. *Robert Ryan: A Biography*. Jefferson, NC: McFarland Classics, 1990, 1997.

Johnston, Gerry. *Lights, Camera, Dynamite*. Dublin: Liberties Press, 2008.

Jones, J.R. *The Lives of Robert Ryan*. Middletown, CT: Wesleyan University Press, 2015.

Kaminsky, Stuart M. *Don Siegel: Director*. New York: Curtis Books, 1974.

——. *John Huston: Maker of Magic*. Boston, MA: Houghton Mifflin Company, 1978.

Katz, Friedrich. *The Life and Times of Pancho Villa*. Palo Alto, CA: Stanford University Press, 1998.

Keil, Robert. *Bosque Bonito*. Alpine TX: Center for Big Bend Studies, 2002.

Kitses, Jim. *Horizons West*. Bloomington, IN: Indiana University Press, 1970.

—— and Gregg Rickman (eds). *The Western Reader*. New York: Limelight Editions, 1998.

Lansford, William Douglas. *Pancho Villa*. Los Angeles: Sherbourne Press, 1965. A paperback reprint from 2001 contains introductory comments from Lansford, which I quote.

Lawrence, D. H. *Studies in Classic American Literature*. Garden City, NY: Doubleday, 1953.

LoBrutto, Vincent. *Selected Takes: Film Editors on Editing*. Westport, CT: Praeger, 1991.

Luck, Richard. *The Pocket Essential Sam Peckinpah*. Harpenden, UK: Pocket Essentials, 2000.

McKinney, Doug. *Sam Peckinpah*. Boston: Twayne Publishers, 1979.

Macklin, Tony, and Nick Pici (eds). *Voices from the Set*. Lanham, MD: The Scarecrow Press, Inc., 2000.

Maltin, Leonard. *Behind the Camera*. New York: Signet, 1971.

Mayo, C. M. *Metaphysical Odyssey into the Mexican Revolution*. Palo Alto, CA: Dancing Chiva Literary Arts, 2014.

Mesce, Bill, Jr. *Peckinpah's Women*. Lanham, MD: Scarecrow Press, Inc., 2001.

Miller, Henry. *The Air-Conditioned Nightmare*. New York: New Directions, 1945–47.

Morgenthaler, Jefferson. *The River Has Never Divided Us: A Border History of La Junta de los Ríos*. Austin TX: University of Texas Press, 2004.

Murray, Gabrielle. *This Wounded Cinema, This Wounded Life*. Wesport, CT: Praeger, 2004.

Nevares, Beatriz Reyes. *The Mexican Cinema*. Albuquerque: University of New Mexico Press, 1976.

Nott, Robert. *Last of the Cowboy Heroes*. Jefferson, NC: McFarland & Co., 2000.

Parra, Max. *Writing Pancho Villa's Revolution*. Austin: University of Texas Press, 2005.

Parrill, William. *Heroes Twilight: The Films of Sam Peckinpah*. Hammond, LA: Bay-Wulf Books, 1980.

Pick, Zuzana M. *Constructing the Image of the Mexican Revolution*. Austin, TX: University of Texas Press, 2010.

Poniatowska, Elena. *Las Soldaderas: Women of the Mexican Revolution*. El Paso: Cinco Puntos Press, 2006.

Prince, Stephen (ed). *Sam Peckinpah's* The Wild Bunch. New York: Cambridge University Press, 1998.

——. *Savage Cinema: Sam Peckinpah and the Rise of Ultraviolet Movies*. Austin TX: University of Texas Press, 1998.

Roberts, Randy, and James S. Olson. *John Wayne: American*. New York: Free Press, 1995.

Rødje, Kjetil. *Images of Blood in American Cinema*. Copehagen, Denmark: University of Copenhagen Press, 2015.

Rosenbaum, Jonathan. *Dead Man*. London: British Film Institute, 2016.

Salas, Elizabeth. *Soldaderas in the Mexican Military*. Austin: University of Texas Press, 1990.

Sarras, Andrew. *The American Cinema*. New York: Da Capo Press, 1996.

——. *The John Ford Movie Mystery*. Bloomington, IN: University of Indiana Press, 1975.

Schroeder, Richard. *Lone Star Picture Shows*. College Station, TX: Texas A&M University Press, 2001.

Schickel, Richard. *Second Sight*. New York: Simon and Schuster, 1972.

Seydor, Paul. *The Authentic Death & Contentious Afterlife of Pat Garrett & Billy the Kid: The Untold Story of Peckinpah's Last Western Film*. Evanston, IL: Northwestern University Press, 2015.

——. *Peckinpah: The Western Films: A Reconsideration*. Urbana, IL: University of Illinois Press, 1980, 1997.

Simkin, Stevie. *Straw Dogs*. New York: Palgrave Macmillan, 2011.

Simmons, Garner. *Peckinpah: A Portrait in Montage*. Austin, TX: University of Texas Press, 1982.

Simons, John L., and Robert Merrill. *Peckinpah's Tragic Westerns*. Jefferson, NC: McFarland & Company, Inc., 2011.

Slater, Jeff. *Enter His House Justified: The Making of the Films of Sam Peckinpah*. Privately printed.

Slotkin, Richard. *Gunfighter Nation: The Myth of the Frontier in Twentieth Century America*. New York: Atheneum, 1992.

Smith, Dean, with Mike Cox. *Cowboy Stuntman*. Lubbock: Texas Tech University Press, 2013.

Sonnichsen, C. L. *From Hopalong to Hud*. College Station, TX: Texas A&M University Press, 1978.

Soto, Shirlene. *Emergence of the Modern Mexican Woman*. Denver: Arden Press, 1990.

Taibo, Paco Ignacio I. *El Indio Fernández*. Mexico City: Editorial Planeta Mexicana, 1986, 1991.

Thomas, Bob. *Golden Boy: The Untold Story of William Holden*. New York: St. Martin's Press, 1983.

Tierney, Dolores. *Emilio Fernandez*. Manchester, UK: Manchester University Press, 2012.

Tuchman, Barbara W. *The Zimmermann Telegram*. New York: Macmillan, 1958.

Turner, Timothy G. *Bullets, Bottles, and Gardenias*. Dallas: South-West Press, 1935.

Tuska, Jon (ed). *Close-Up: The Contemporary Director*. Metuchen, NJ: Scarecrow Press, Inc., 1981.

——. *Encounters with Filmmakers: Eight Career Studies*. Westwood, CT: Greenwood Press, 1991.

Ward, Robert. *Renegades: My Wild Trip from Professor to New Journalist with Outrageous Visits from Clint Eastwood, Reggie Jackson, Larry Flynt, and other American Icons*. New York: Gallery Books, 2012.

Warshow, Robert. *The Immediate Experience*. Cambridge, MA: Harvard University Press, 2001.

Weddle, David. *If They Move . . . Kill 'Em!: The Life and Times of Sam Peckinpah*. New York: Grove Press. 1994.

Wellman, William Jr. *Wild Bill Wellman: Hollywood Rebel*. New York: Pantheon Books, 2015.

Willsmer, Trevor (ed). *Sam Peckinpah*. Twickenham, UK: Aclea Enterprises Ltd., undated.

Wolfe, Tom. *The Electric Kool-Aid Acid Test*. New York: Farrar, Straus and Giroux, 1968.

Wunder, John R. (ed). *Working the Range*. Westport, CT: Greenwood Press, 1985.

NOTES

Introduction: Son of Liberty Valance

1   Roger Ebert, "The Man Who Shot Liberty Valence," review, Roger Ebert website, retrieved November 23, 2017.
2   *The Man Who Shot Liberty Valance* (1962), Turner Classic Movies website, retrieved November 23, 2017.
3   Thomas Doherty, *Hollywood's Censor: Joseph I. Breen and the Production Code Administration*.
4   Billy Bob Thornton interview, *Sam Peckinpah's West: Legacy of a Hollywood Renegade* (documentary).
5   Audience reaction cards, *The Wild Bunch*, Peckinpah Collection, Margaret Herrick Library.
6   Ken Kesey as quoted by Tom Wolfe, *The Electric Kool-Aid Acid Test*.
7   Kris Kristofferson, "The Pilgrim: Chapter 33" (1971), Monument Records.
8   Monte Hellman, author interview.
9   Max Evans, author interview.
10 Henry Miller, *The Air-Conditioned Nightmare*.
11 William Butler Yeats, "The Second Coming," *The Collected Poems of W. B. Yeats*.

Part I: "A Wild Bunch"

1   Buck Holland, author interview.
2   James Crumley, "The Heavy," *Whores*.
3   Haycox's novel *The Wild Bunch* was published in 1946 by Triangle Books.
4   David Weddle, *If They Move . . . Kill 'Em!: The Life and Times of Sam Peckinpah*.
5   Ibid.
6   Gordon Dawson, author interview.
7   Weddle, *If They Move*.
8   In total, Sickner appeared in ten Marlboro Man commercials between 1966 and 1970, never alone but as part of an ensemble.
9   The University of California, San Francisco (UCSF), maintains the online Industry Documents Library (www.industrydocumentslibrary.ucsf.edu). It is an essential resource for researching the American tobacco industry. It contains scanned copies of primary source material pertaining to the Marlboro Man campaign, including a list of TV commercials, actors appearing in them, and the date they were first broadcast. Katherine M. West's research piece "The Marlboro Man: The Making

of an American Image" is posted on the Florida Gulf Coast University website and contains useful information about the advertising campaign. I also relied on Jim Carrier's eight-part series on the Marlboro Man, which began running in the *Denver Post* in 1991.

10 Robert Ward, Renegedes.
11 Dwayne Epstein, *Lee Marvin: Point Blank.*
12 Walon Green, author interview.
13 Elena Poniatowska, *Las Soldaderas.*
14 Barbara Tuchman, *The Zimmerman Telegram.*
15 Walon Green, Nat Segaloff, "Greenland," *Film Commentary*, Jan.–Feb. 1993.
16 Ibid.
17 Green, author interview.
18 Green, author interview.
19 Jefferson Morgenthaler, *The River Has Never Divided Us.*
20 Green, Segaloff, "Greenland."
21 Green, author interview.
22 Green, Segaloff, "Greenland."
23 Green, author interview.
24 One such outlaw group, Uvalde County's Newton brothers, hit their first bank in 1914 at Cline, Texas, maybe sixty miles as the crow flies from the Rio Grande. From that start, the Newtons rode on to become America's most successful bank and train robbers. Eventually director Richard Linklater told their story in his movie *The Newton Boys.*
25 Robert Keil, *Bosque Bonito*; also Walter Prescott Webb, *The Texas Rangers.*
26 Carell never produced another picture and faded out of the business. Eventually he owned a company that installed radiant barriers in houses. He died in 2003.

Part II: "Who the Hell Is They?"

1   *Sam Peckinpah's West: A Study of the Filmmaker.* KPFK, 1969.
2   Ibid.
3   Dianne Solis, author interview. Solis, an award-winning *Dallas Morning News* writer, grew up in Fresno.
4   *Sam Peckinpah's West.*
5   Diana Serra Cary, *The Hollywood Posse.*
6   L. Q. Jones, author interview.
7   Randy Roberts and James S. Olson, *John Wayne: American.*
8   Tony Macklin and Nick Pici, *Voices from the Set.*
9   William Wellman Jr., *Wild Bill Wellman.*
10 Weddle, *If They Move.*
11 Kevin J. Hayes, *Sam Peckinpah Interviews.*
12 Don Hyde, author interview.
13 Sam Peckinpah interview, *Playboy*, August 1972.
14 Ibid.
15 Jim Kitses, Gregg Rickman, *The Western Reader.*

16   Jim Silke, author interview.

17   Ibid. Silke was a friend of both Peckinpah's and George Stevens's.

18   Elsa Cárdenas, author interview. Cárdenas befriended Peckinpah in the 1950s and became his lover in the late 1960s.

19   Weddle, *If They Move*.

Part III: "We're Gonna Stick Together Just Like It Used to Be"

1   Deneen Peckinpah, author interview.

2   Max Evans, *Sam Peckinpah, Master of Violence*.

3   Max Evans with Robert Nott, *Goin' Crazy with Sam Peckinpah and All Our Friends*.

4   Jim Silke (uncredited), "Wanted: Sam Peckinpah," interview with Peckinpah, *Cinema* 1, no. 4, undated.

5   Jim Silke, author interview.

6   Jim Silke, author interview.

7   Years after Peckinpah's death, *The Hi-Lo Country* finally was made into a movie using a fresh screenplay by Walon Green. One of the producers was Martin Scorsese; the director, Stephen Frears. An interesting film, it came and then disappeared with relatively little notice after its distributor opted to put the bulk of its promotional resources for that year behind a Cate Blanchett costumer.

8   Weddle, *If They Move*.

9   Author interview, Gentleman Jim Brewer. Brewer was a professional boxer and actor who attended the University of Texas shortly after Parker, McQueen, and Woodward and knew all three men.

10   *Ben Johnson: Third Cowboy on the Right*.

11   Some of this material came from my own interviews and original research done in the Osage during my newspaper days. I'm greatly indebted to my friend Kathryn Jones, who shared much of her forthcoming biography of Ben Johnson with me. Her book promises to be authoritative.

12   Harry "Dobe" Carey, author interview. Carey, a fellow cowboy actor, was Johnson's best friend for decades.

13   In writing the definitive biography of Johnson, Kathryn Jones discovered he occasionally took credit for things he simply did not do, such as writing the screenplay for *One-Eyed Jacks*. Johnson made the claim in *Ben Johnson: Third Cowboy on the Right* and elsewhere. No evidence exists to suggest that he actually scripted Brando's movie, though he did make significant contributions.

14   Garner Simmons, *Peckinpah: A Portrait in Montage*.

15   Paul Seydor, e-mail to the author.

16   L. Q. Jones, author interview.

17   Gregorio Rocha, *The Lost Reels of Pancho Villa*.

18   Margarita de Orellana, *Filming Pancho Villa*.

19   William Douglas Lansford, *Pancho Villa* (2001 reprint).

20   Ibid.

21   Ibid.

22 William Douglas Lansford, author interview.

23 Weddle, *If They Move.*

24 Peter Biskind, *Easy Riders, Raging Bulls.*

25 *New York*, September 7, 1970.

26 "Stay Tuned" by Stan Cornyn, Rhino website, April 11, 2013.

27 Weddle, *If They Move.*

28 Ibid.

29 Silke, author interview.

30 Christopher Frayling, *Sergio Leone: Something to Do with Death.*

31 Weddle, *If They Move.*

32 Ibid.

33 IRS letter, Peckinpah Collection.

34 Silke, author interview.

35 Deneen Peckinpah, author interview.

36 Sydney Field, "Lonely Are the Brave," *Film Quarterly* 16, no. 4.

37 Syd Field, *Going to the Movies.*

38 Deneen Peckinpah, author interview.

39 Field, *Going to the Movies.*

40 Sam Peckinpah, Q&A, Sam Peckinpah Retrospective, Rice University, April 1984.

41 Field, *Going to the Movies.*

42 Ibid.

43 Ibid.

44 Robert Culp, "Sam Peckinpah, the Storyteller and *The Wild Bunch*," *Entertainment World*, January 16, 1970.

45 Ibid.

46 Jason Culp, author interview.

47 David Peckinpah, "Losing It on High Street," unpublished manuscript. David Peckinpah wrote this remembrance in hopes of publishing it in a magazine. However, he was unsuccessful. A literary agent provided me with a copy.

48 Ibid.

49 Ibid.

50 It is known as the Colorado Street Bridge; however, the roadway it carries was renamed Colorado Boulevard decades ago.

51 Bob Thomas, *Golden Boy.*

52 Ibid.

53 "Oscar-winning star Ernest Borgnine dies at 95," Associated Press, July 8, 2010.

54 R. J. Jones, *The Lives of Robert Ryan.*

55 She used the pen name Adrien Joyce for both scripts.

56 Strother Martin's popularity would so grow that he'd eventually host an episode of *Saturday Night Live.*

57 William R. Horner, *Bad at the Bijou.*

58 Billy Hart, author interview.

59 Ibid.

60 Jaime Sánchez, author interview.

61 Ibid.

Part IV: "This Time We Do It Right!"

1   Andrew Sarris as quoted in Andrew Horton, *The Films of George Roy Hill*.

2   Jeff Wilson, author interview. Wilson, who went on to become a respected Associated Press reporter, worked as a busboy at the restaurant when it was popular with movie people. He provided me with descriptions of the atmosphere there during the mid- to late 1960s.

3   Chalo González, author interview.

4   Elsa Cárdenas, author interview.

5   González, author interview.

6   Ibid.

7   Ibid.

8   Lupita Peckinpah interview, in Mike Siegel, *Passion and Poetry: The Ballad of Sam Peckinpah*.

9   Ibid.

10 Weddle, *If They Move*.

11 Over time, *M* would be replaced by *PG* and *PG-13*, while *X* wound up used exclusively to designate porn flicks. For mainstream movies with content with adult content that exceeded *R*, the MPAA created the *NC-17* rating in 1990.

12 Weddle, *If They Move*.

13 Ballard met Henry Hathaway on *Morocco*. Hathaway would go on to become an important director of Westerns. Ballard would eventually be Hathaway's director of photography on *The Sons of Katie Elder*, *Nevada Smith*, and, most important, *True Grit*, which was released in 1969, the same year as *The Wild Bunch*.

14 Budd Boetticher interview.

15 Leonard Maltin, *The Art of the Cinematographer*.

16 Carroll Ballard, author interview.

17 Bob Thomas, *Directors in Action: Selections from* Action, *the Official Magazine of the Directors Guild of America*.

18 González, author interview.

19 Ibid.

20 Gordon Dawson, author interview.

21 Ibid.

22 Ibid.

23 Stephen Ferry and Dawson, author interviews.

24 Brendan O'Brien, author interview. Also, insurance documents, Peckinpah Collection.

25 Edmond O'Brien letter to Sam Peckinpah, Peckinpah Collection. This citation applies to the previous quotes from O'Brien as well.

26 Ibid.

27 O'Brien, author interview.

28 C. Courtney Joyner, *The Westerners*.

29 Simmons, *Peckinpah: A Portrait in Montage*.

30 Weddle, *If They Move*.

31 Sánchez, author interview.

Part V: "I Wouldn't Have It Any Other Way Either"

1   James Strong, "Daley Backed by Wilson," *Chicago Tribune*, April 17, 1968.

2   Morgan Smith, author interview. Smith is the son of Crayton Smith, *The Wild Bunch*'s script supervisor.

3   "Emilio 'El Indio' Fernández encumbró al cine mexicano," *Novedades de Tabasco* website, retrieved December 4, 2017; translated by the author.

4   Lilia Castillo, author interview.

5   R. G. Armstrong interview, in Siegel, *Passion and Poetry*.

6   Cliff Coleman, author interview.

7   Buck Holland and L. Q. Jones, author interviews.

8   Holland and Gordon Dawson, author interviews.

9   Memo, Peckinpah Collection.

10 Cliff Coleman, author interview.

11 Ibid.

12 Ibid.

13 Sam Peckinpah interview, in Siegel, *Passion and Poetry*.

14 The hymn's proper name is "Hanson Place," but is rarely called that. "Shall We Gather at the River?" or simply "At the River" are more common alternative names. The song was written by Robert Lowry in 1864 and published the next year, and it would be associated with a number of Westerns during the second half of the twentieth century, although it was composed in Brooklyn on a hot summer day by a Baptist preacher who spent his whole life on the East Coast. Lowry was also a professor at Bucknell University and operated a religious publishing house.

15 Asbjørn Grønstad, "Gathering at the River: Ford, Peckinpah, and the Failure of the Communal," *American Studies in Scandanavia* 35 (2003).

16 Lex Rawlins, author interview. Rawlins is Phil Rawlins's son.

17 Ernest Borgnine interview in Siegel, *Passion and Poetry*.

18 Hart, author interview.

19 Edward S. Feldman, *Tell Me How You Love the Picture*.

20 Jerry Holt dissertation.

21 Peckinpah would tell an audience at a retrospective of his work at Rice University that the river crossing was shot by his second-unit crew. He was not present. Had he been, he said, he would have caught the error. However, the same error occurs during the bridge explosion sequence later in the movie, which was definitely not shot by the second unit. Therefore, it is likely that Peckinpah didn't notice the error at all during the filming.

22 Weddle, *If They Move*.

23 Ibid.

24 Kathryn Lane, author interview.

25 Alfonso Arau, author interview.

26 Ibid.

27 Ibid.

28 *The Wild Bunch: An Album in Montage*.

29 Paco Calderón is a Mexican political cartoonist. He posted his comments about *The Wild Bunch* on Amazon.com.

30   Bo Hopkins interview, "Baptism in Blood: Bo Hopkins Gets Squibbed for *The Wild Bunch*," *A Word on Entertainment*, YouTube, retrieved December 27, 2017.

31   Ibid.

32   Cárdenas, author interview.

33   Castillo, author interview. Castillo was the roommate of the actress in question.

34   Hart, author interview.

35   Arau, author interview.

36   Tony Cano and Ann Sochat. *Bandido: The Story of Chico Cano, the Last Western Bandit.*

37   "Investigation of Mexican Affairs, Preliminary Report and Hearings of the Committee on Foreign Relations, United States Senate"; also Tony Cano and Anne Sochat.

38   Edgar Pablos, author interview.

39   Juan Tejeda, author interview.

40   González, author interview.

41   Jones, author interview.

42   Ibid.

43   Ralph Prieto Jr., author interview.

44   The Internet Movie Car Database says it is a 1914 Packard, which could make it an anachronism for a movie set in late 1913 or early 1914.

45   Ralph Prieto Jr., author interview.

46   Ibid.

47   Ibid.

48   Lou Lombardo interview in Vincent LoBrutto, *Selected Takes.*

49   Ibid.

50   Vincent LoBrutto, *Selected Takes.*

51   Ibid.

52   David A. Cook, "Ballistic Balletics," Stephen Prince, *Sam Peckinpah's* The Wild Bunch.

53   Edward Feldman, *Tell Me How You Love the Picture.*

54   Phil Feldman memo, Peckinpah Collection.

55   Ibid.

56   Memo, Peckinpah Collection.

57   This material is primarily derived from memos in the Sam Peckinpah Collection at the Margaret Herrick Library as well as the author interview with Chalo González and interviews from Edgar Pablos's documentary *Legacy*, a near-final cut of which Pablos was so generous as to share with me prior to its release. In my interview and in Edgar's film, Chalo avoided naming Faralla as the offending party. However, González named Faralla as the source of his difficulty in an interview conducted by Mike Siegel for *Passion and Poetry: The Ballad of Sam Peckinpah.*

58   Memos, Peckinpah Collection.

59   González, author interview.

60   Phil Feldman memo, Peckinpah Collection.

61   Memo, Peckinpah Collection.

62   Ibid.

63 Sam Peckinpah letter, Peckinpah Collection. Peckinpah endlessly attempted to get Hollywood to hire moviemaking talent he'd encountered in Mexico—including cinematographer Alex Phillips Jr. and director Felipe Cazals—usually to no avail.

64 Sonia Amelio, author interview.

65 Castillo, author interview.

66 Ibid.

67 Ibid.

68 Ibid.

69 *Warren Oates: Across the Border.*

70 Susan A. Compo, *Warren Oates.*

71 Ibid.

72 Ibid.

73 Castillo, author interview.

74 Ibid.

75 Margarita de Orellana, *Filming Pancho Villa.*

76 Prieto Jr., author interview.

77 Walon Green, Nat Segaloff, "Greenland."

78 Arau, author interview.

79 Coleman, author interview.

80 González, author interview.

81 Jones, author interview.

82 Sánchez, author interview.

83 Phil Feldman memo, Peckinpah Collection.

84 Coleman, author interview.

85 Cliff Coleman interview, *The Wild Bunch: An Album in Montage.*

86 Weddle, *If They Move.*

87 "Ernest Borgnine on *The Wild Bunch*," American Film Institute channel, YouTube, retrieved November 29, 2017.

88 Kjetil Rødje, *Images of Blood in American Cinema.*

89 Gordon Dawson interview, in Siegel, *Passion and Poetry.*

90 Prieto Jr., author interview.

91 Dawson, author interview.

92 Brendan O'Brien, author interview.

93 Peckinpah Collection, Margaret Herrick Library.

94 Arau, author interview.

95 Sánchez, author interview. Also, Bob Thomas, *Golden Boy: The Untold Story of William Holden.*

96 Thomas, *Golden Boy.*

97 Coleman, Castillo, and Arau, author interviews.

98 Ryan and Brendan O'Brien, author interviews.

99 González, author interview.

100 My friend Mark Belanger, a railroad buff, performed the research on the NM 650. In addition to turning up other information, he found a helpful article in a Puebla, Mexico, newspaper concerning the restoration of the engine: "El MNFM restaura una de las siete locomotoras de vapor NM 650 que sobreviven en el país," April 27, 2007, *La Jornada de Oriente* website, retrieved December 31, 2017. After *The Wild*

Bunch, the locomotive was used for a number of other pictures, including *Rio Lobo*, *Big Jake*, *The Train Robbers*, and *The Mask of Zorro*, by which time it was no longer able to power itself. Happily, Engine 650 wound up at El Museo del Ferrocarril de México, the Mexican National Railroad Museum, in Puebla, where, restored, it is now on permanent exhibit: El Museo del Ferrocarril de México website, retrieved December 31, 2017.

101 Steve Ferry, and Hart, author interviews.

102 David Weddle, "Dead Man's Clothes: The Making of *The Wild Bunch*," *Film Comment*, May–June 1994.

103 Ibid.; also Garner Simmons, *Peckinpah: A Portrait in Montage*.

104 Susan Compo, *Warren Oates: A Wild Life*.

105 Coleman, author interview.

106 Peckinpah Collection, Margaret Herrick Library.

107 Hart, author interview.

108 Simmons, *Peckinpah*.

109 Hart, author interview.

110 Ibid.

111 Simmons, *Peckinpah*.

112 Prieto Jr., author interview.

113 *The Wild Bunch: An Album in Montage*.

Part VI: "It Ain't Like It Used to Be. But It'll Do"

1   Weddle, *If They Move*.

2   The Acid Western concept is discussed in Jonathan Rosenbaum's *Dead Man*.

3   Weddle, *If They Move*.

4   González, author interview.

5   Nick Redman, author interview.

6   Peter Lehman and Jonathan Rosenbaum, "Film Music: An Interview with Jerry Fielding and Dan Carlin," *Wide Angle* 4, no. 3 (1980).

7   David Raksin, "A Conversation with Jerry Fielding," *Soundtrack* 23 (1980).

8   *Sight and Sound* 5, issues 7–12.

9   Weddle, *If They Move*.

10 Ibid.

11 Ibid.

12 Ibid.

13 "Sam Peckinpah Interview," December 1, 1976, YouTube, retrieved February 14, 2016.

14 The account of the Grand Bahama Island junket is drawn from Roger Ebert, "Sam Peckinpah: Dying Is Not Fun and Games," *Chicago Sun-Times*, June 29, 1969.

15 Ibid.

16 Ibid.

17 Ibid.

18 Ibid.

19 Marshall Fine, *Bloody Sam*.

20 "Wild Bunch," Movie Film Review website, retrieved June 25, 2018.

21 Ibid.

22 C. Courtney Joyner, author interview.

23 "Wild Bunch," Movie Film Review website.

24 "New Movies: Man and Myth," *Time*, June 20, 1969.

25 Vincent Canby, "Violence and Beauty Mesh in 'Wild Bunch,'" *New York Times*, June 26, 1969.

26 Richard Schickel, Movie Review, *Life*, July 25, 1969.

27 Andrew Sarris, *Wild Bunch* review, *Village Voice*, July 10, 1969.

28 Pauline Kael, "The Wild Bunch," *New Yorker* online, retrieved June 25, 2018.

29 Stanley Kauffmann, *Wild Bunch* review, *New Republic*, July 19, 1969.

30 Stanley Kauffmann interview, in Bert Cardullo, ed., *Conversations with Stanley Kauffmann*.

31 Robert Marks, "*The Wild Bunch* Stomach-Knotting," *High Point (NC) Enterprise*, August 10, 1969.

32 Weddle, *If They Move*.

33 John Milius, author interview.

34 Ron Shelton, author interview.

35 William Skidelsky, "Kathryn Bigelow: Director with a Different Take," *Guardian*, August 15, 2009.

36 Quentin Tarantino, "Go Ahead, Take Your Best Shot: Quentin Tarantino on the Story Behind His Western *Django Unchained*," *Daily Mail*, January 12, 2013.

37 Sam Peckinpah, Q&A, Sam Peckinpah Retrospective, Rice University, April 1984.

38 Arau, Amelio, Castillo, and Cárdenas, author interviews. *El Topo* was filmed at some of the same locations as *The Wild Bunch*, and Jodorowsky employed some of the Mexican crew members who had earlier worked on *The Wild Bunch*.

39 Richard Vasquez, "Chicano Protest on Movie Image Backed by Guild," *Los Angeles Times*, August 27, 1970.

40 Bob Thomas, "Chicanos Seek Improvement of Mexican Image in Films, Television Through Groups," *Gettysburg (PA) Times*, October 31, 1970 (Associated Press wire story).

41 The filmmaker requested to remain anonymous.

42 As David Weddle points out in *If They Move . . . Kill 'Em!: The Life and Times of Sam Peckinpah*, Warner Bros.' creative accounting has made it impossible to tell just how much money *The Wild Bunch* made over the years. The cost of the picture was likely inflated as WB charged expenses from other movies to *The Wild Bunch*, so it was probably more profitable than it seems.

43 Horner, *Bad at the Bijou*.

44 Jim Kitses, *Horizons West*.

45 Sam Peckinpah interview, *Playboy*, August 1972.

46 Carol O'Connor, author interview.

47 Sam Peckinpah Retrospective, Rice University, April 1984.

48 "Sam Peckinpah's Bloodless Years with L. Q. Jones," A Word on Westerns, YouTube, retrieved June 25, 2018.

49 Joyner, *The Westerners*.

INDEX

The letter *p* following a page number denotes a photograph.

A NOTE ON THE AUTHOR

W. K. Stratton is the author of five books of nonfiction and three of poetry. He has written for *Sports Illustrated*, *Outside*, *GQ*, and *Texas Monthly* and was named a Fellow of the Texas Institute of Letters in 2017. He is a longtime resident of Austin, Texas.